PIANO · VOCAL · GUITAR

THE **BIG** BOOK OF

2nd EDITION

CHRISTMAS SONGS

ISBN-13: 978-0-7935-0783-2
ISBN-10: 0-7935-0783-9

HAL•LEONARD®
CORPORATION

7777 W. BLUEMOUND RD. P.O. BOX 13819 MILWAUKEE, WI 53213

In Australia Contact:
Hal Leonard Australia Pty. Ltd.
4 Lentara Court
Cheltenham, Victoria, 3192 Australia
Email: ausadmin@halleonard.com

Visit Hal Leonard Online at
www.halleonard.com

CONTENTS

ALL MY HEART THIS NIGHT REJOICES

Words by PAUL GERHARDT
Translated by CATHERINE WINKWORTH
Traditional Music

ALL THROUGH THE NIGHT

Welsh Folksong

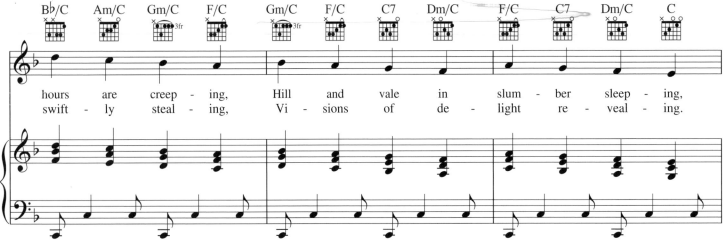

hours are creep - ing, Hill and vale in slum - ber sleep - ing,
swift - ly steal - ing, Vi - sions of de - light re - veal - ing.

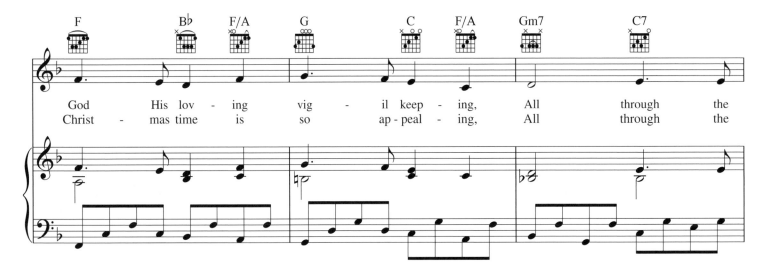

God His lov - ing vig - il keep - ing, All through the
Christ - mas time is so ap - peal - ing, All through the

night.
night. You, my God, a Babe of won - der,

All through the night; Dreams you dream can't

ANGELS FROM HEAVEN

Traditional Hungarian

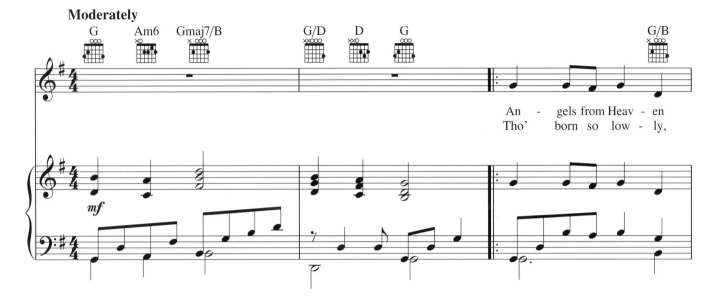

An - gels from Heav - en
Tho' born so low - ly,

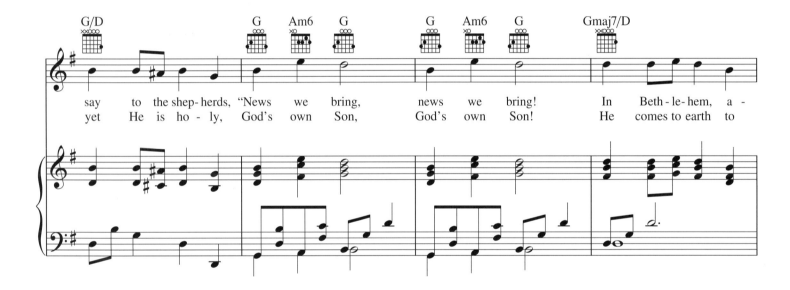

say to the shep - herds, "News we bring, news we bring! In Beth - le - hem, a -
yet He is ho - ly, God's own Son, God's own Son! He comes to earth to

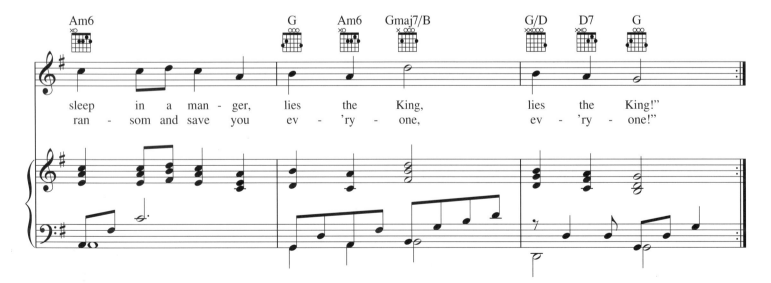

sleep in a man - ger, lies the King, lies the King!"
ran - som and save you ev - 'ry - one, ev - 'ry - one!"

AS EACH HAPPY CHRISTMAS

Traditional

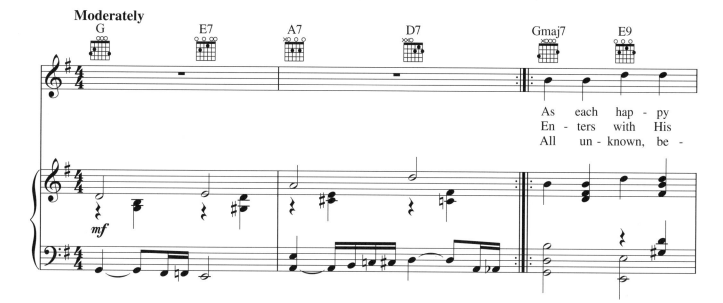

As each hap - py
En - ters with His
All un - known, be -

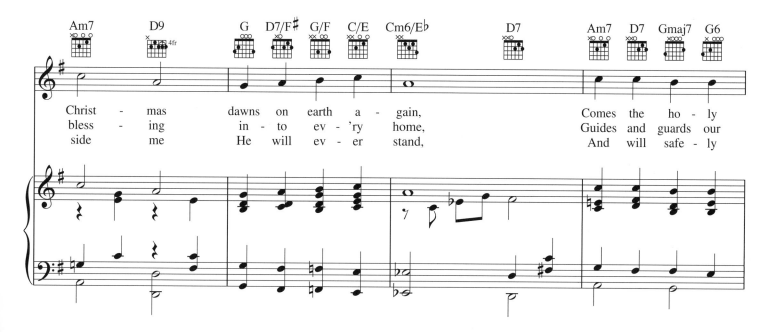

Christ - mas dawns on earth a - gain, Comes the ho - ly
bless - ing in - to ev - 'ry home, Guides and guards our
side me He will ev - er stand, And will safe - ly

Christ - child to the hearts of men.
foot - steps as we go and come.
lead me with His own right hand.

ANGELS FROM THE REALMS OF GLORY

Words by JAMES MONTGOMERY
Music by HENRY T. SMART

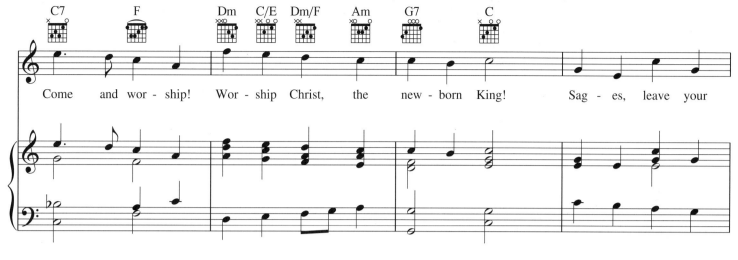

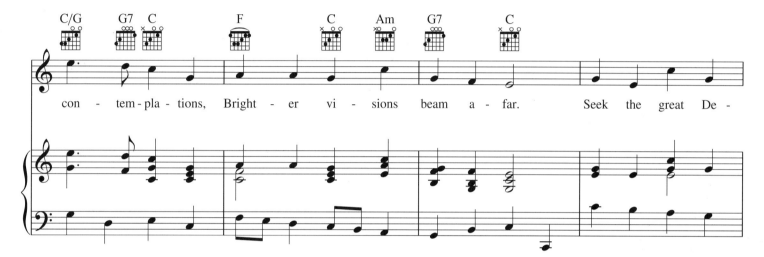

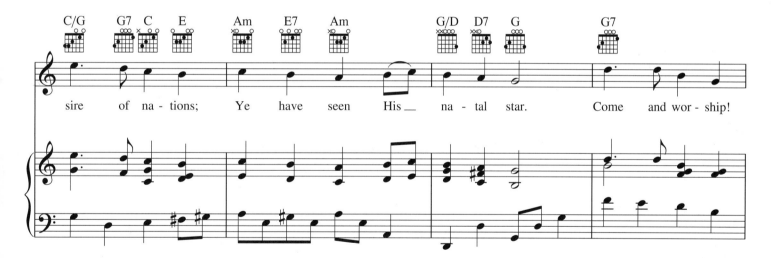

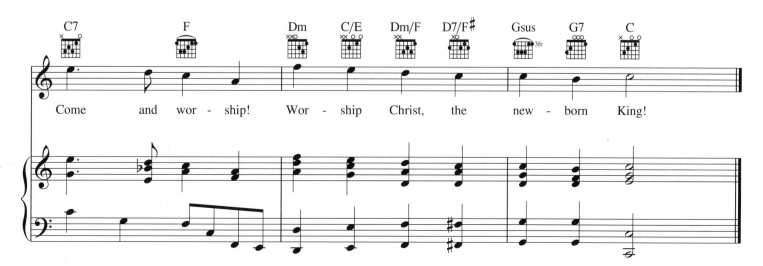

ANGELS WE HAVE HEARD ON HIGH

Traditional French Carol
Translated by JAMES CHADWICK

An - gels we have heard on high Sweet - ly sing - ing
Shep - herds, why this ju - bi - lee? Why your joy - ous
Come to Beth - le - hem and see Him whose birth the
See with - in a man - ger laid Je - sus, Lord of

o'er the plains, And the moun - tains in re - ply
strains pro - long? What the glad - some tid - ings be
an - gels sing. Come a - dore on bend - ed knee
heav'n and earth! Come Mar - y, Jo - seph, lend your aid,

Ech - o - ing their joy - ous strains.
Which in - spire your heav'n - ly song? Glo -
Christ the Lord, the new - born King!
With us sing our Sav - ior's birth.

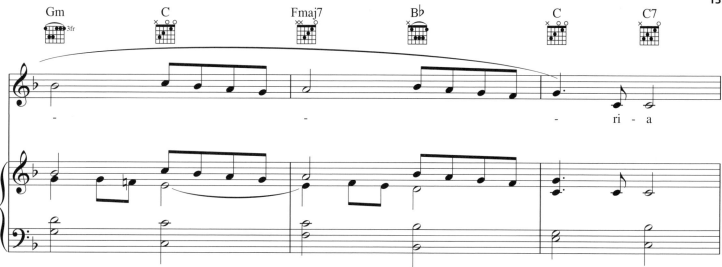

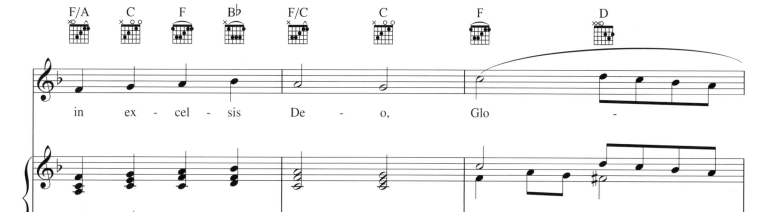

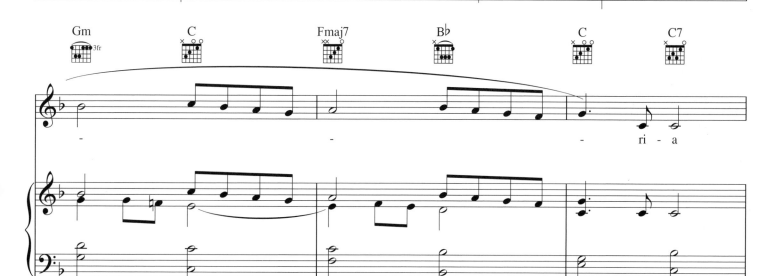

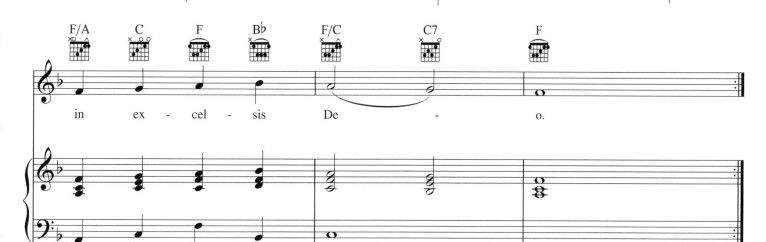

AS LATELY WE WATCHED

19th Century Austrian Carol

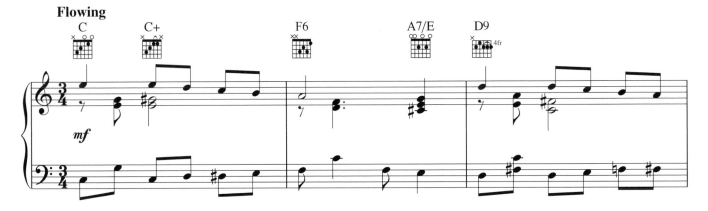

As late - ly we watched o'er our
King of such beau - ty was
shep - herds, be joy - ful; sa -

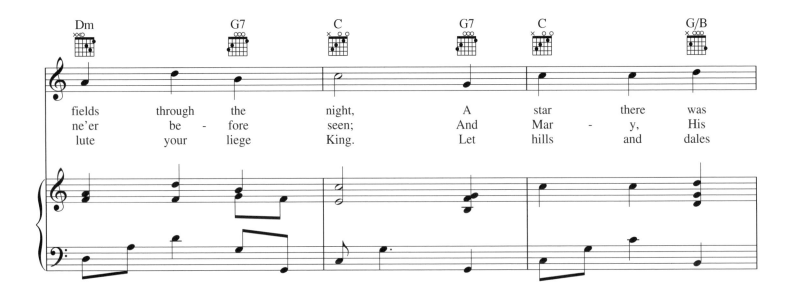

fields through the night, A star there was
ne'er be - fore seen; And Mar - y, His
lute your liege King. Let hills and His dales

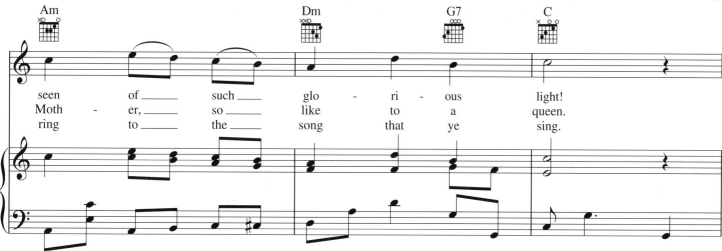

seen   of ____ such ____   glo - ri - ous   light!
Moth - er, ____ so ____   like   to   a   queen.
ring   to ____ the ____   song   that   ye   sing.

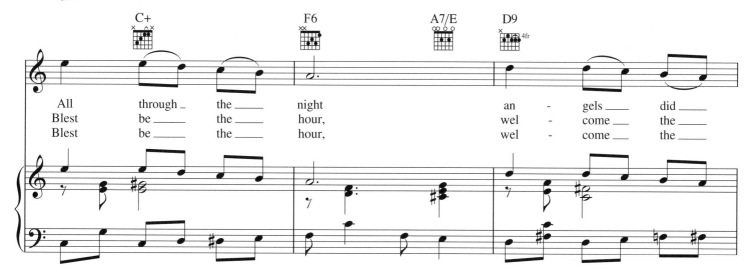

All   through _ the ____   night   an - gels ____ did ____
Blest   be ____ the ____ hour,   wel - come ____ the ____
Blest   be ____ the ____ hour,   wel - come ____ the ____

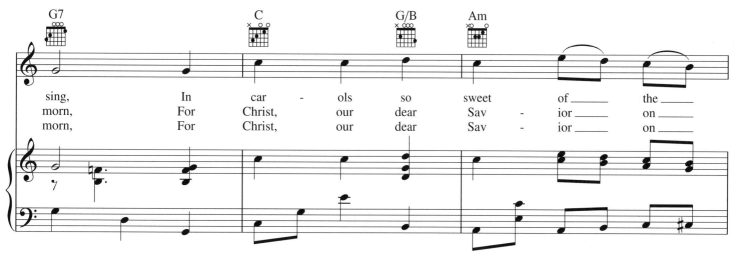

sing,   In   car - ols   so   sweet   of ____ the ____
morn,   For   Christ,   our   dear   Sav - ior ____ on ____
morn,   For   Christ,   our   dear   Sav - ior ____ on ____

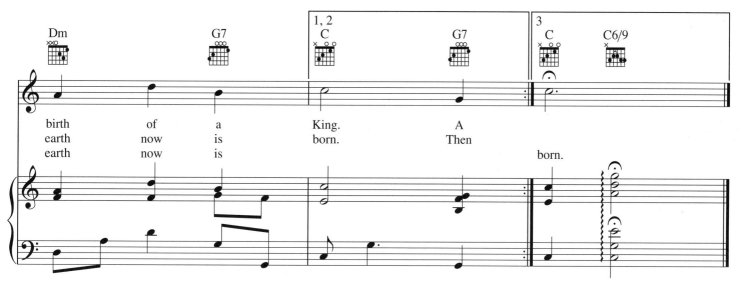

birth   of   a   King.   A
earth   now   is   born.   Then
earth   now   is   born.

AS WITH GLADNESS MEN OF OLD

Words by WILLIAM CHATTERTON DIX
Music by CONRAD KOCHER

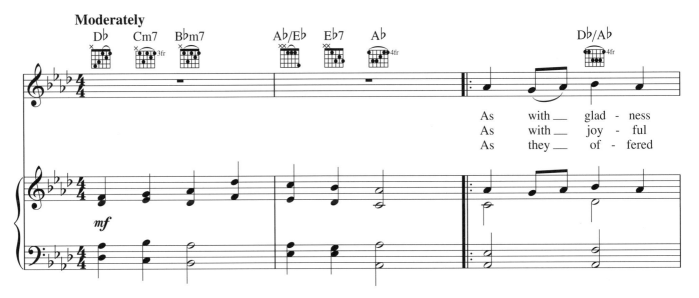

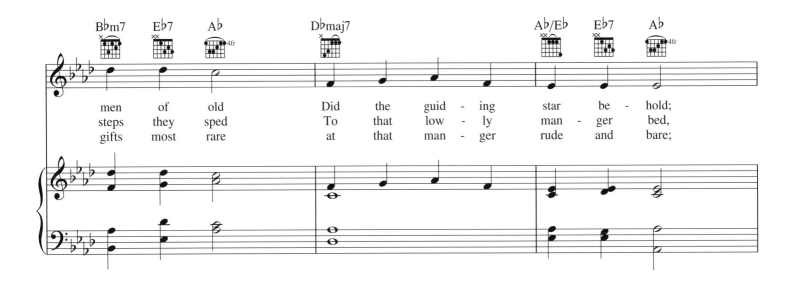

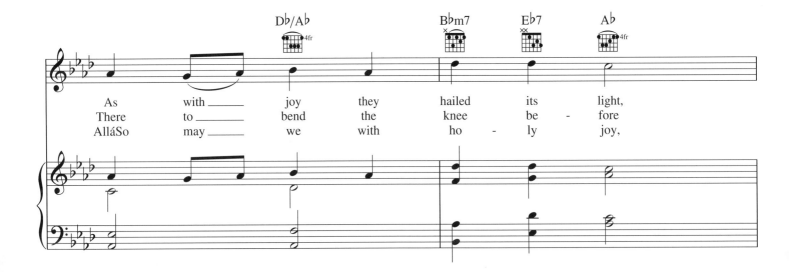

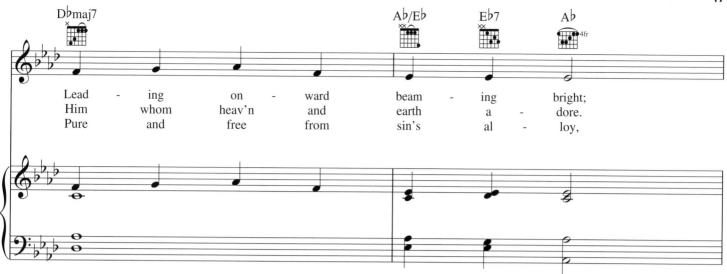

Lead - ing on - ward beam - ing bright;
Him whom heav'n and earth a - dore.
Pure and free from sin's al - loy,

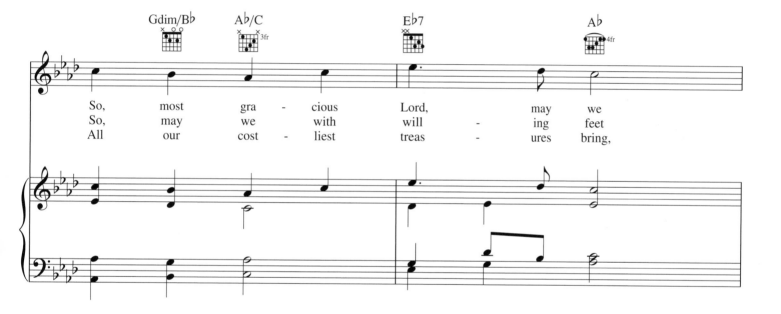

So, most gra - cious Lord, may we
So, may we with will - ing feet
All our cost - liest treas - ures bring,

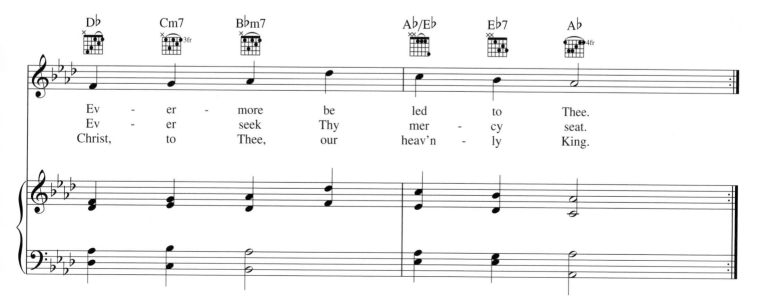

Ev - er - more be led to Thee.
Ev - er seek Thy mer - cy seat.
Christ, to Thee, our heav'n - ly King.

AT THE HOUR OF MIDNIGHT

Traditional

La la la la la la la la la la la la la la la la la la la

la la la la la la la la la la la la la. La la.

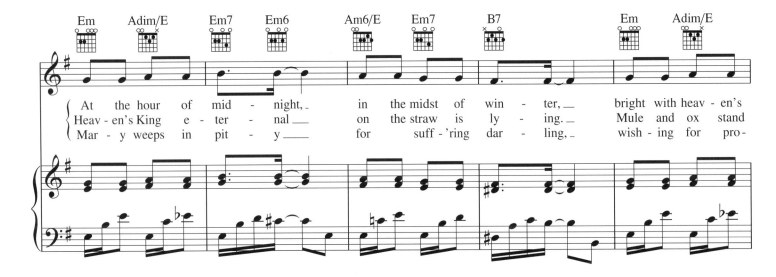

At the hour of mid - night, _____ in the midst of win - ter, _____ bright with heav - en's

Heav - en's King e - ter - nal _____ on the straw is ly - ing. _____ Mule and ox stand

Mar - y weeps in pit - y _____ for suff - 'ring dar - ling, _____ wish - ing for pro-

AULD LANG SYNE

Words by ROBERT BURNS
Traditional Scottish Melody

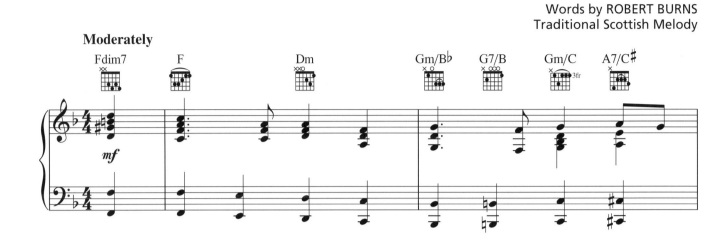

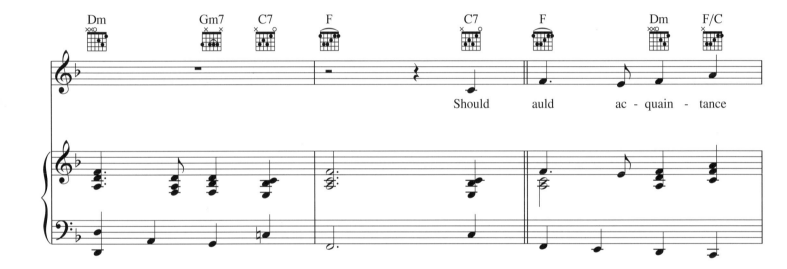

Should auld ac - quain - tance

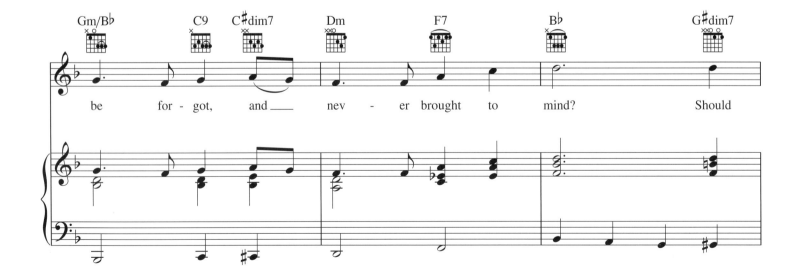

be for - got, and ___ nev - er brought to mind? Should

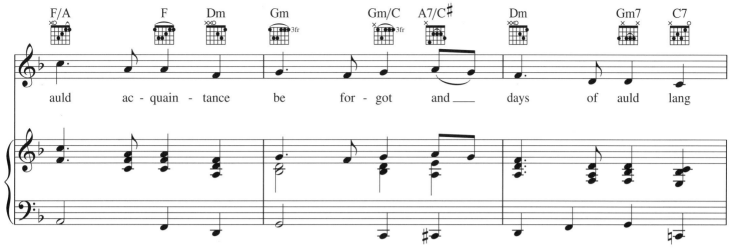

auld ac-quain-tance be for-got and ___ days of auld lang

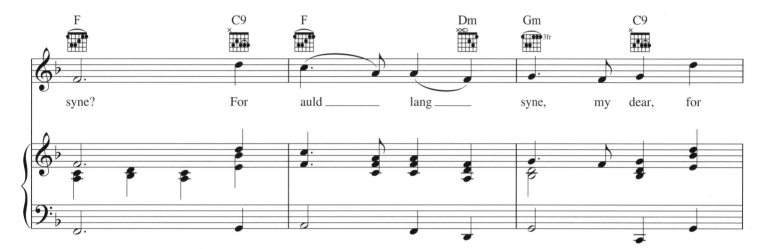

syne? For auld ___ lang ___ syne, my dear, for

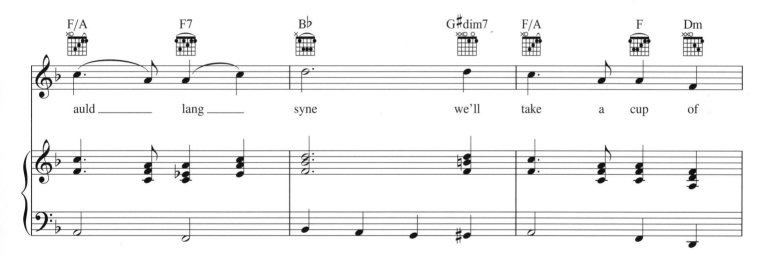

auld ___ lang ___ syne we'll take a cup of

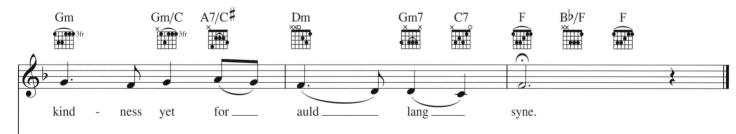

kind-ness yet for ___ auld ___ lang ___ syne.

AWAY IN A MANGER

Traditional
Words by JOHN T. McFARLAND (v.3)
Music by WILLIAM J. KIRKPATRICK

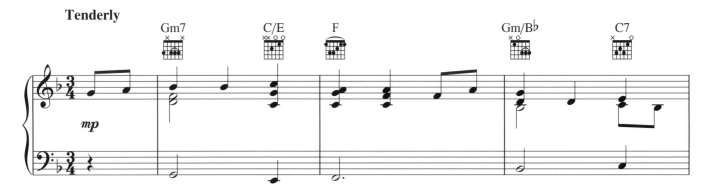

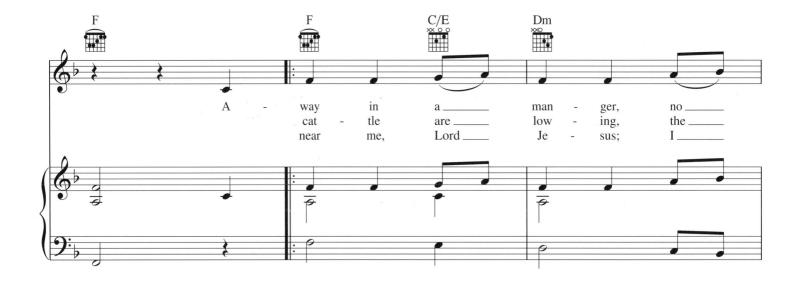

A - way in a _____ man - ger, no _____
cat - tle are _____ low - ing, the _____
near me, Lord _____ Je - sus; I _____

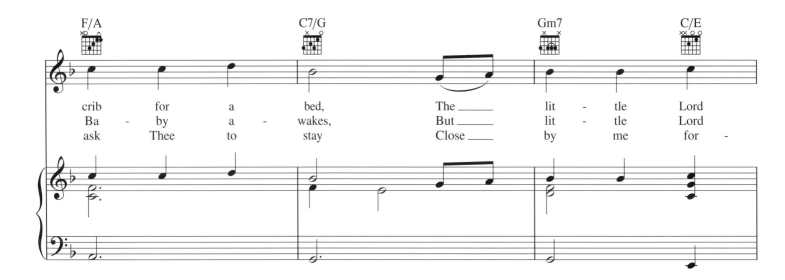

crib for a bed, The _____ lit - tle Lord
Ba - by a - wakes, But _____ lit - tle Lord
ask Thee to stay Close _____ by me for -

23

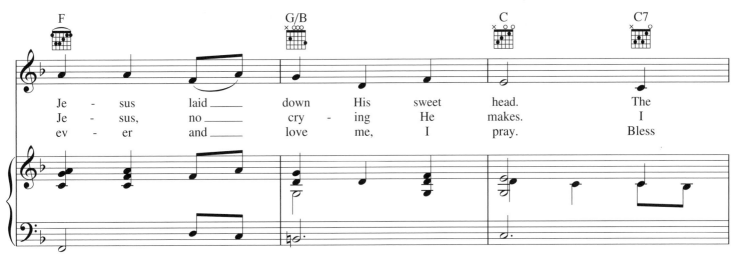

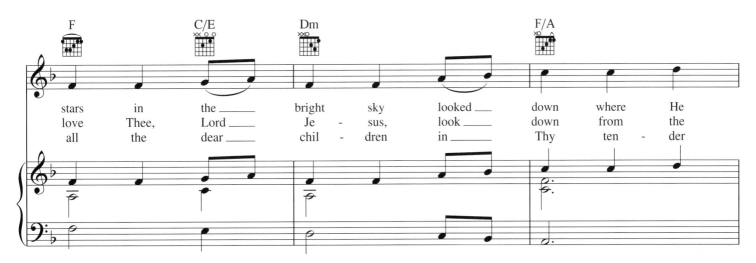

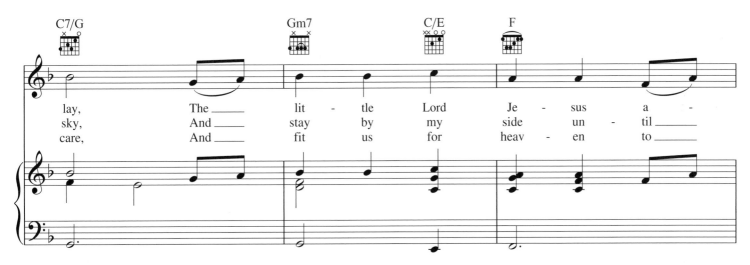

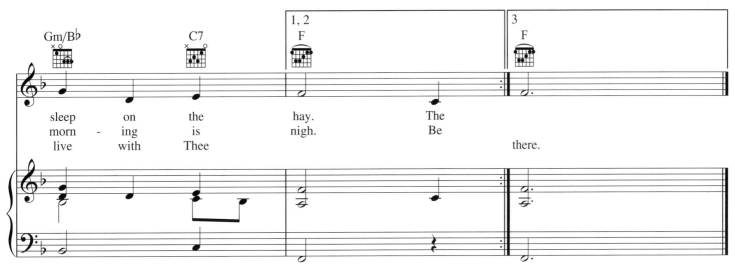

AWAY IN A MANGER

Traditional
Words by JOHN T. McFARLAND (v.3)
Music by JAMES R. MURRAY

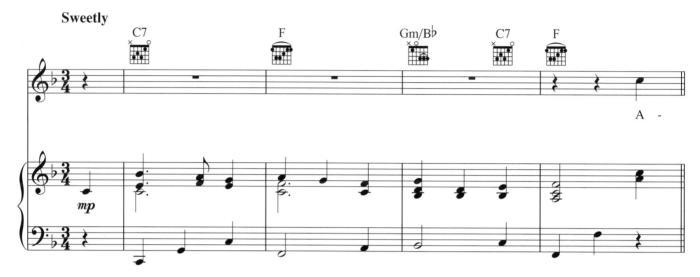

A-

way in a man - ger, no crib for a

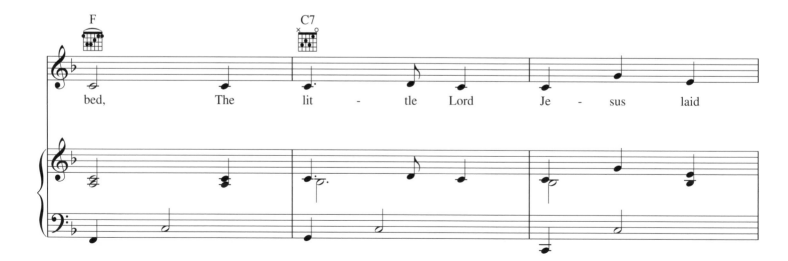

bed, The lit - tle Lord Je - sus laid

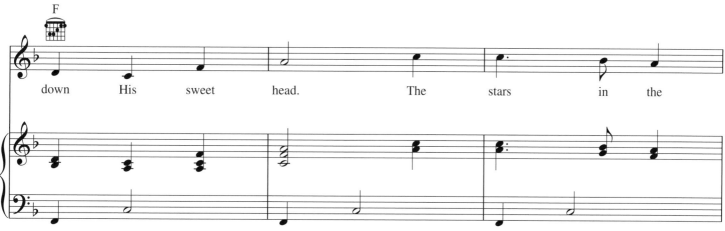

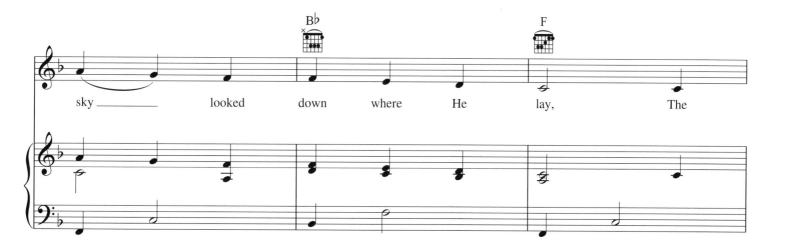

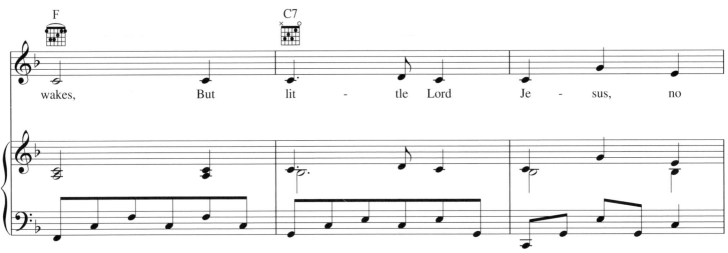

wakes, But lit - tle Lord Je - sus, no

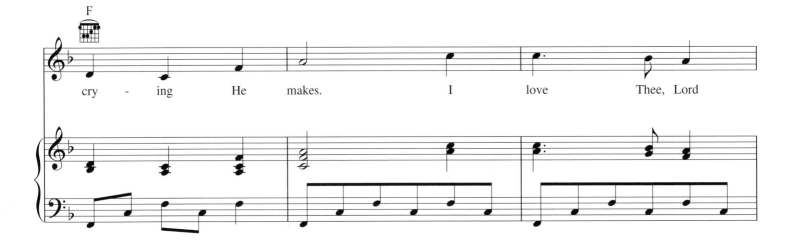

cry - ing He makes. I love Thee, Lord

Je - sus, look down from the sky,
And

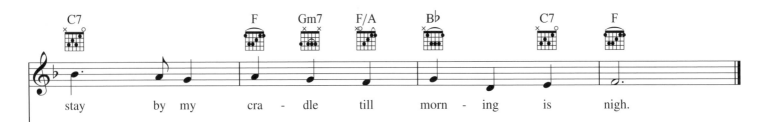

stay by my cra - dle till morn - ing is nigh.

BELLS OVER BETHLEHEM

Traditional Andalusian Carol

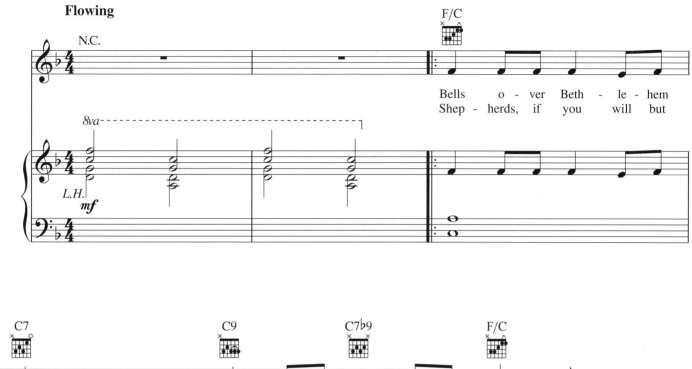

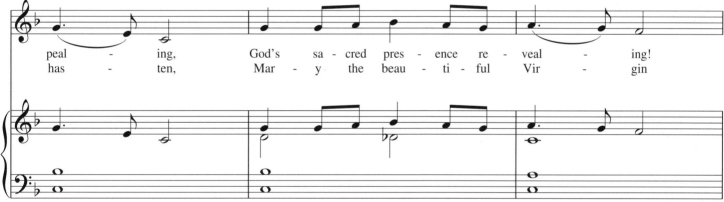

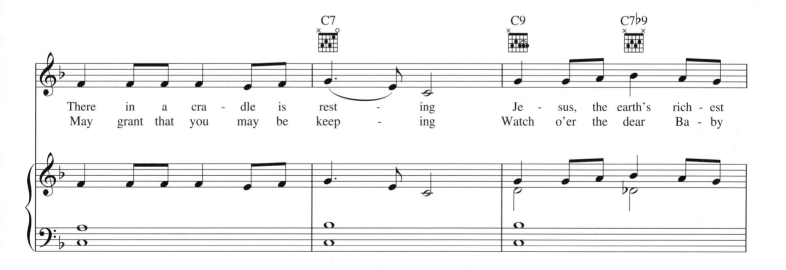

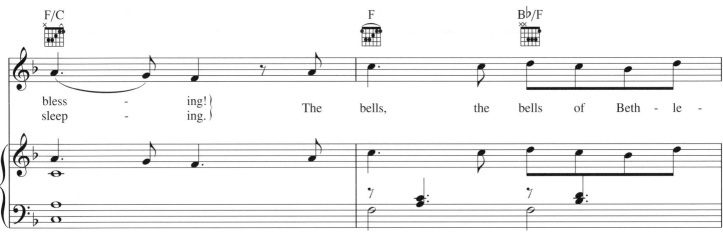

bless - ing!
sleep - ing. } The bells, the bells of Beth - le -

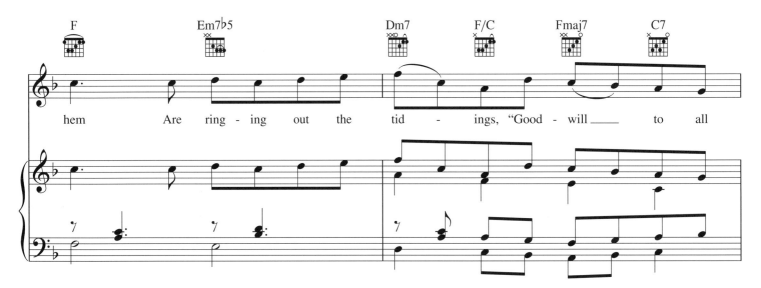

hem Are ring - ing out the tid - ings, "Good - will ____ to all

men!" Leave your sheep ___ and come, O shep - herds,

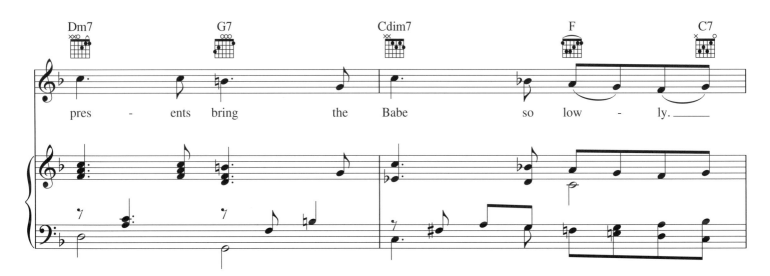

pres - ents bring the Babe so low - ly. ____

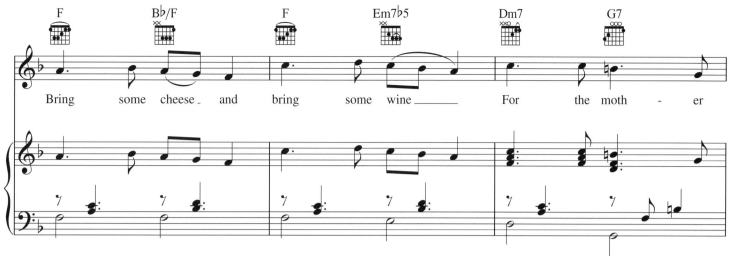

Bring some cheese and bring some wine ____ For the moth - er

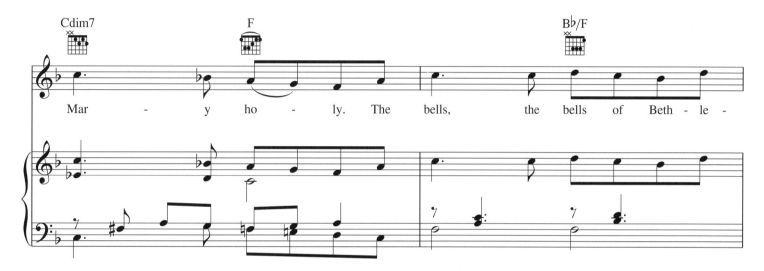

Mar - y ho - ly. The bells, the bells of Beth - le -

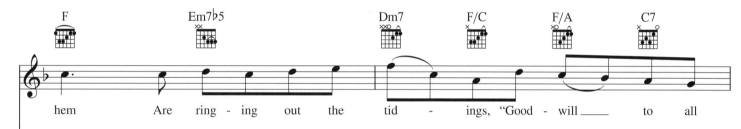

hem Are ring - ing out the tid - ings, "Good - will ____ to all

men!"

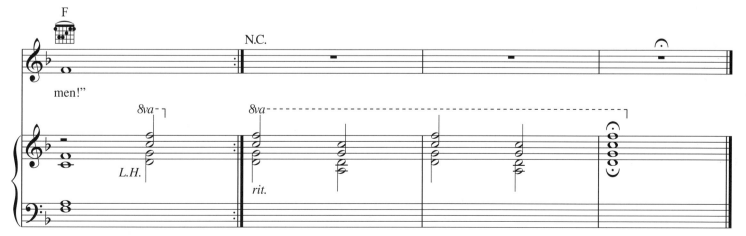

THE BABE OF BETHLEHEM

Traditional

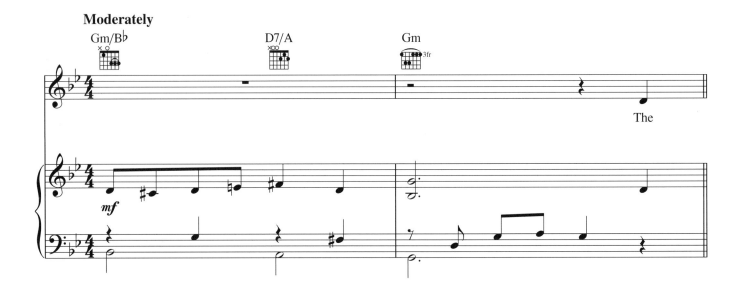

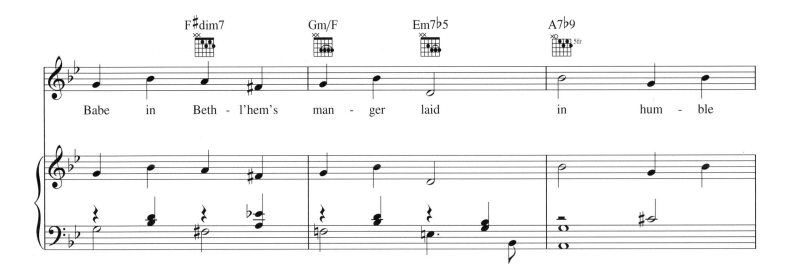

Babe in Beth - l'hem's man - ger laid in hum - ble

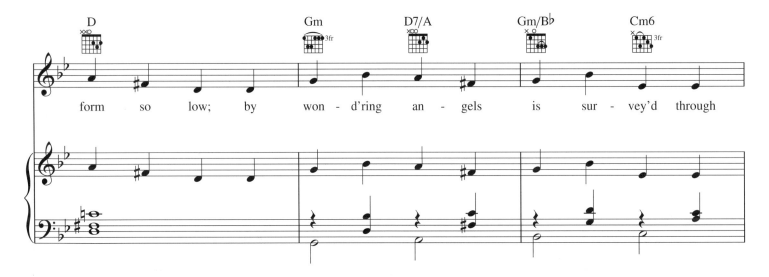

form so low; by won - d'ring an - gels is sur - vey'd through

A BABY IN THE CRADLE

By D.G. CORNER

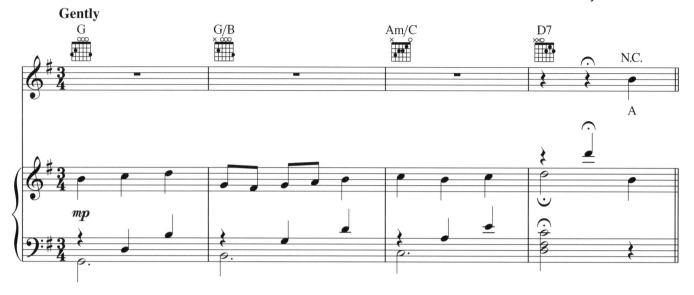

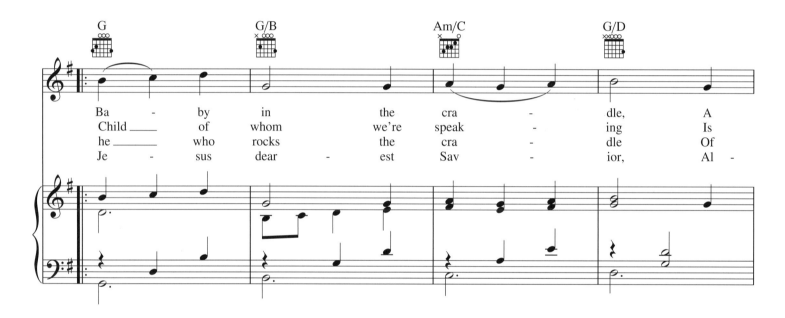

Ba — by in the cra — dle, A
Child ___ of whom we're speak — ing Is
he ___ who rocks the cra — dle Of
Je — sus dear — est Sav — ior, Al —

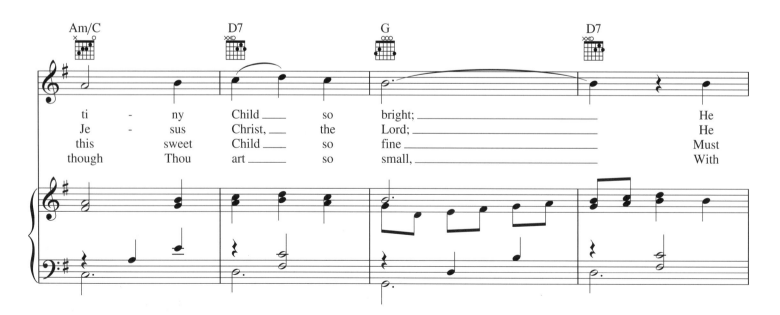

ti — ny Child ___ so bright; ___ He
Je — sus Christ, ___ the Lord; ___ He
this sweet Child ___ so fine ___ Must
though Thou art ___ so small, ___ With

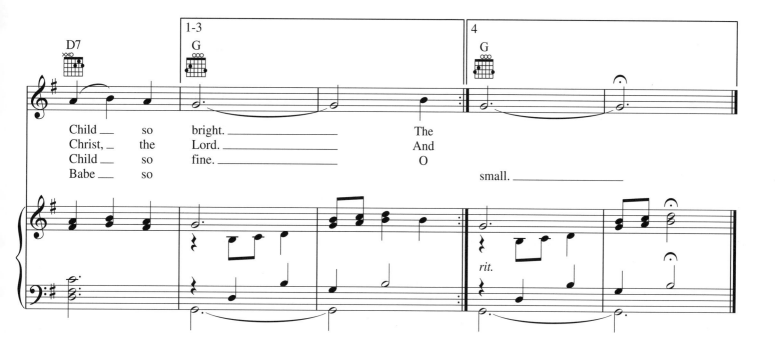

BESIDE THY CRADLE HERE I STAND

Words by PAUL GERHARDT
Translated by REV. J. TROUTBECK
Music from the *Geistliche Gesangbuch*

Slowly, with feeling

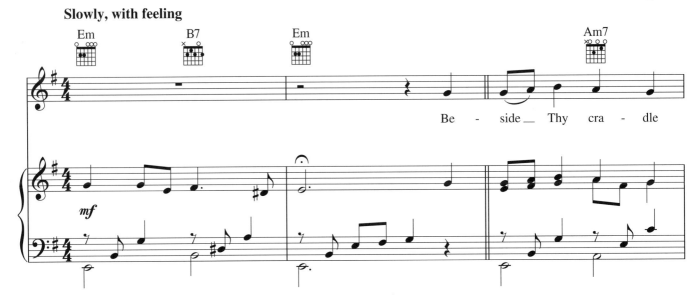

Be- side__ Thy cra- dle

here I stand, O_____ Thou that ev- er_____

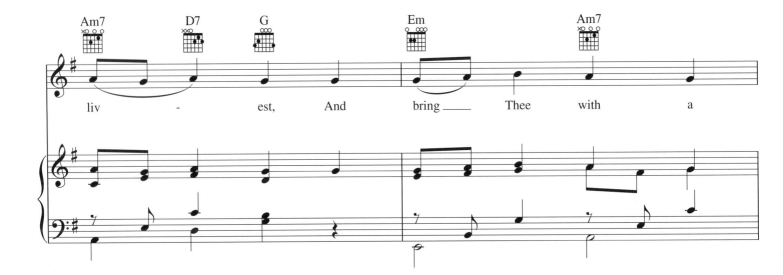

liv - est, And bring_____ Thee with a

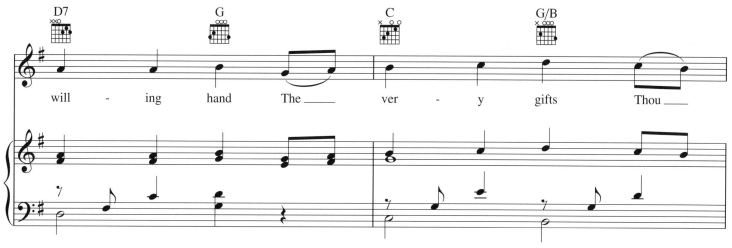

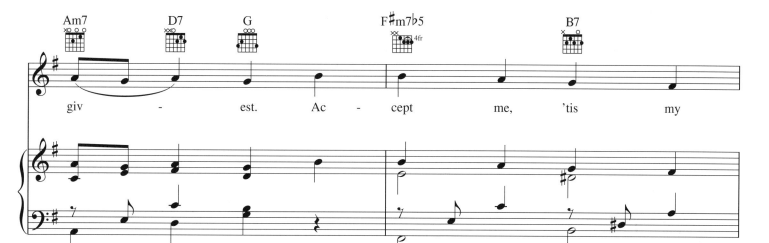

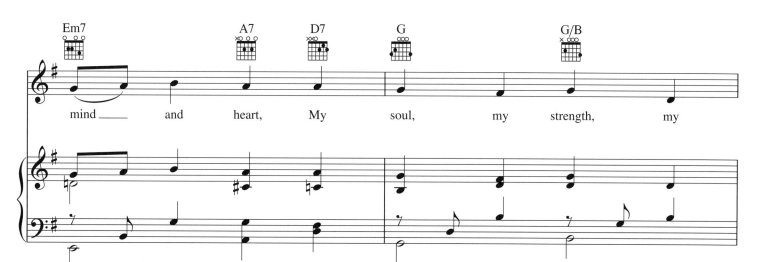

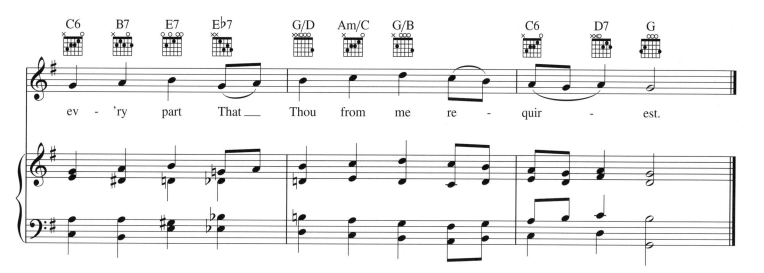

THE BIRTHDAY OF A KING

Words and Music by
WILLIAM H. NEIDLINGER

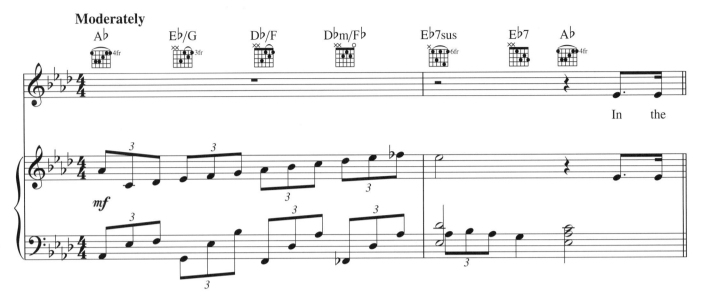

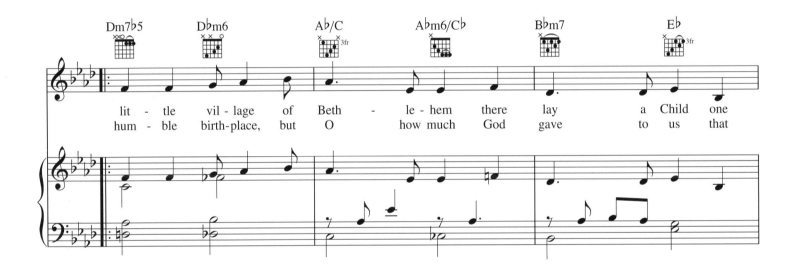

THE BOAR'S HEAD CAROL

Traditional English

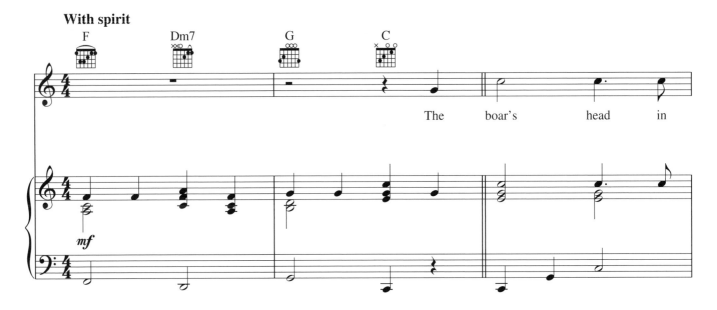

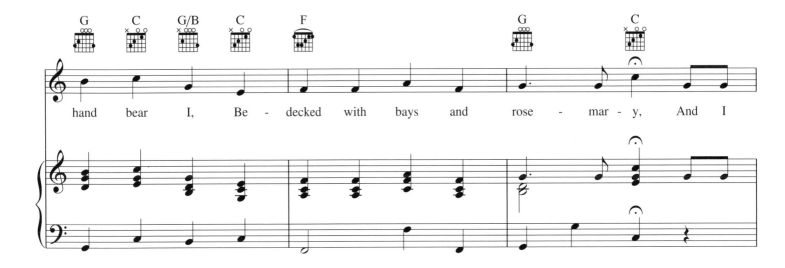

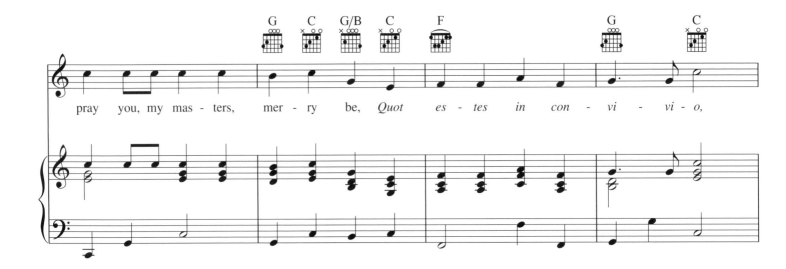

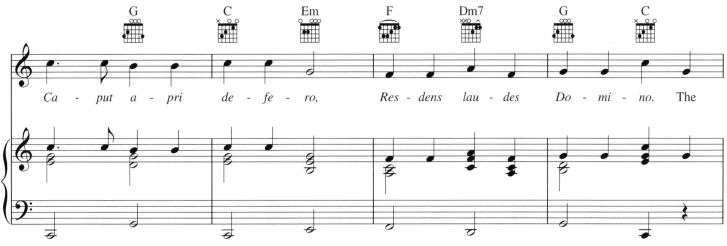

Ca - put a - pri de - fe - ro, Res - dens lau - des Do - mi - no. The

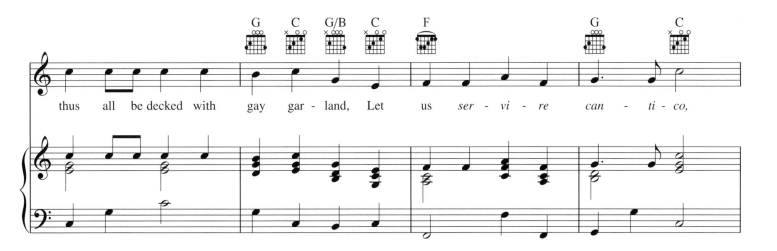

boar's head I un - der - stand, The fin - est dish in all the land. Which is

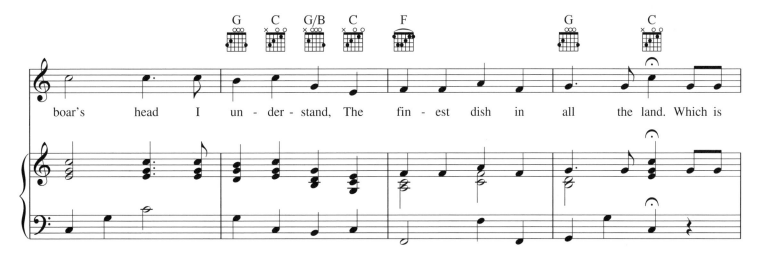

thus all be decked with gay gar - land, Let us *ser - vi - re can - ti - co,*

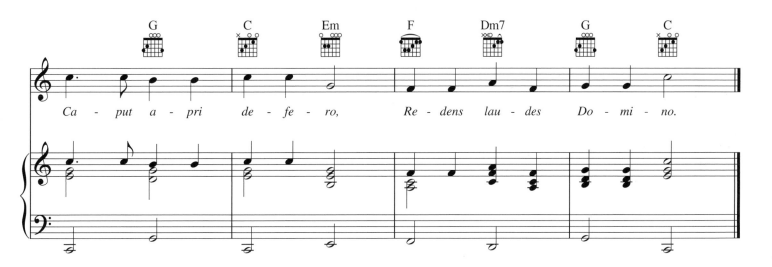

Ca - put a - pri de - fe - ro, *Re - dens lau - des Do - mi - no.*

A BOY IS BORN IN BETHLEHEM

Traditional

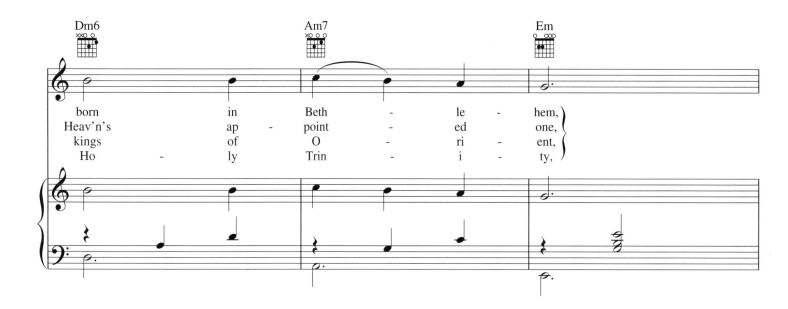

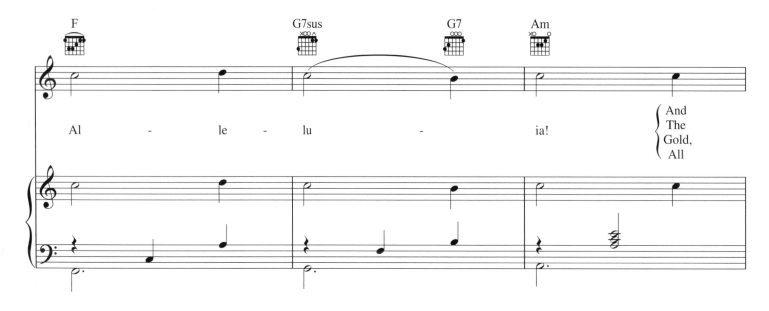

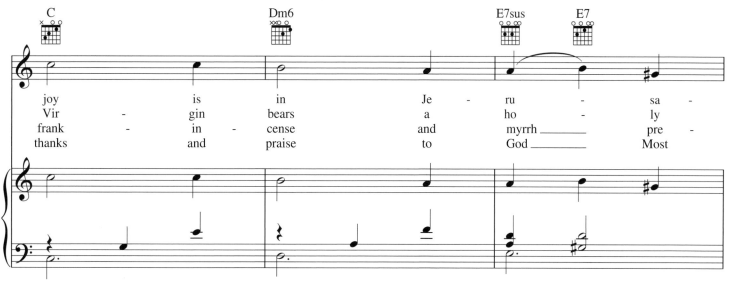

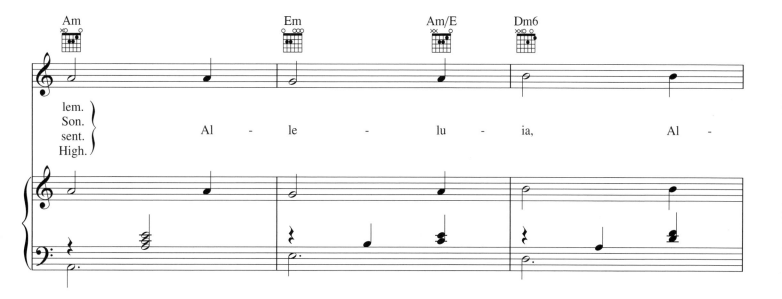

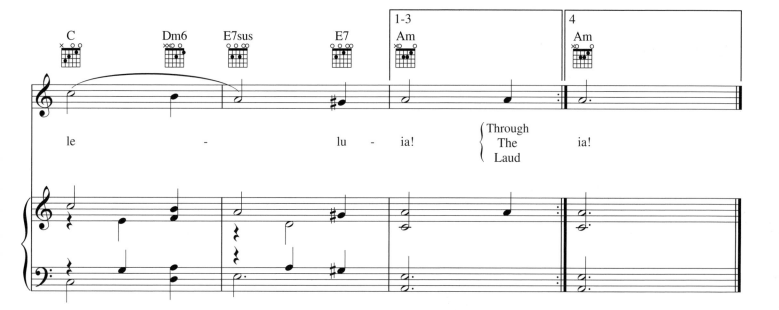

BREAK FORTH, O BEAUTEOUS, HEAVENLY LIGHT

Words by JOHANN RIST
Translated by REV. J. TROUTBECK
Melody by JOHANN SCHOP
Arranged by J.S. BACH

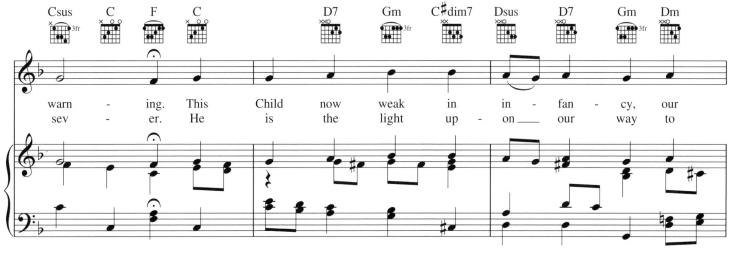

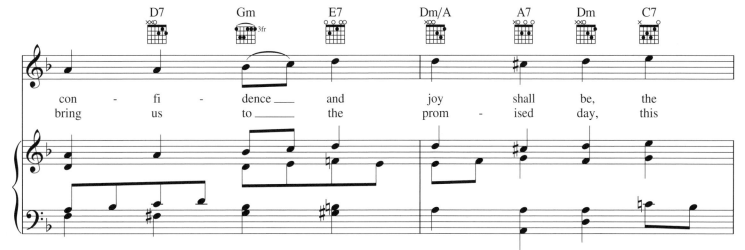

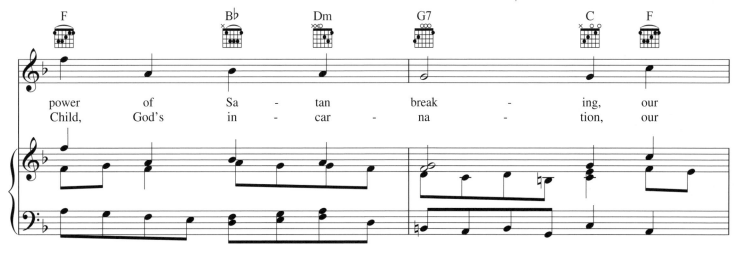

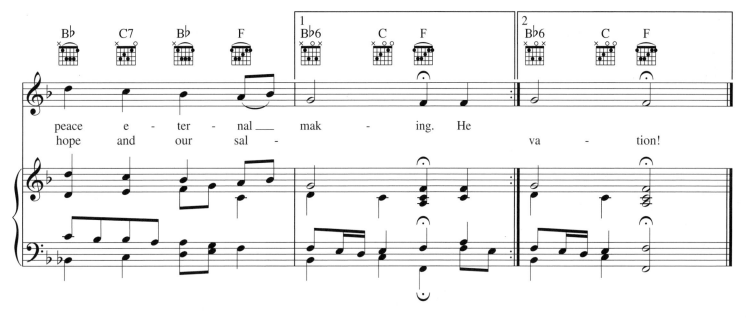

BRING A TORCH, JEANNETTE, ISABELLA

17th Century French Provençal Carol

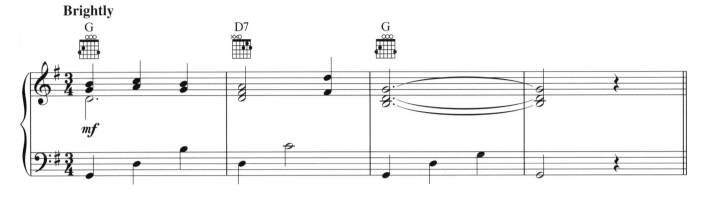

Bring a torch, ___ Jean - nette, Is - a - bel - la,
Has - ten now, ___ good folk of the vil - lage,

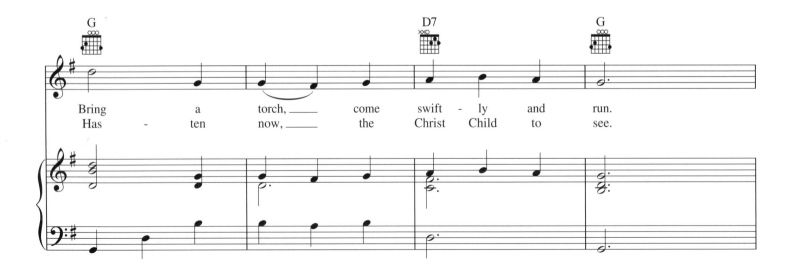

Bring a torch, ___ come swift - ly and run.
Has - ten now, ___ come the Christ Child to see.

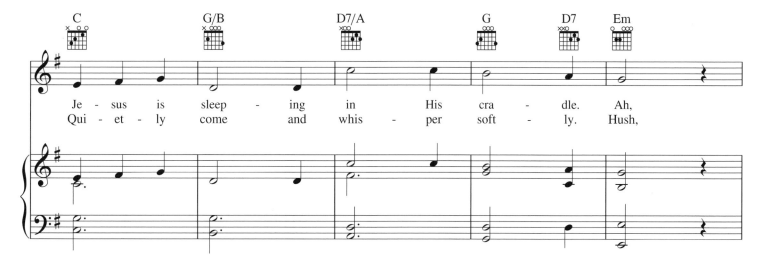

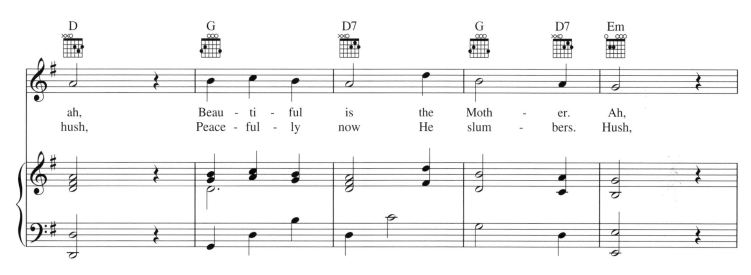

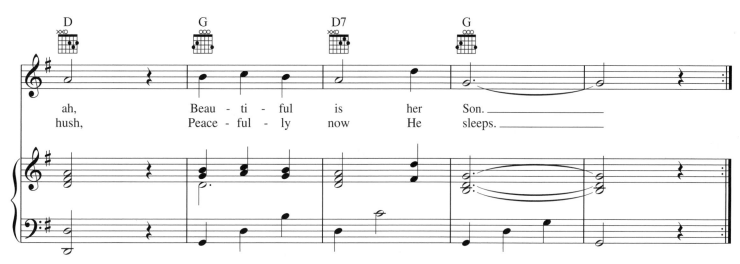

CAROL OF THE BELLS

Ukrainian Christmas Carol

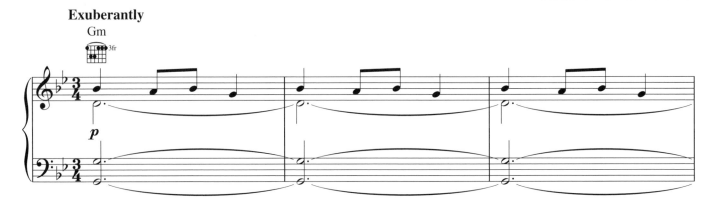

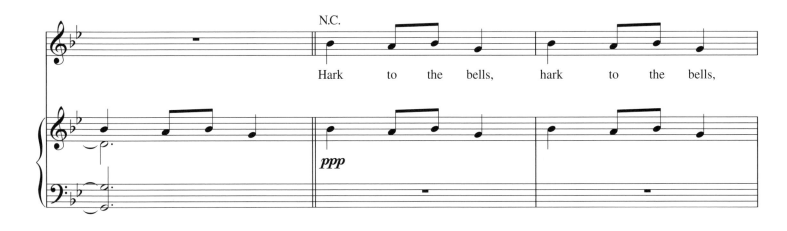

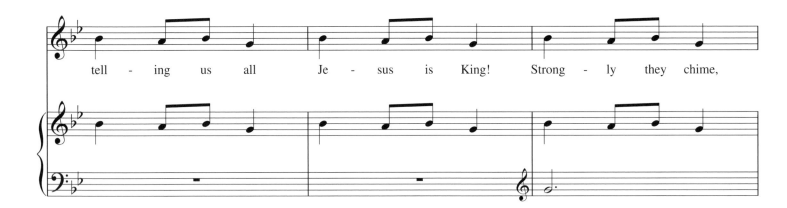

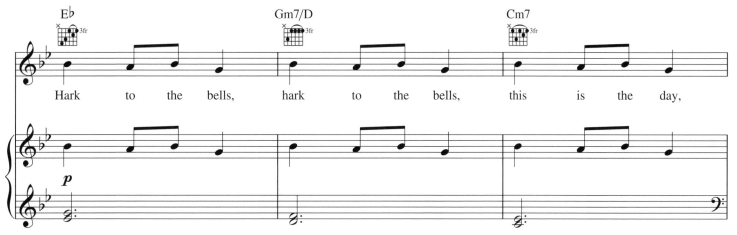

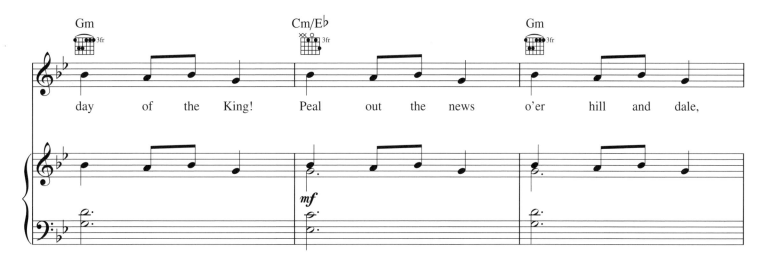

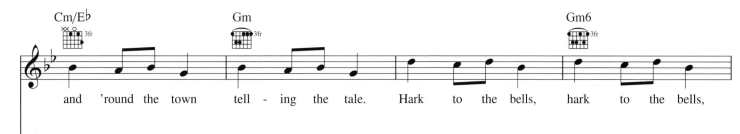

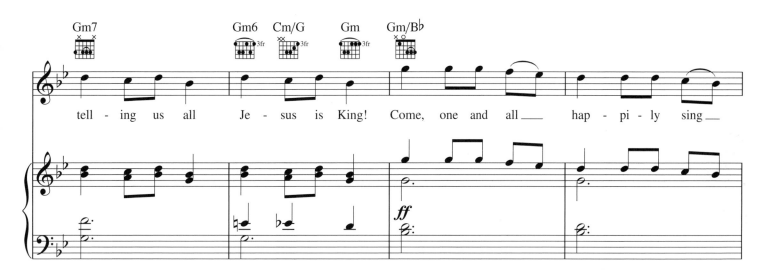

songs of good will, __ O let them sing! Ring, _____ sil - v'ry bells,

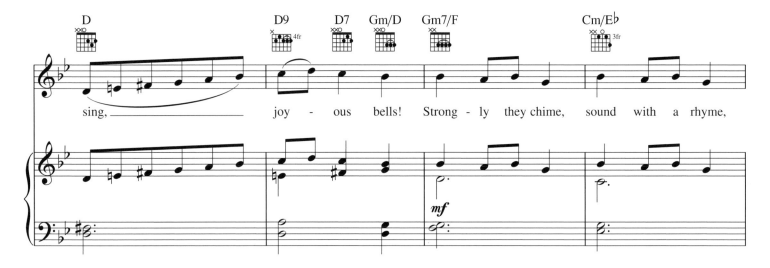

sing, _____ joy - ous bells! Strong - ly they chime, sound with a rhyme,

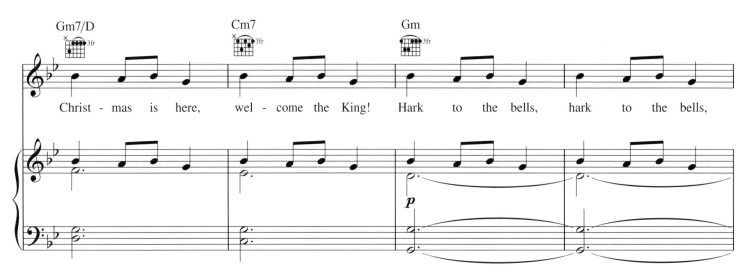

Christ - mas is here, wel - come the King! Hark to the bells, hark to the bells,

tell - ing us all Je - sus is King! Ring! Ring! __ bells. _____

A CHILD IS BORN IN BETHLEHEM

14th-Century Latin Text adapted by
NICOLAI F.S. GRUNDTVIG
Traditional Danish Melody

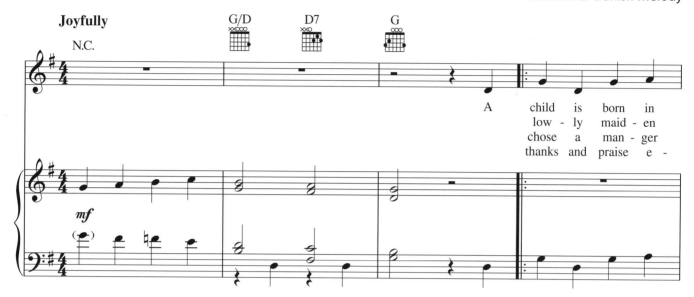

A child is born in
lowly maiden chose a manger
thanks and praise e-

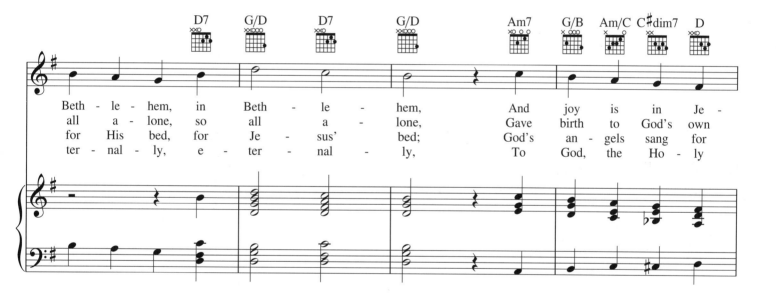

Beth - le - hem, in Beth - le - hem, And joy is in Je -
all a - lone, so all a - lone, Gave birth to God's own
for His bed, for Je - sus' bed; God's an - gels sang for
ter - nal - ly, e - ter - nal - ly, To God, the Ho - ly

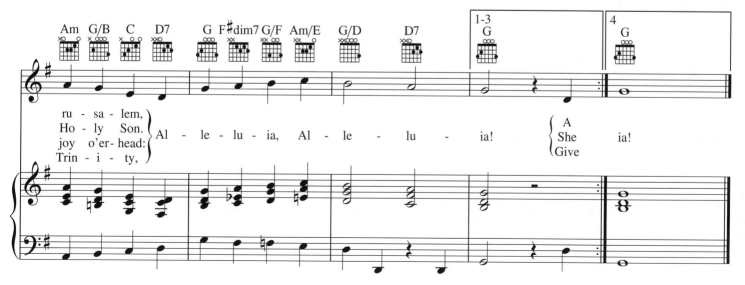

ru - sa - lem,
Ho - ly Son. Al - le - lu - ia, Al - le - lu - ia! A She ia!
joy o'er-head: Give
Trin - i - ty,

CAROL OF THE BIRDS

Traditional Catalonian Carol

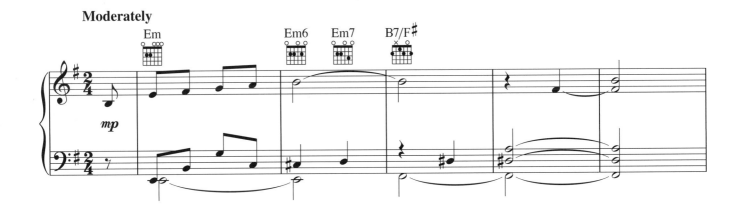

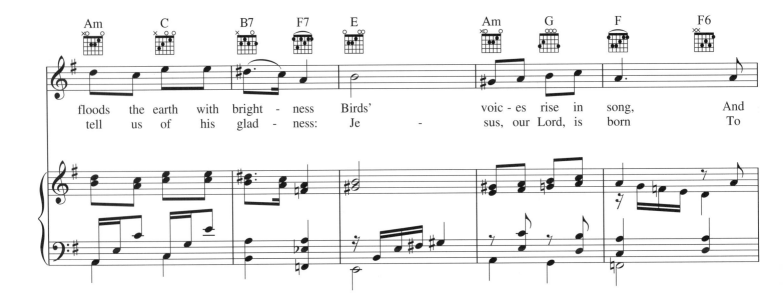

1. Up - on this ho - ly night, When God's great star ap - pears, And
2. night - in - gale is first To bring his song of cheer, And
3., 4. *(See additional lyrics)*

floods the earth with bright - ness Birds' voic - es rise in song, And
tell us of his glad - ness: Je - sus, our Lord, is born To

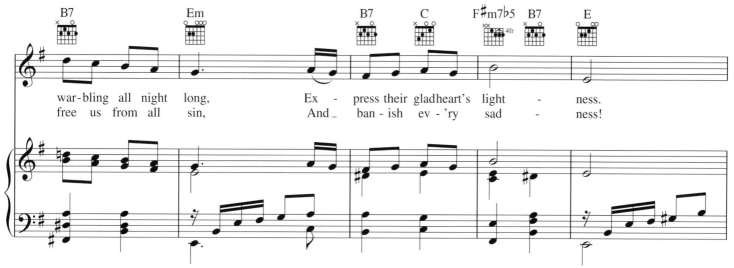

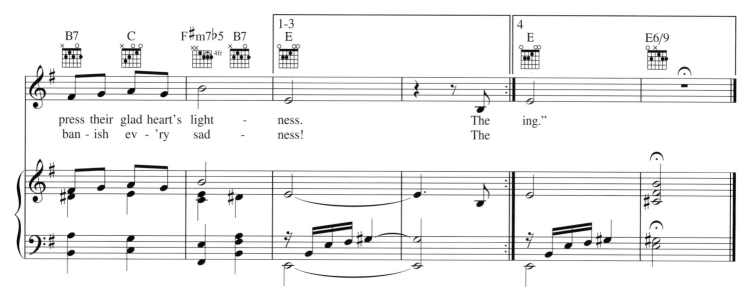

Additional Lyrics

3. The answ'ring Sparrow cries:
   "God comes to earth this day
   Amid the angels flying."
   Trilling in sweetest tones,
   The Finch his Lord now owns:
   "To Him be all thanksgiving."
   Trilling in sweetest tones,
   The Finch his Lord now owns:
   "To Him be all thanksgiving."

4. The Partridge adds his note:
   "To Bethlehem I'll fly,
   Where in the stall He's lying.
   There, near the manger blest,
   I'll build myself a nest,
   And sing my love undying.
   There, near the manger blest,
   I'll build myself a nest,
   And sing my love undying."

CHILD JESUS CAME TO EARTH THIS DAY

Traditional Carol

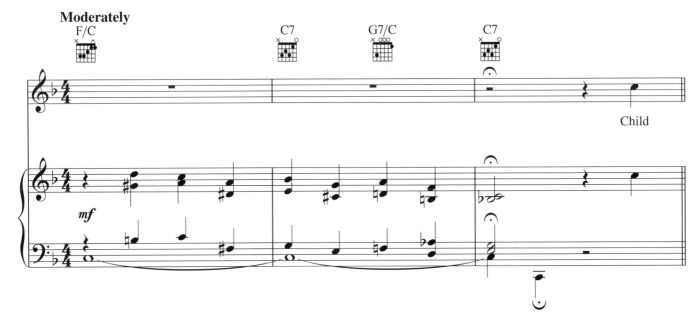

Child

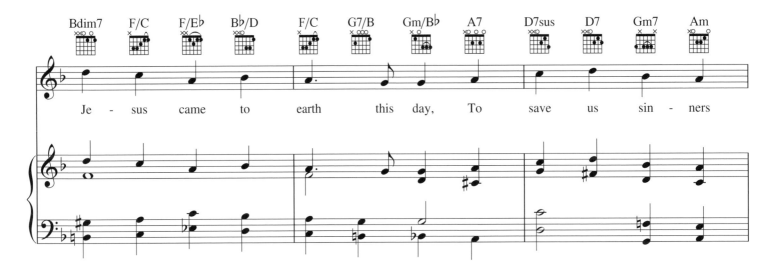

Je - sus came to earth this day, To save us sin - ners

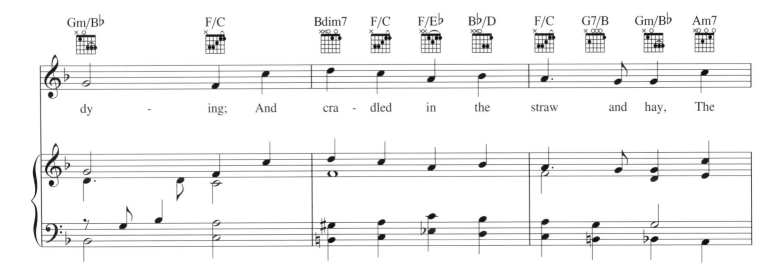

dy - ing; And cra - dled in the straw and hay, The

CHILDREN, GO WHERE I SEND THEE

Traditional Spiritual

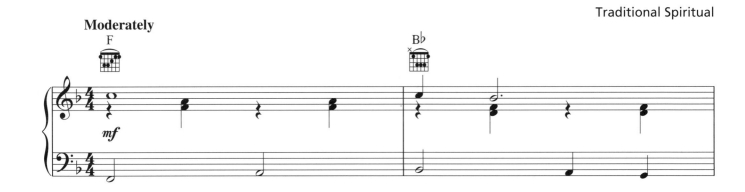

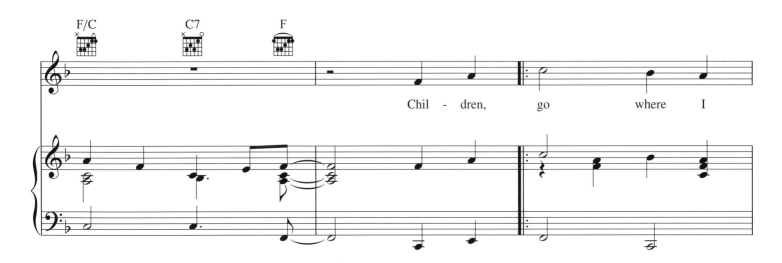

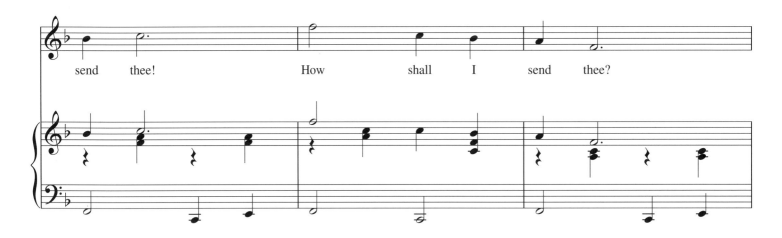

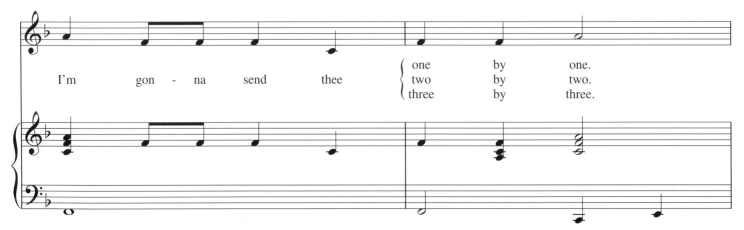

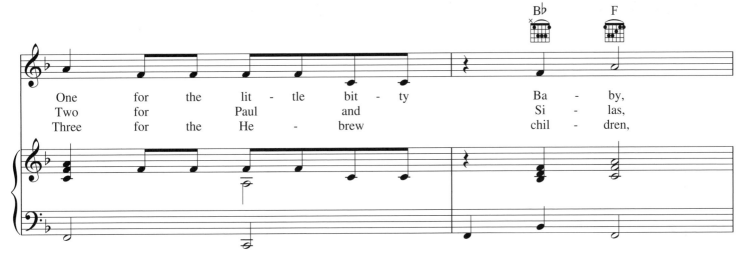

One for the lit - tle bit - ty Ba - by,
Two for Paul and Si - las,
Three for the He - brew chil - dren,

one for the lit - tle bit - ty Ba - by.
two for Paul and Si - las.
three for the He - brew chil - dren.

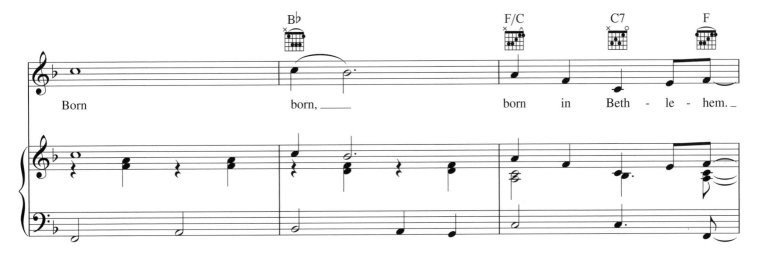

Born born, _____ born in Beth - le - hem. _

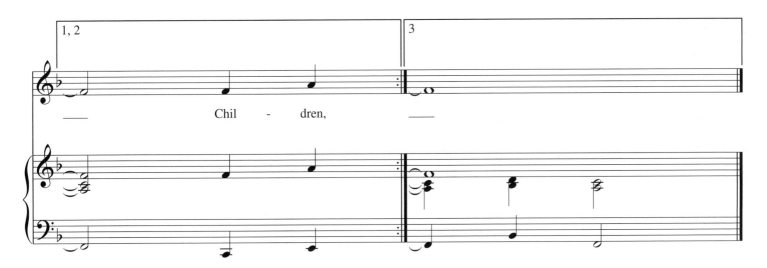

Chil - dren, _____

CHRIST IS BORN THIS EVENING

Traditional

Not too fast

Christ is born this
Shep - herds, has - ten

eve - ning,
yon - der,
Let us go re - joic - ing!
Where the Babe most ho - ly,

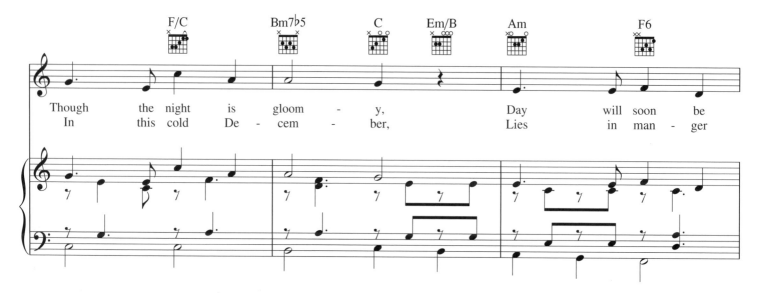

Though the night is gloom - y,
In this cold De - cem - ber,
Day will soon be
Lies in man - ger

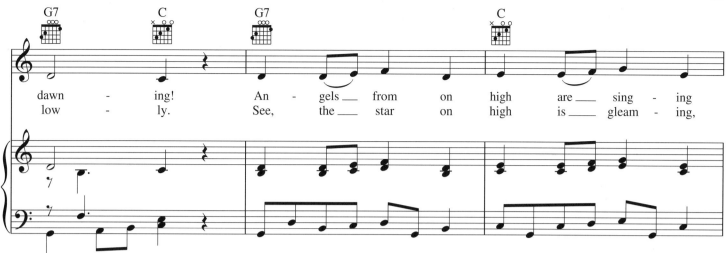

dawn - ing! An - gels __ from on high are __ sing - ing
low - ly. See, the __ star on high is __ gleam - ing,

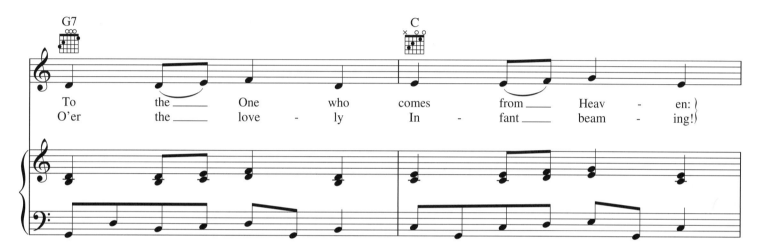

To the __ One who comes from __ Heav - en: ⎰
O'er the __ love - ly In - fant __ beam - ing! ⎱

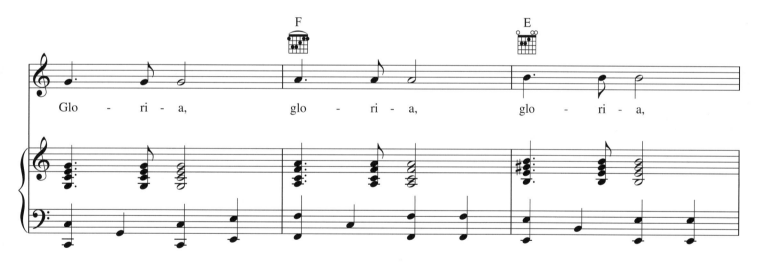

Glo - ri - a, glo - ri - a, glo - ri - a,

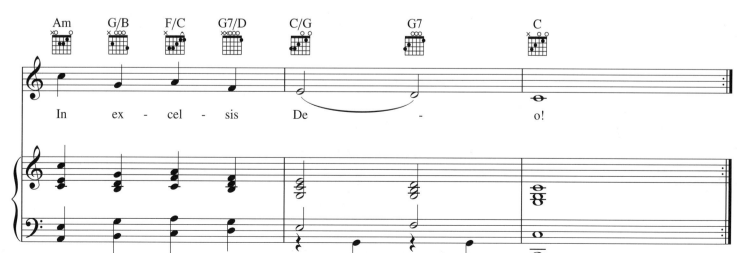

In ex - cel - sis De - o!

CHRIST WAS BORN
ON CHRISTMAS DAY

Traditional

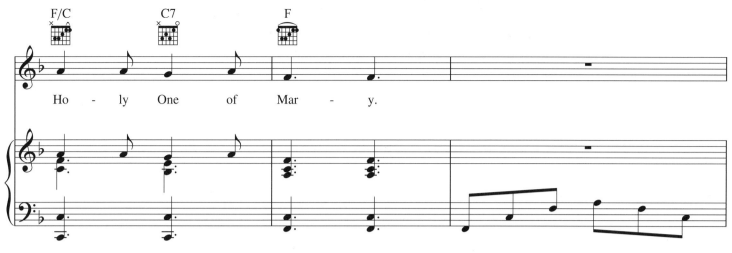

Ho - ly One of Mar - y.

Christ was born on Christ - mas day, Wreath the hol - ly,

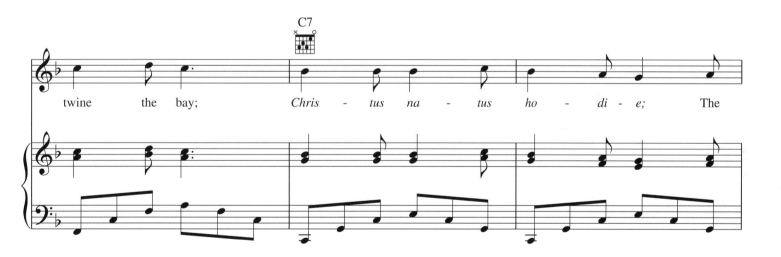

twine the bay; *Chris - tus na - tus ho - di - e;* The

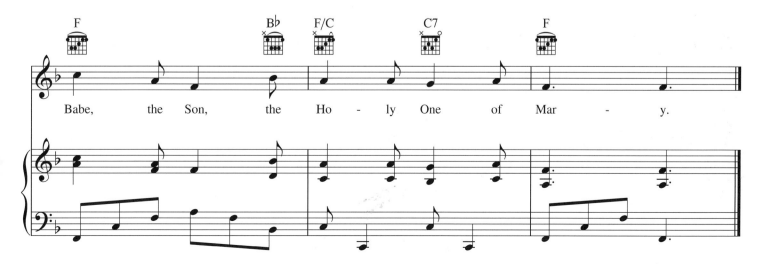

Babe, the Son, the Ho - ly One of Mar - y.

CHRISTIANS, AWAKE!
SALUTE THE HAPPY MORN

Words by JOHN BYROM
Music by JOHN WAINWRIGHT

CHRISTMAS COMES ANEW
(Noël nouvelet)

Traditional French Carol

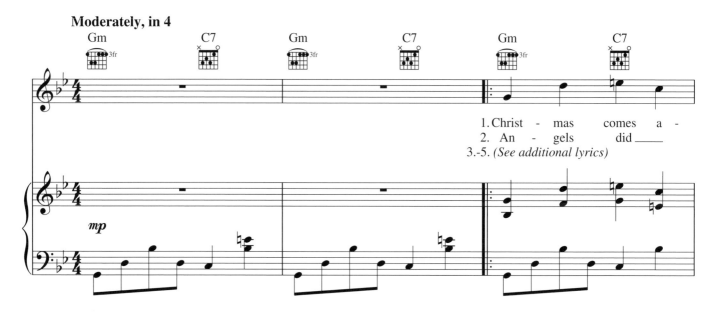

1. Christ - mas comes a -
2. An - gels did _____
3.-5. *(See additional lyrics)*

new, O let us _____ sing No - ël!
say, "O shep - herds _____ come and see,

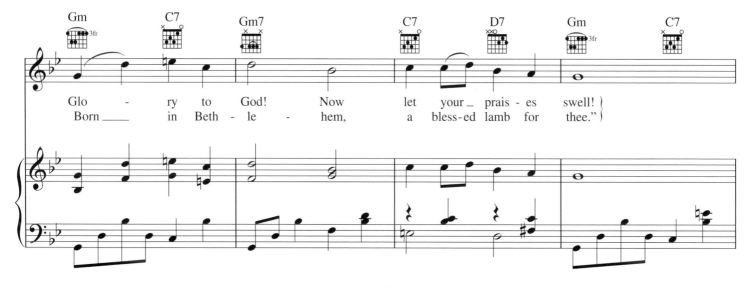

Glo - ry to God! Now let your _ prais - es swell!)
Born _____ in Beth - le - hem, a bless - ed lamb for thee.")

Chorus

Sing we No-ël for Christ, the new-born King, No-ël!

Sing we No-ël for Christ, the new-born King.

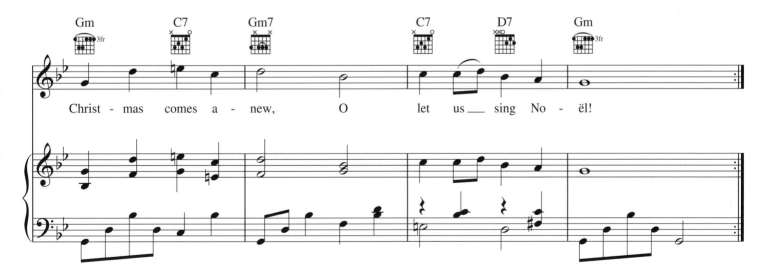

Christ-mas comes a-new, O let us sing No-ël!

Additional Lyrics

3. In the manger bed,
   The shepherds found the child;
   Joseph was there,
   And the Mother Mary mild.
   Chorus

4. Soon came the kings
   From following the star,
   Bearing costly gifts
   From Eastern lands afar.
   Chorus

5. Brought to Him gold
   And incense of great price;
   Then the stable bar
   Resembled paradise.
   Chorus

CHRISTMAS GREETING

Traditional

Brightly

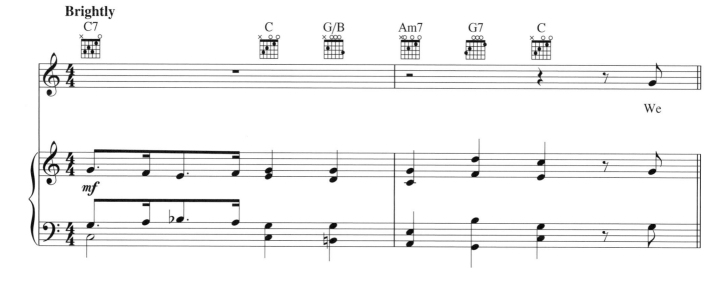

We

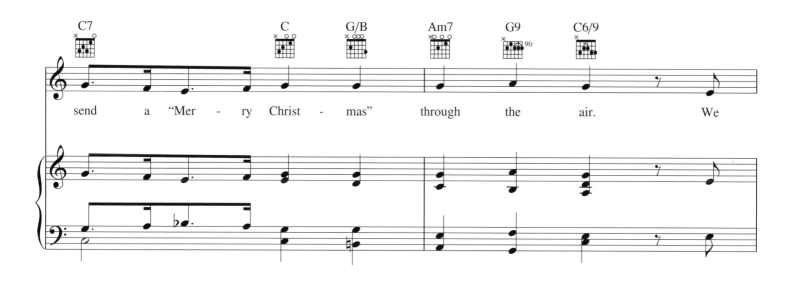

send a "Mer - ry Christ - mas" through the air. We

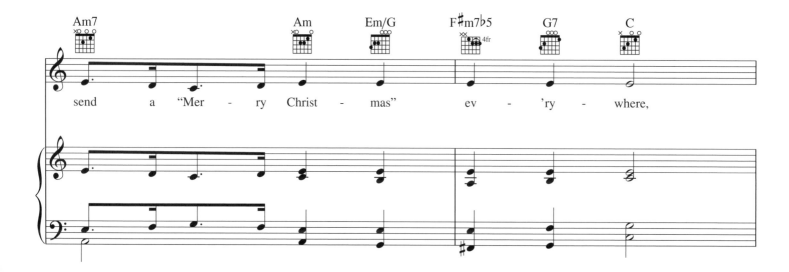

send a "Mer - ry Christ - mas" ev - 'ry - where,

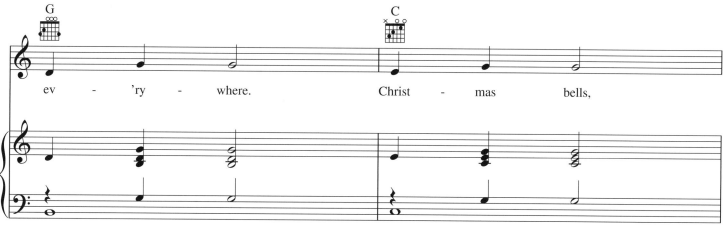

ev - 'ry - where. Christ - mas bells,

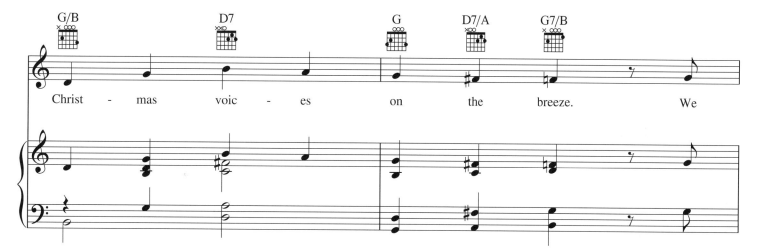

Christ - mas voic - es on the breeze. We

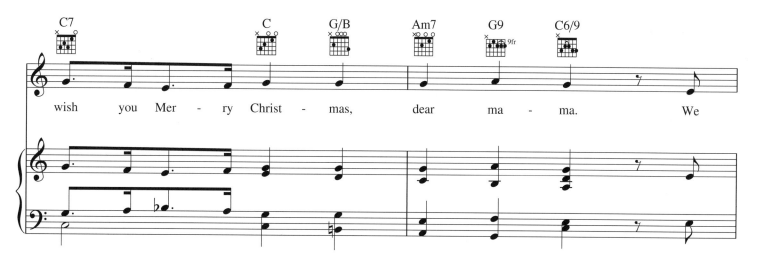

wish you Mer - ry Christ - mas, dear ma - ma. We

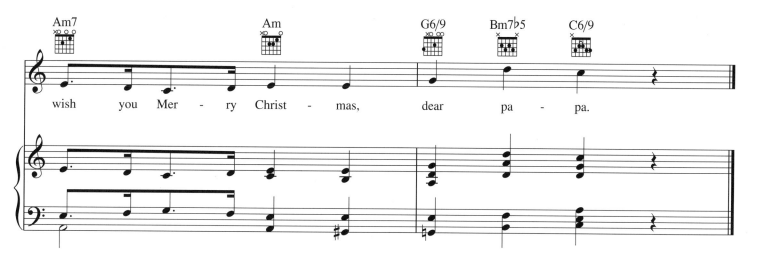

wish you Mer - ry Christ - mas, dear pa - pa.

THE CHRISTMAS TREE WITH ITS CANDLES GLEAMING

Traditional Czech Text
Traditional Bohemian-Czech Tune

The Christ-mas tree, with its can-dles
stand 'round the glit-t'ring
heart _____ you of-fer

gleam-ing, A glow is kin-dling in all our _ hearts. It speaks of God's _____ pure love-light
treas-ure; Their eyes are spar-kling, their spir-its _ bright. O sweet re-mind-er of love's full
bless-ing, For ev-'ry par-ent as well as _ child. For young and old, _____ your bea-cons

stream-ing; It brings us hope, _____ and joy im-parts. The chil-dren
meas-ure, Our shin-ing sym-bol of heav'n-ly _ light! For ev-'ry
beck-'ning Lead us to Je-sus, _ sweet and _ mild.

COME, THOU LONG-EXPECTED JESUS

Words by CHARLES WESLEY
Music by ROWLAND HUGH PRICHARD

68

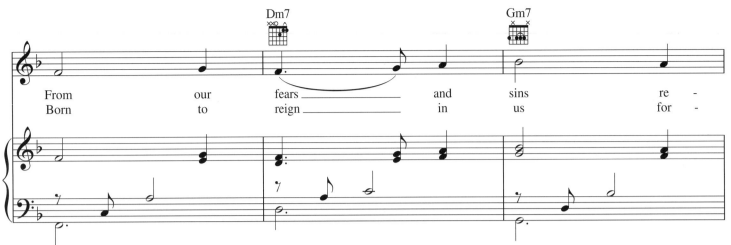

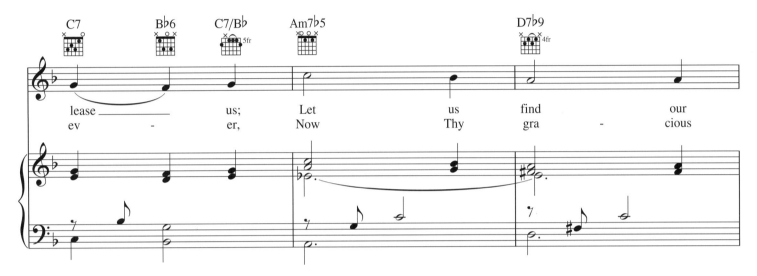

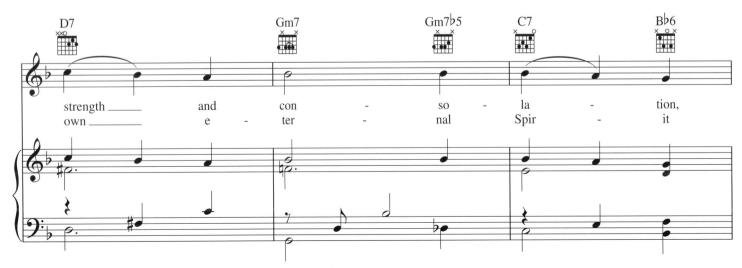

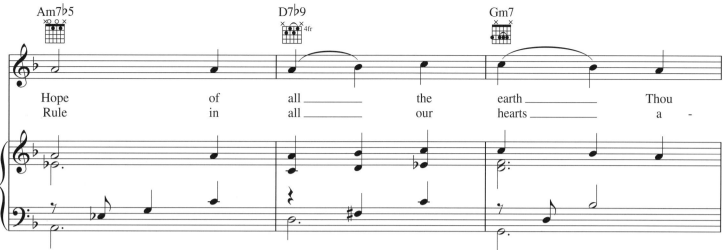

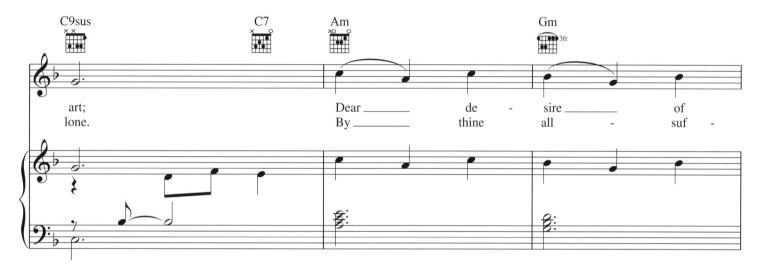

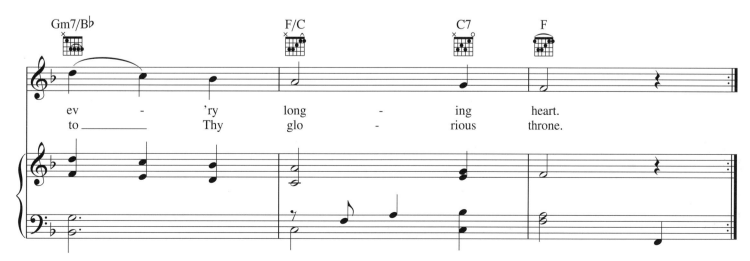

COME, HEAR THE WONDERFUL TIDINGS

Traditional Czech Text
Traditional Bohemian-Czech Tune

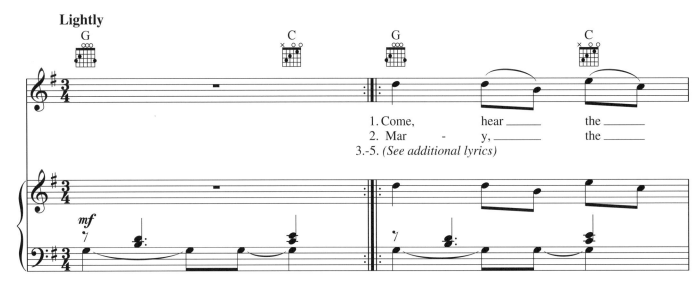

1. Come, hear the
2. Mar y, the

3.-5. *(See additional lyrics)*

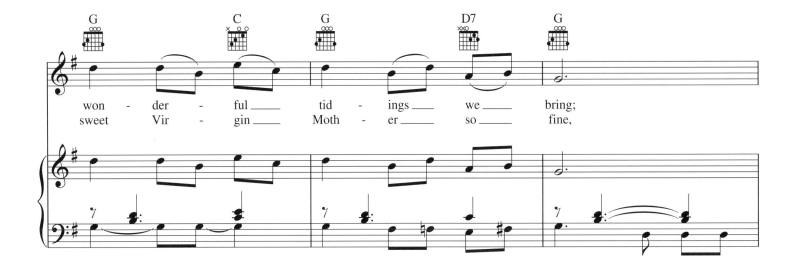

won - der - ful tid - ings we bring;
sweet Vir - gin Moth - er so fine,

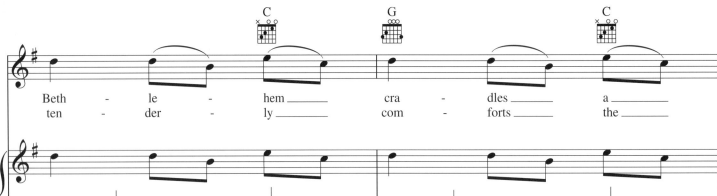

Beth - le - hem cra - dles a
ten - der - ly com - forts the

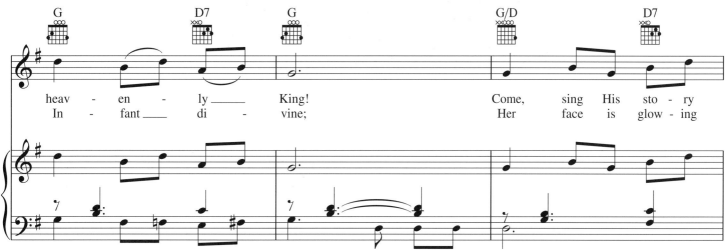

heav - en - ly ____ King! Come, sing His sto - ry
In - fant ____ di - vine; Her face is glow - ing

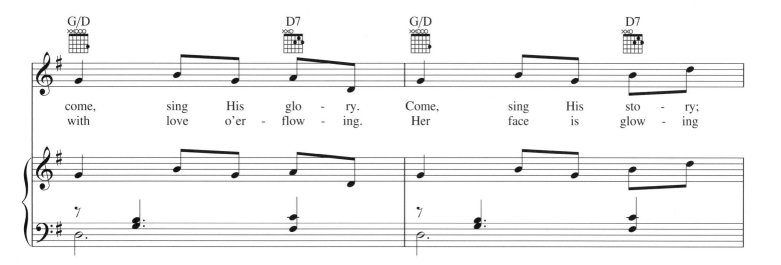

come, sing His glo - ry. Come, sing His sto - ry;
with love o'er - flow - ing. Her face is glow - ing

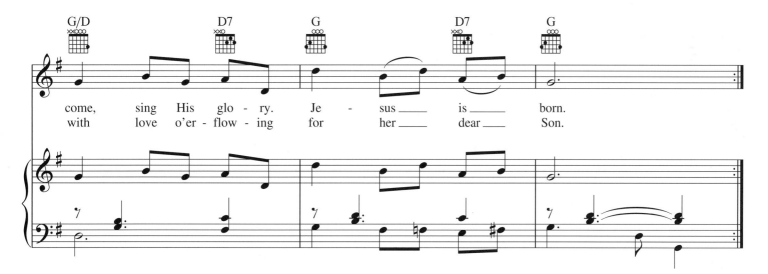

come, sing His glo - ry. Je - sus ____ is ____ born.
with love o'er - flow - ing for her ____ dear ____ Son.

Additional Lyrics

3. Angels from Heaven are singing His praise
   Shepherds in wonder and joy on Him gaze;
   Bringing Him honor, presents they offer,
   Bringing Him honor, presents they offer,
   Jesus their Lord.

4. Over the desert shines God's radiant star
   Guiding the kings who come journeying far
   Here to discover, in lowly manger,
   Here to discover, in lowly manger,
   Wisdom divine.

5. Prophecy now is fulfilled in this hour;
   Darkness is scattered by Heaven's great pow'r
   God's glory beaming, o'er Jesus streaming,
   God's glory beaming, o'er Jesus streaming,
   Shines through the night.

COVENTRY CAROL

Words by ROBERT CROO
Traditional English Melody

Tenderly

1. Lul - lay, thou lit - tle ti - ny Child, by, by, lul -
2. O sis - ters too, how may we do for to pre -
3., 4. *(See additional lyrics)*

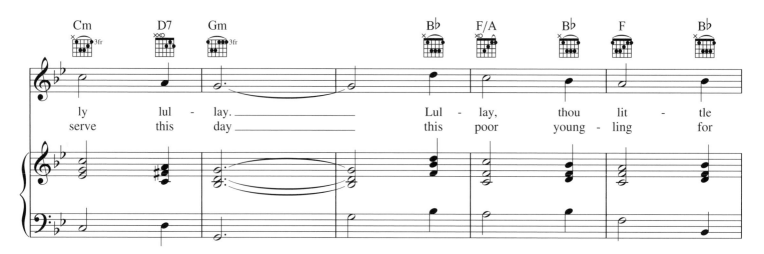

ly lul - lay._____ Lul - lay, thou lit - tle
serve this day_____ this poor young - ling for

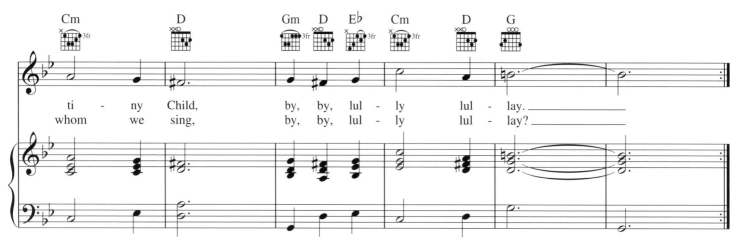

ti - ny Child, by, by, lul - ly lul - lay._____
whom we sing, by, by, lul - ly lul - lay?_____

Additional Lyrics

3. Herod the king,
   In his raging,
   Charged he hath this day.
   His men of might,
   In his own sight,
   All young children to slay.

4. That woe is me,
   Poor child for thee!
   And ever morn and day,
   For thy parting
   Neither say nor sing
   By, by, lully lullay!

DANCE OF THE SUGAR PLUM FAIRY

By PYOTR IL'YICH TCHAIKOVSKY

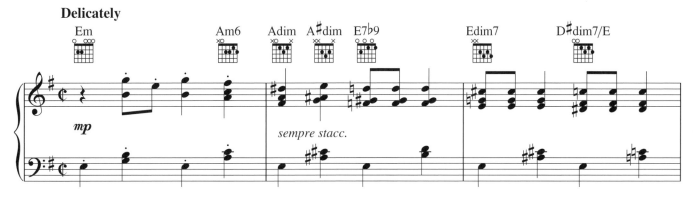

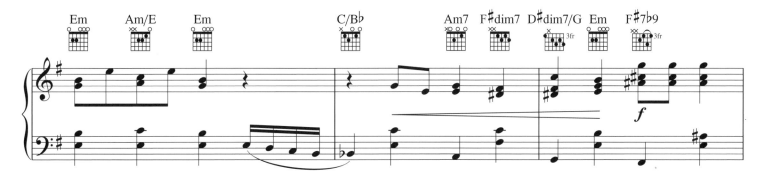

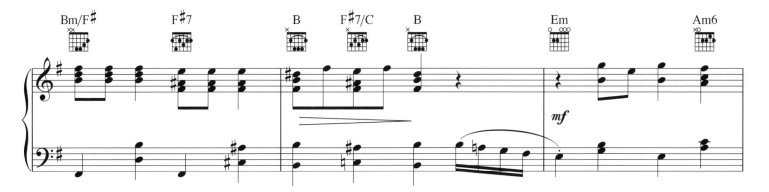

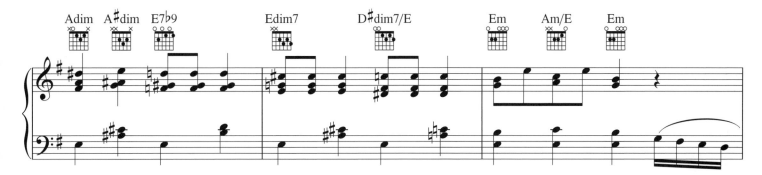

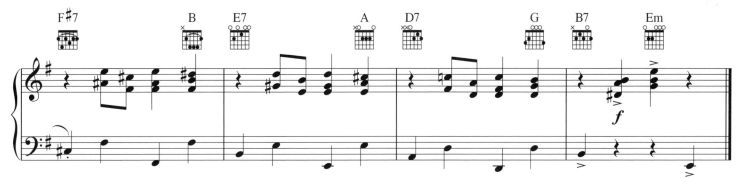

A DAY, BRIGHT DAY OF GLORY

Traditional

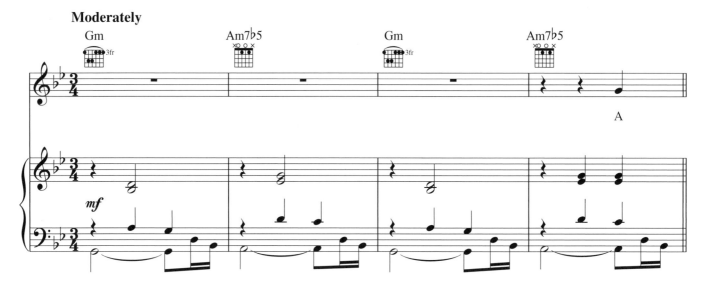

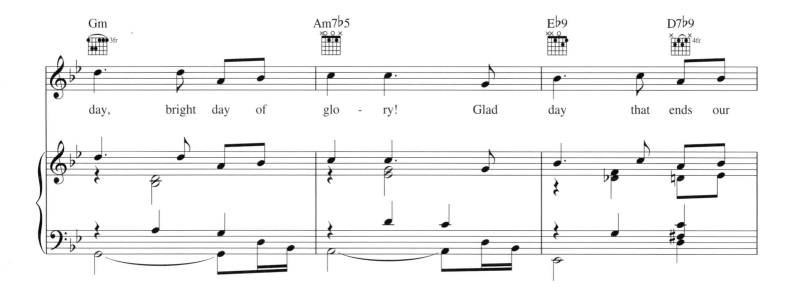

DECK THE HALL

Traditional Welsh Carol

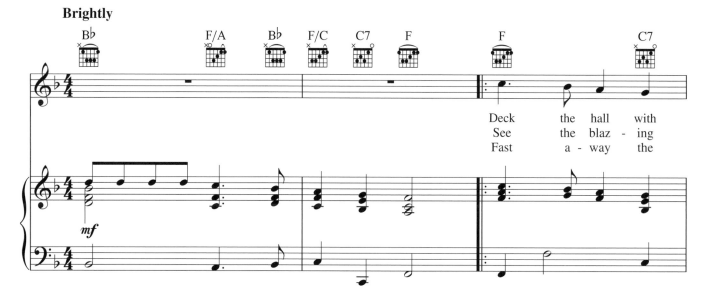

Brightly

Deck the hall with
See the blaz - ing
Fast a - way the

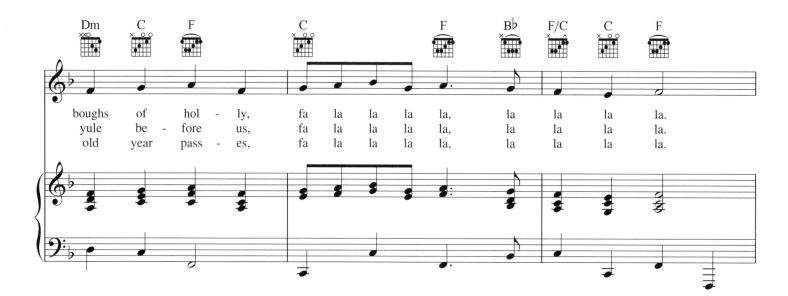

boughs of hol - ly, fa la la la la, la la la la.
yule be - fore us, fa la la la la, la la la la.
old year pass - es, fa la la la la, la la la la.

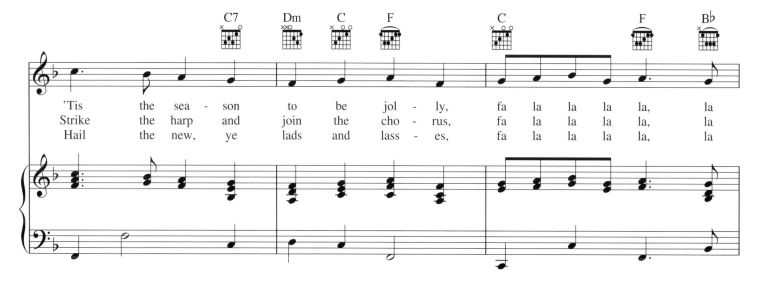

'Tis the sea - son to be jol - ly, fa la la la la, la
Strike the harp and join the cho - rus, fa la la la la, la
Hail the new, ye lads and lass - es, fa la la la la, la

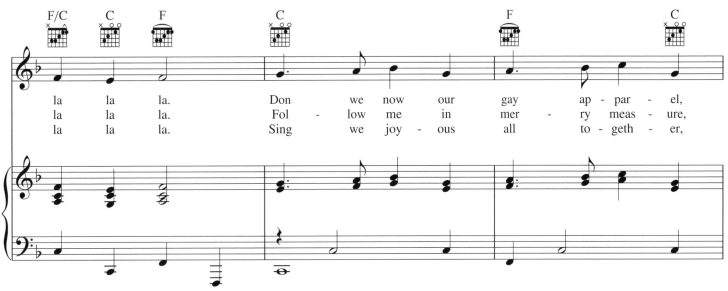

la la la. Don we now our gay ap- par- el,
la la la. Fol - low me in mer - ry meas - ure,
la la la. Sing we joy - ous all to- geth - er,

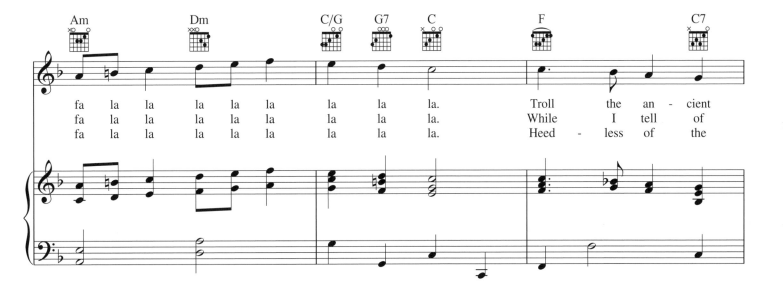

fa la la la la la la la la. Troll the an - cient
fa la la la la la la la la. While I tell of
fa la la la la la la la la. Heed - less of the

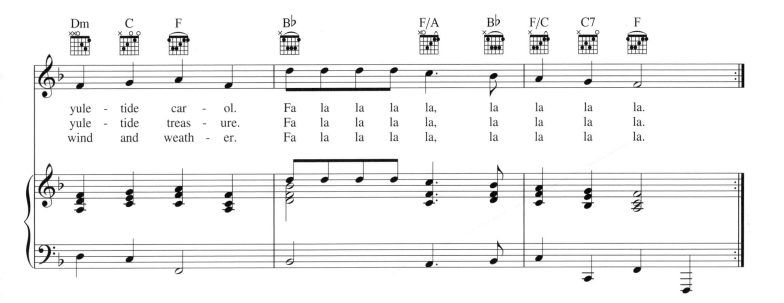

yule - tide car - ol. Fa la la la la, la la la la.
yule - tide treas - ure. Fa la la la la, la la la la.
wind and weath - er. Fa la la la la, la la la la.

DING DONG! MERRILY ON HIGH!

French Carol

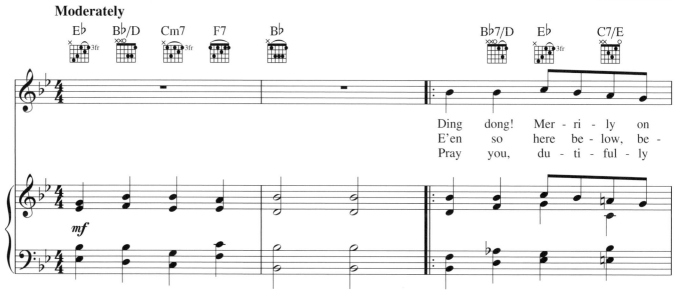

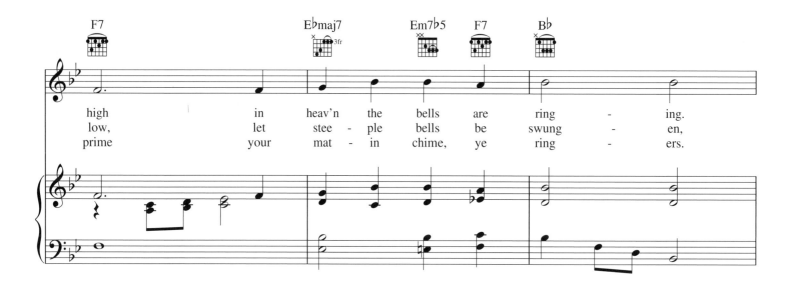

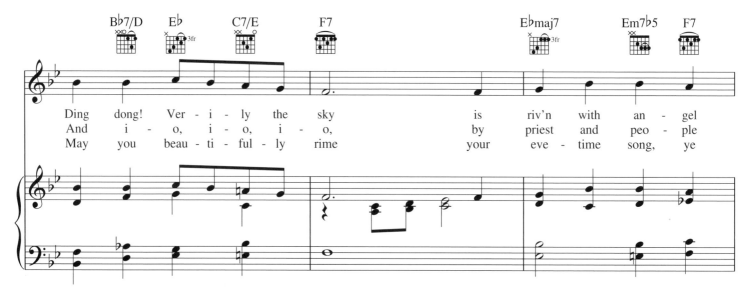

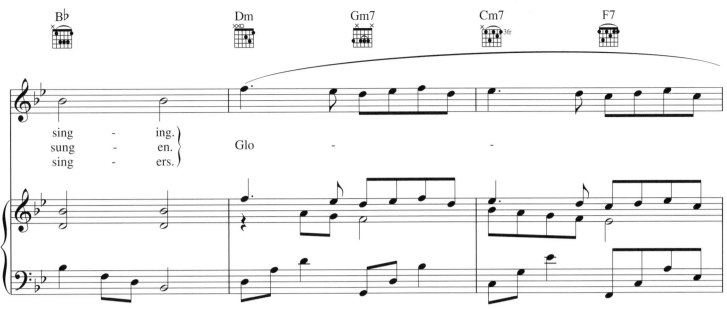

sing - ing.
sung - en. }
sing - ers. }   Glo - - -

- - -

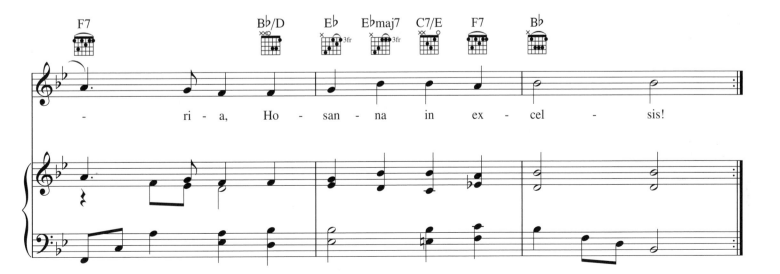

- ri - a, Ho - san - na in ex - cel - sis!

EVERYWHERE, EVERYWHERE, CHRISTMAS TONIGHT

By LEWIS H. REDNER
and PHILLIPS BROOKS

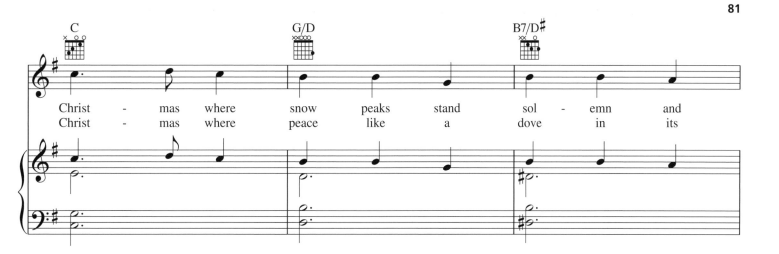

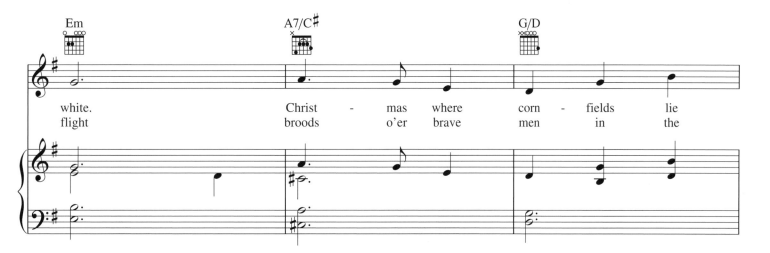

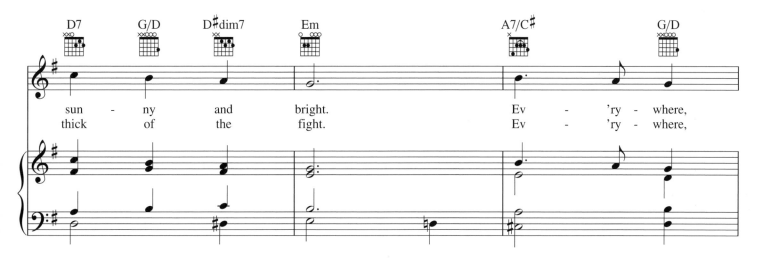

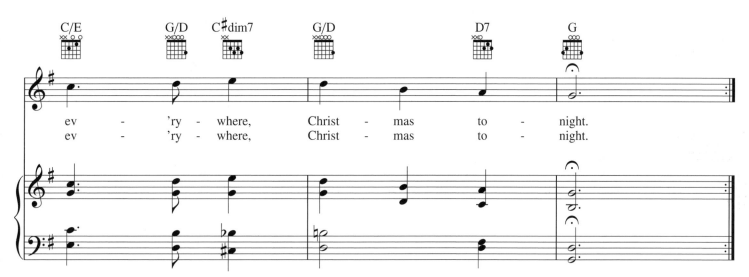

THE FIRST NOËL

17th Century English Carol
Music from W. Sandys' *Christmas Carols*

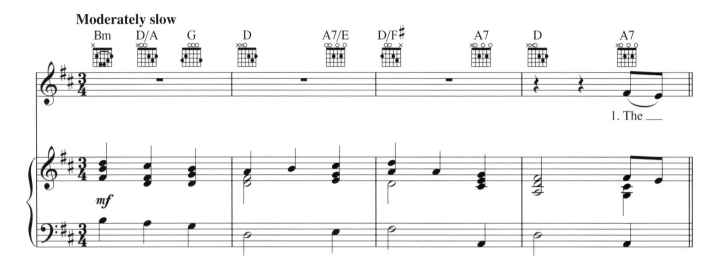

1. The __

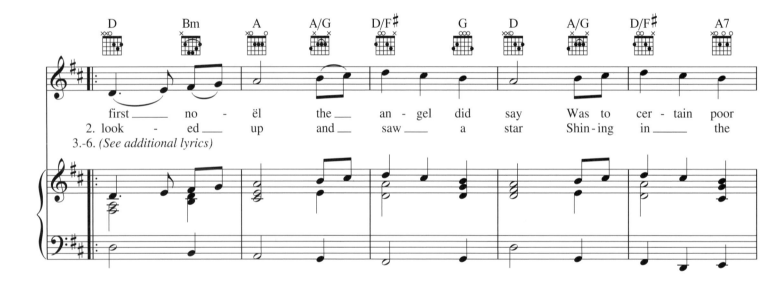

first __ no - ël the __ an - gel did say Was to cer - tain poor

2. look - ed __ up and __ saw __ a star Shin - ing in __ the

3.-6. *(See additional lyrics)*

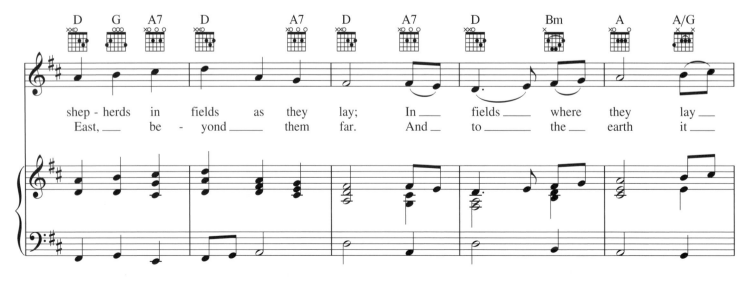

shep - herds in fields as they lay; In __ fields __ where they lay __

East, __ be - yond __ them far. And __ to __ the __ earth it __

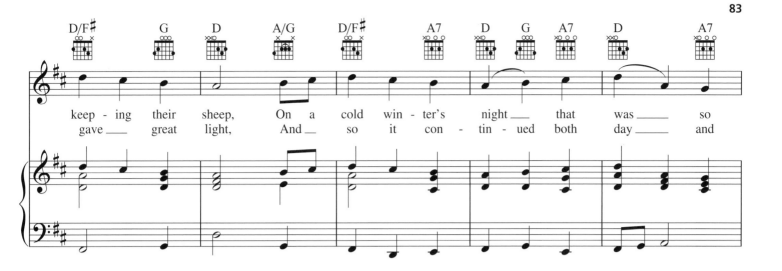

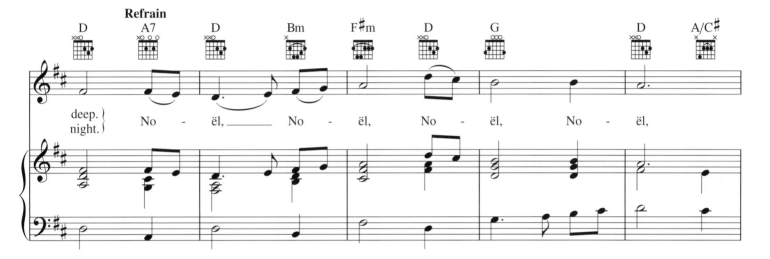

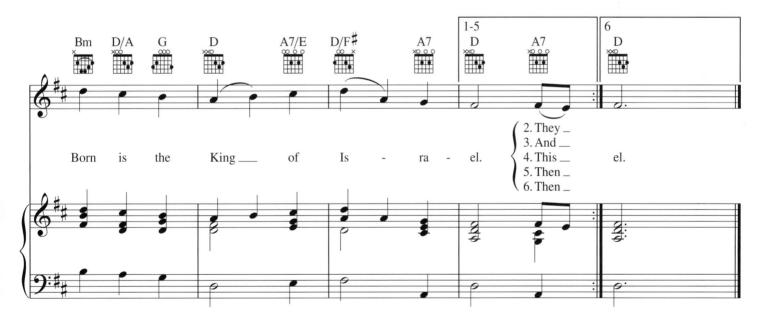

Additional Lyrics

3. And by the light of that same star,
   Three wise men came from country far.
   To seek for a King was their intent,
   And to follow the star wherever it went.
   Refrain

4. This star drew nigh to the northwest;
   O'er Bethlehem it took its rest.
   And there it did both stop and stay,
   Right over the place where Jesus lay.
   Refrain

5. Then entered in those wise men three,
   Full rev'rently upon their knee;
   And offered there in His presence,
   Their gold and myrrh and frankincense.
   Refrain

6. Then let us all with one accord
   Sing praises to our heav'nly Lord,
   That hath made heav'n and earth of naught,
   And with His blood mankind hath bought.
   Refrain

THE FRIENDLY BEASTS

Traditional English Carol

1. Je - sus our broth - er, kind and
2.-6. *(See additional lyrics)*

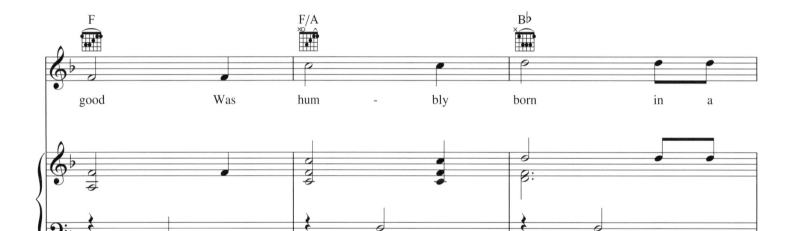

good Was hum - bly born in a

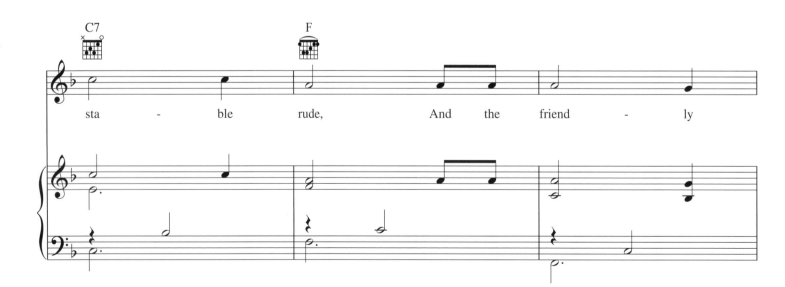

sta - ble rude, And the friend - ly

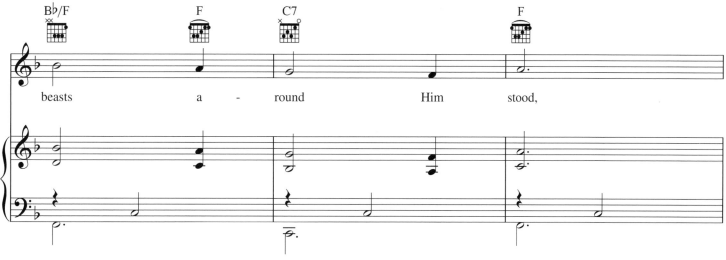

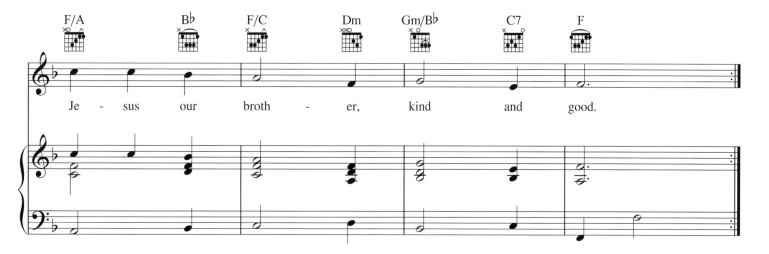

Additional Lyrics

2. "I," said the donkey, shaggy and brown,
"I carried His mother up hill and down;
I carried her safely to Bethlehem town."
"I," said the donkey, shaggy and brown.

3. "I," said the cow all white and red,
"I gave Him my manger for His bed;
I gave him my hay to pillow His head."
"I," said the cow all white and red.

4. "I," said the sheep with curly horn,
"I gave Him my wool for His blanket warm;
He wore my coat on Christmas morn."
"I," said the sheep with curly horn.

5. "I," said the dove from the rafters high,
"I cooed Him to sleep so He would not cry;
We cooed Him to sleep, my mate and I."
"I," said the dove from the rafters high.

6. Thus every beast by some good spell,
In the stable dark was glad to tell
Of the gift he gave Emmanuel,
The gift he gave Emmanuel.

FROM HEAVEN ABOVE TO EARTH I COME

Words by MARTIN LUTHER
Music from *Geistliche Lieder*, 1539

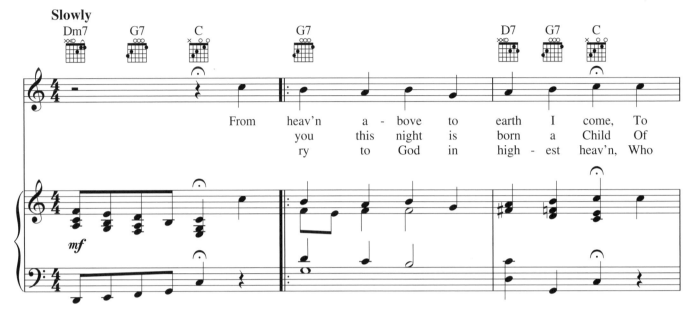

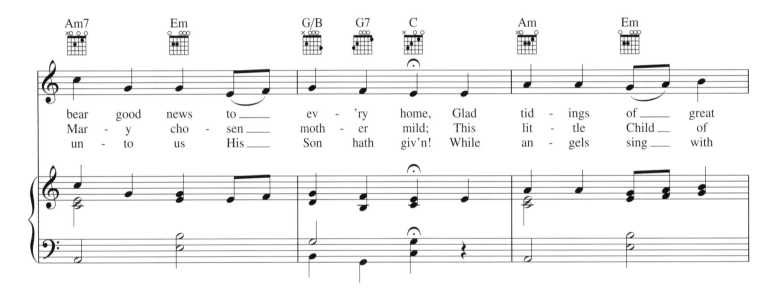

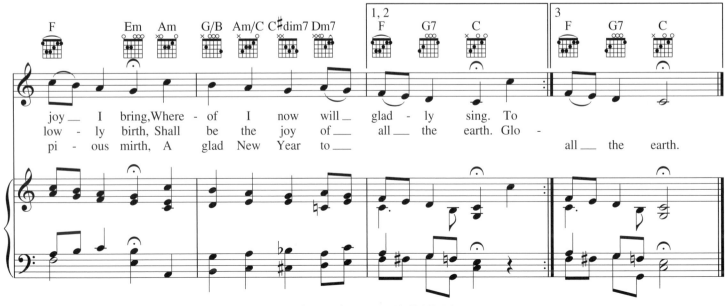

FUM, FUM, FUM

Traditional Catalonian Carol

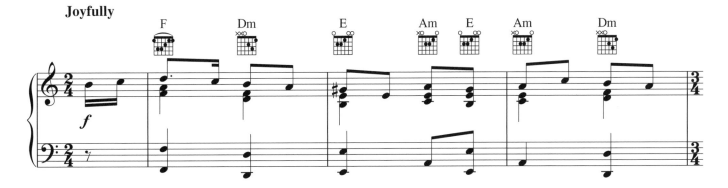

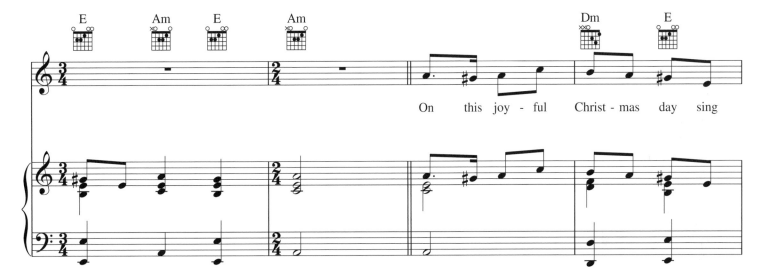

On this joy - ful Christ - mas day sing

Fum, Fum, Fum. On this joy - ful Christ - mas day sing

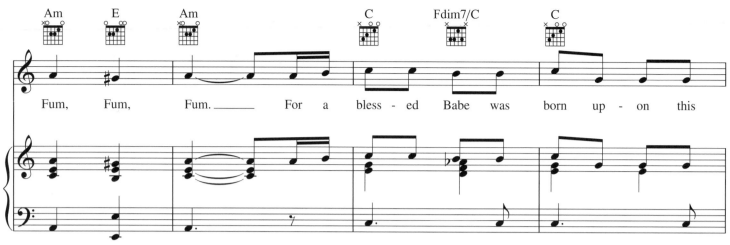

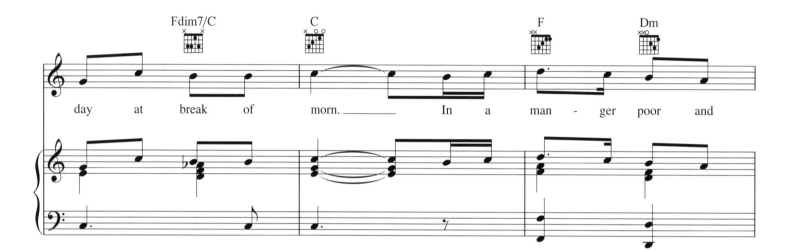

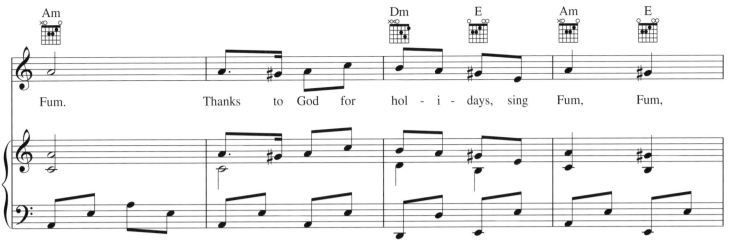

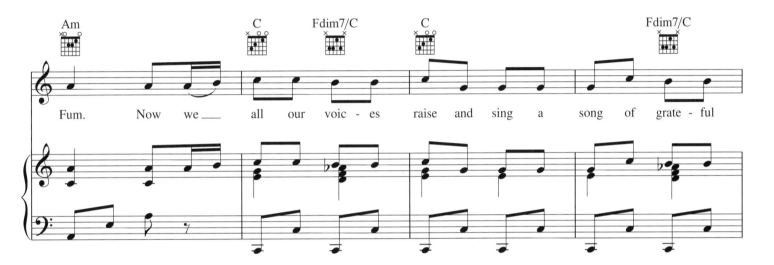

FROM THE EASTERN MOUNTAINS

Words by GODFREY THRING
Traditional Melody

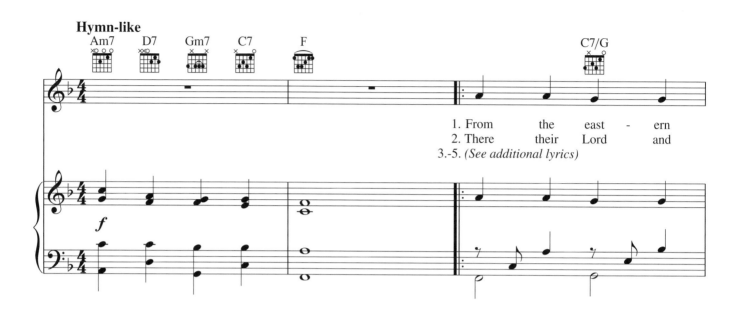

1. From the east - ern
2. There their Lord and
3.-5. *(See additional lyrics)*

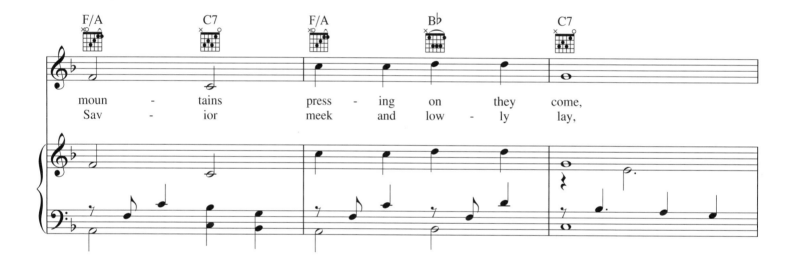

moun - tains press - ing on they come,
Sav - ior meek and low - ly lay,

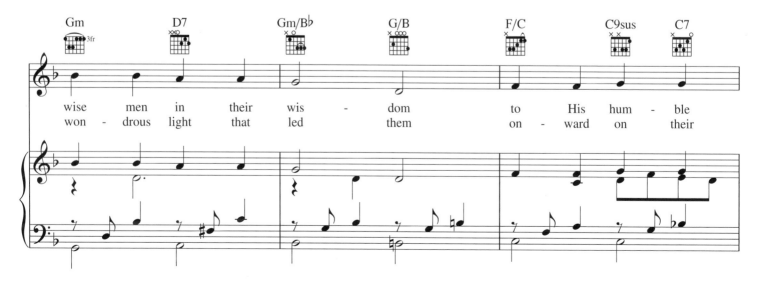

wise men in their wis - dom to His hum - ble
won - drous light that led them on - ward on their

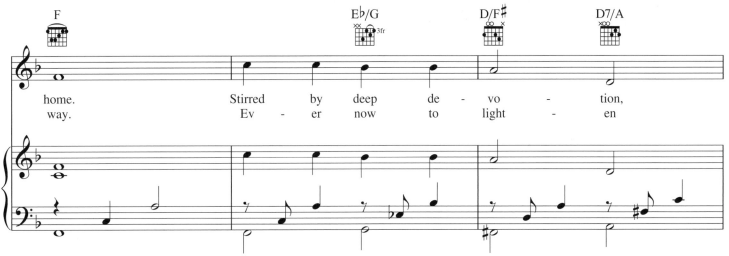

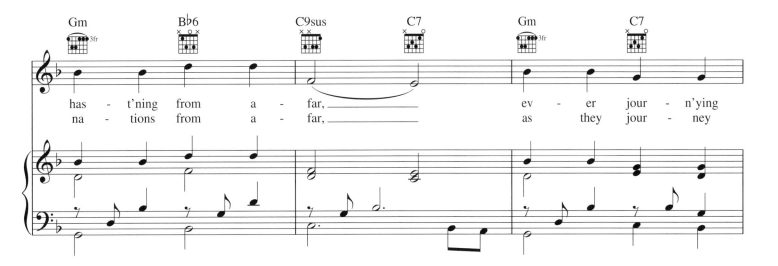

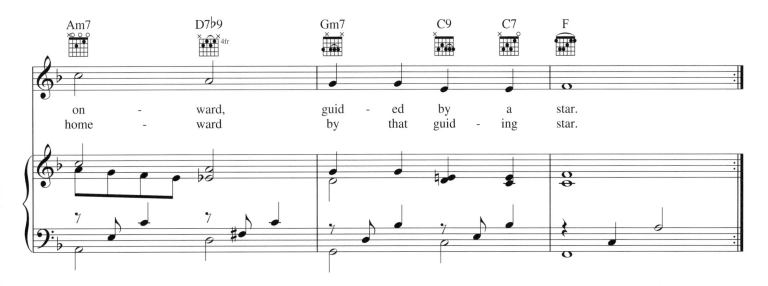

Additional Lyrics

3. Thou who in a manger
   Once hast lowly lain,
   Who dost now in glory
   O'er all kingdoms reign,
   Gather in the heathen
   Who in lands afar
   Ne'er have seen the brightness
   Of Thy guiding star.

4. Gather in the outcasts,
   All who have astray,
   Throw Thy radiance o'er them,
   Guide them on their way,
   Those who never knew Thee,
   Those who have wandered far,
   Guide them by the brightness
   Of Thy guiding star.

5. Onward through the darkness
   Of the lonely night,
   Shining still before them
   With Thy kindly light,
   Guide them, Jew and Gentile,
   Homeward from afar,
   Young and old together,
   [Something] guiding star.

GATHER AROUND
THE CHRISTMAS TREE

Words and Music by
JOHN H. HOPKINS

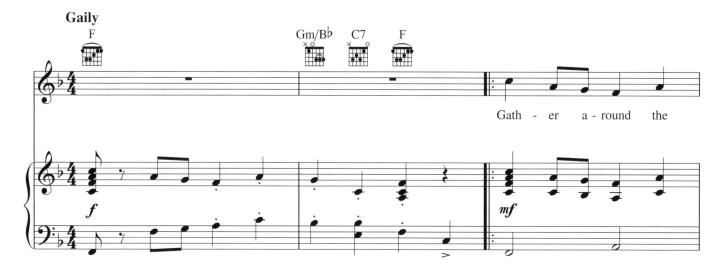

Gath - er a - round the

Christ - mas tree! Gath - er a - round the Christ - mas tree!

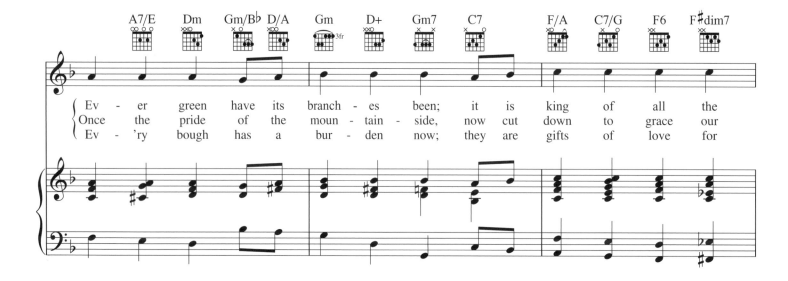

Ev - er green have its branch - es been; it is king of all the
Once the pride of the moun - tain - side, now cut down to grace our
Ev - 'ry bough has a bur - den now; they are gifts of love for

93

GLAD CHRISTMAS BELLS

Traditional American Carol

Additional Lyrics

3. Nor raiment gay as there He lay,
   Adorn'd the infant stranger;
   Poor humble child of mother mild
   She laid Him in a manger.

4. But from afar, a splendid star
   The wise men westward turning;
   The livelong night saw pure and bright,
   Above His birthplace burning.

I AM SO GLAD ON CHRISTMAS EVE

Words by MARIE WEXELSEN
Music by PEDER KNUDSEN

GO, TELL IT ON THE MOUNTAIN

African-American Spiritual
Verses by JOHN W. WORK, JR.

shep - herds kept their watch - ing o'er si - lent flocks by
shep - herds feared and trem - bled when, lo! a - bove the
in a low - ly man - ger the hum - ble Christ was

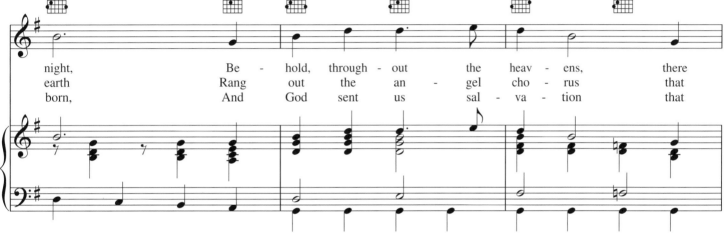

night, Be - hold, through - out the heav - ens, there
earth Rang out the an - gel cho - rus that
born, And God sent us sal - va - tion that

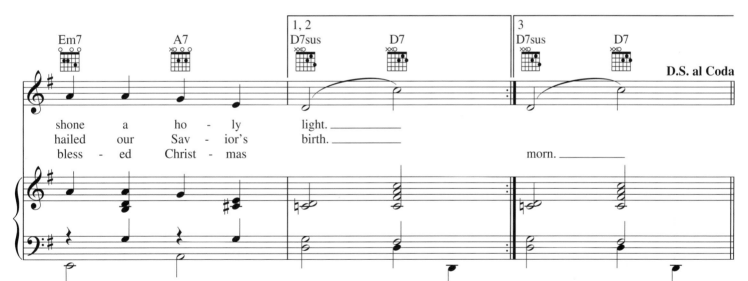

shone a ho - ly light. _____
hailed our Sav - ior's birth. _____
bless - ed Christ - mas morn. _____

D.S. al Coda

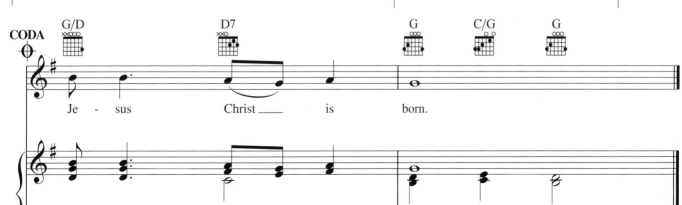

CODA

Je - sus Christ ___ is born.

GOD REST YE MERRY, GENTLEMEN

19th Century English Carol

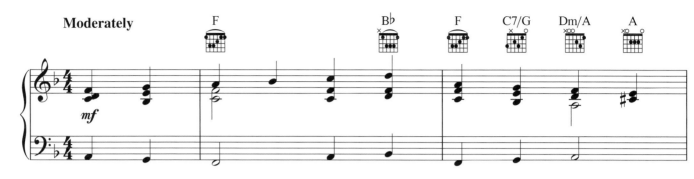

God rest ye mer - ry, gen - tle - men, let
Beth - le - hem, in Jew - ry let this
God our Heav'n - ly Fa - ther a
shep - herds at those tid - ings re -

noth - ing you dis - may, For Je - sus Christ our
bless - ed Babe was born, And laid with - in a
bless - ed an - gel came, And un - to cer - tain
joic - ed much in mind, And left their flocks a -

Sav - ior was born up - on this day, To
man - ger, up - on this bless - ed morn; To
shep - herds brought tid - ings of the same; How
feed - ing in tem - pest, storm, and wind; And

GOOD CHRISTIAN MEN, REJOICE

14th Century Latin Text
Translated by JOHN MASON NEALE
14th Century German Melody

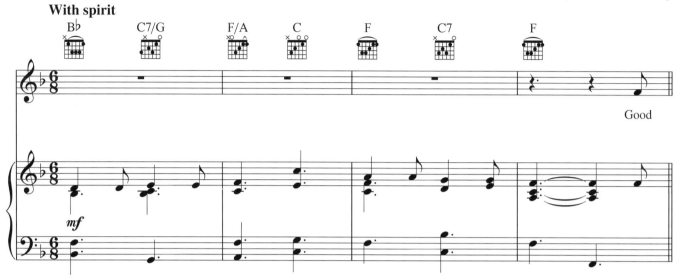

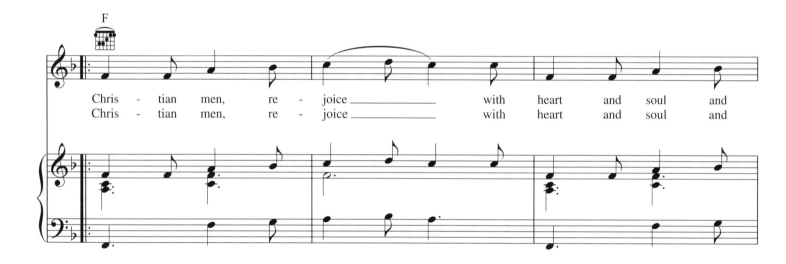

Chris - tian men, re - joice _____ with heart and soul and
Chris - tian men, re - joice _____ with heart and soul and

voice, _____ Give ye heed to what we say:
voice, _____ Now ye hear of end - less bliss;

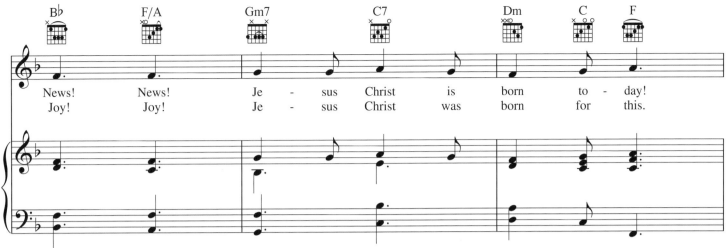

News! News! Je - sus Christ is born to - day!
Joy! Joy! Je - sus Christ was born for this.

Ox and ass be - fore Him bow, And He is in the
He hath ope'd the heav'n - ly door, And man is bless - ed

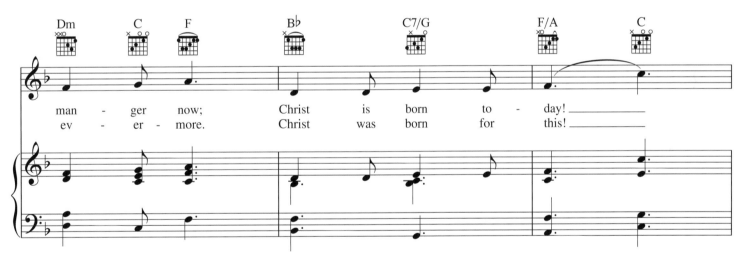

man - ger now; Christ is born to - day! _____
ev - er - more. Christ was born for this! _____

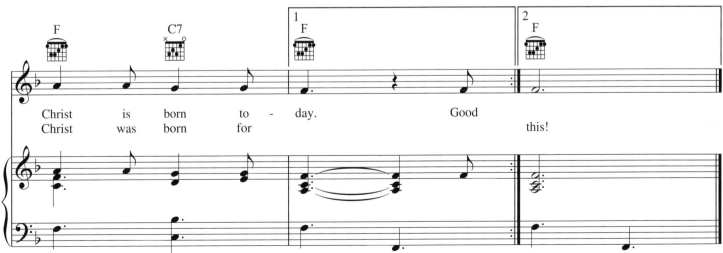

Christ is born to - day. Good
Christ was born for this!

GOOD KING WENCESLAS

Words by JOHN M. NEALE
Music from *Piae Cantiones*

1. Good King Wen - ces - las looked out On the feast of
2.-5. *(See additional lyrics)*

Ste - phen, When the snow lay 'round a - bout, Deep and crisp and

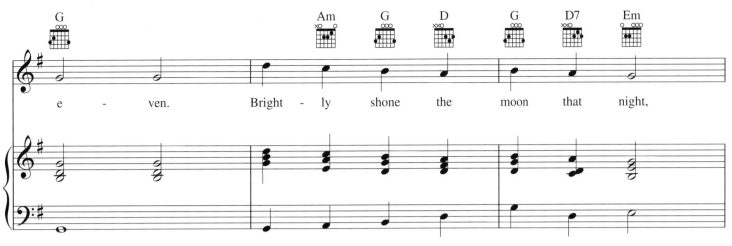

e - ven. Bright - ly shone the moon that night,

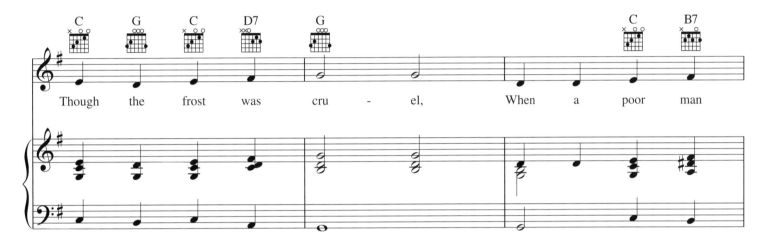

Though the frost was cru - el, When a poor man

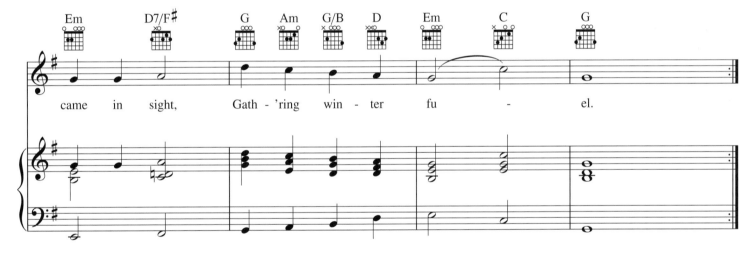

came in sight, Gath - 'ring win - ter fu - el.

Additional Lyrics

2. "Hither page, and stand by me,
   If thou know'st it, telling,
   Yonder peasant, who is he?
   Where and what his dwelling?"
   "Sire, he lives a good league hence,
   Underneath the mountain;
   Right against the forest fence,
   By Saint Agnes' fountain."

3. "Bring me flesh, and bring me wine,
   Bring me pine-logs hither;
   Thou and I will see him dine,
   When we bear them thither."
   Page and monarch forth they went,
   Forth they went together;
   Through the rude winds wild lament:
   And the bitter weather.

4. "Sire, the night is darker now,
   And the wind blows stronger;
   Fails my heart, I know not how,
   I can go no longer."
   "Mark my footsteps, my good page,
   Tred thou in them boldly:
   Thou shalt find the winter's rage
   Freeze thy blood less coldly."

5. In his master's steps he trod,
   Where the snow lay dinted;
   Heat was in the very sod
   Which the saint had printed.
   Therefore, Christian men, be sure,
   Wealth or rank possessing,
   Ye who now will bless the poor,
   Shall yourselves find blessing.

HALLELUJAH CHORUS

By GEORGE FRIDERIC HANDEL

Hal - le - lu - jah! Hal - le - lu - jah! Hal-le - lu - jah! Hal-le-lu - jah! Hal -

le - lu - jah! Hal - le - lu - jah! Hal - le - lu - jah! Hal-le -

lu - jah! Hal - le - lu - jah! Hal - le - lu - jah! For the Lord

God om-ni - po-tent reign - eth. Hal-le-lu-jah! Hal-le-lu-jah! Hal-le-

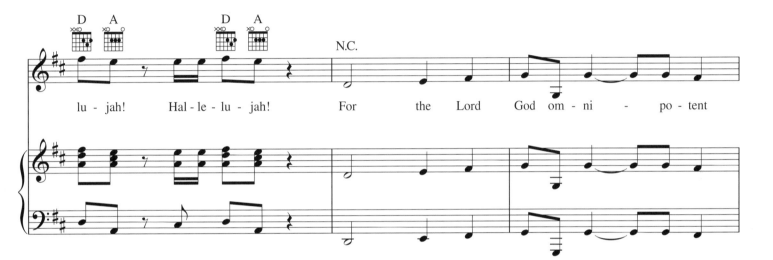

lu-jah! Hal-le-lu-jah! For the Lord God om-ni - po-tent

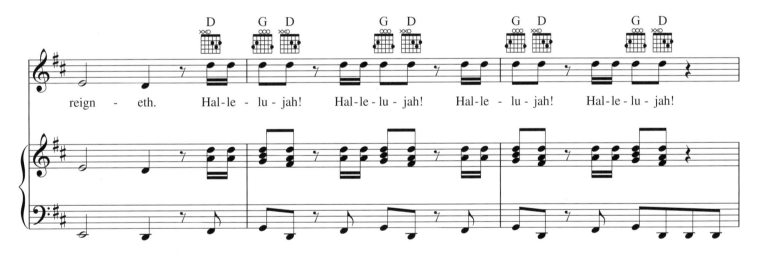

reign - eth. Hal-le-lu-jah! Hal-le-lu-jah! Hal-le-lu-jah! Hal-le-lu-jah!

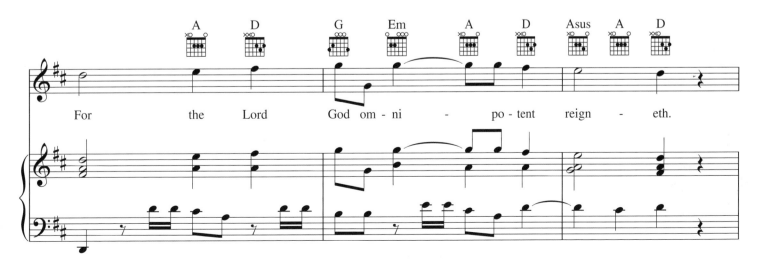

For the Lord God om-ni - po-tent reign - eth.

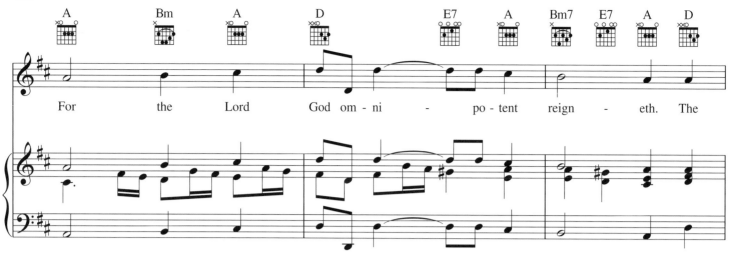

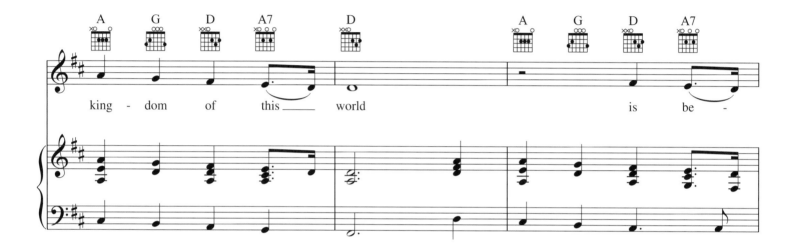

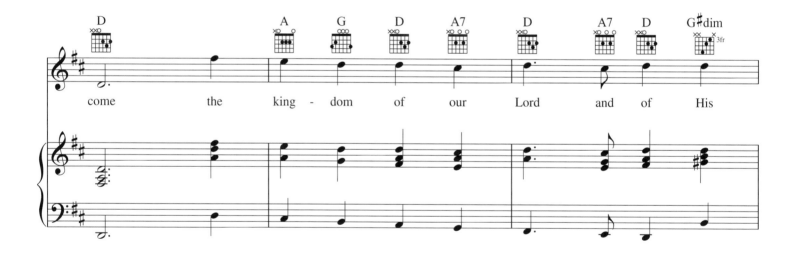

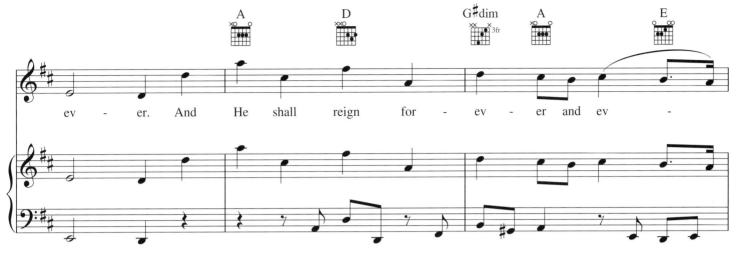

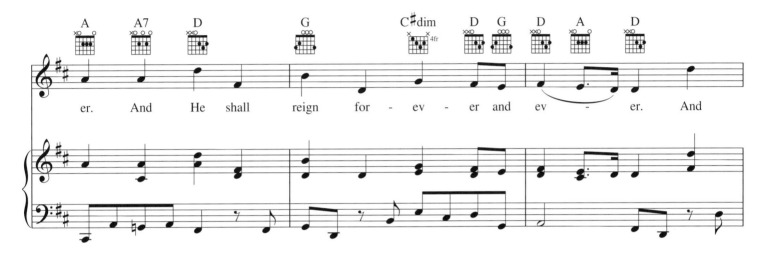

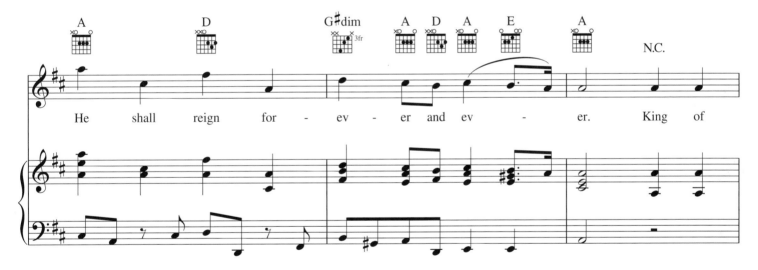

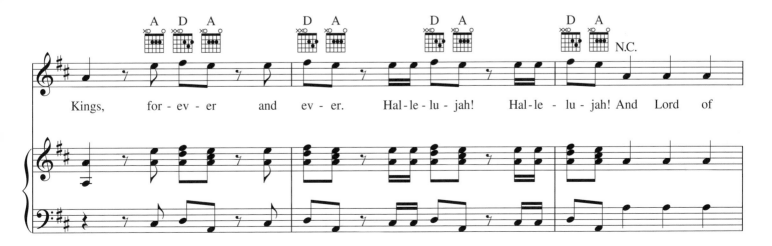

Lords, for-ev-er and ev-er. Hal-le-lu-jah! Hal-le-lu-jah! King of

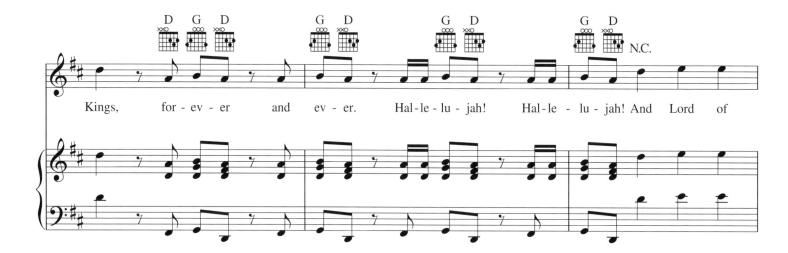

Kings, for-ev-er and ev-er. Hal-le-lu-jah! Hal-le-lu-jah! And Lord of

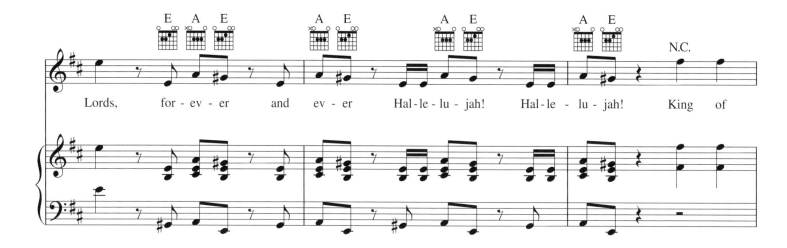

Lords, for-ev-er and ev-er Hal-le-lu-jah! Hal-le-lu-jah! King of

Kings, for-ev-er and ev-er. Hal-le-lu-jah! Hal-le-lu-jah! And Lord of

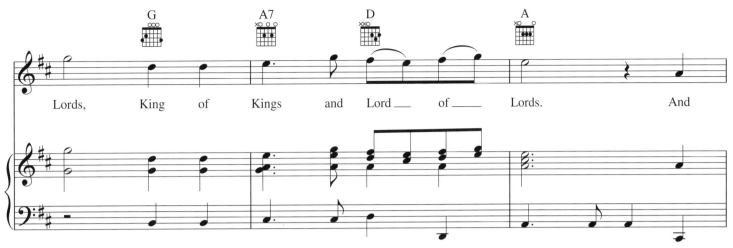

Lords, King of Kings and Lord of Lords. And

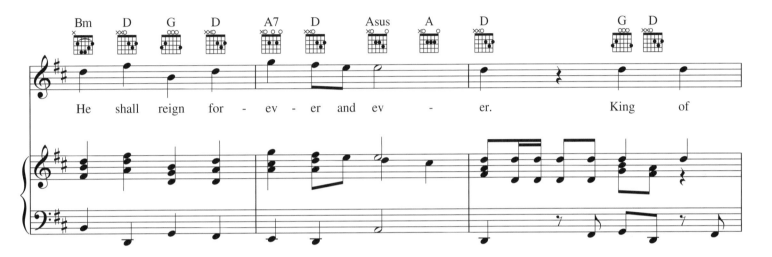

He shall reign for - ev - er and ev - er. King of

Kings and Lord of Lords. Hal-le-lu-jah! Hal-le-lu-jah! Hal-le-lu-jah! Hal-le-

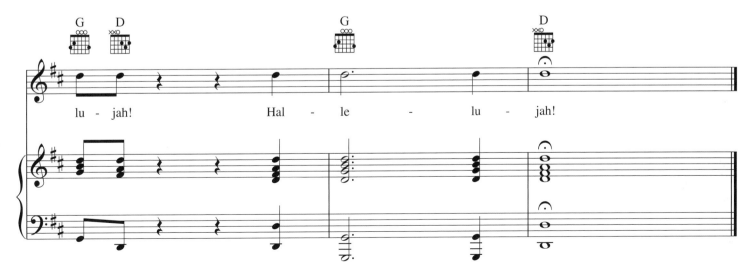

lu-jah! Hal - le - lu - jah!

THE HAPPY CHRISTMAS COMES ONCE MORE

Words by NICOLAI F.S. GRUNDTVIG
Music by C. BALLE

Flowing Waltz, not too fast

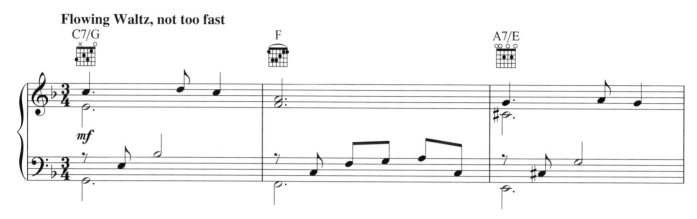

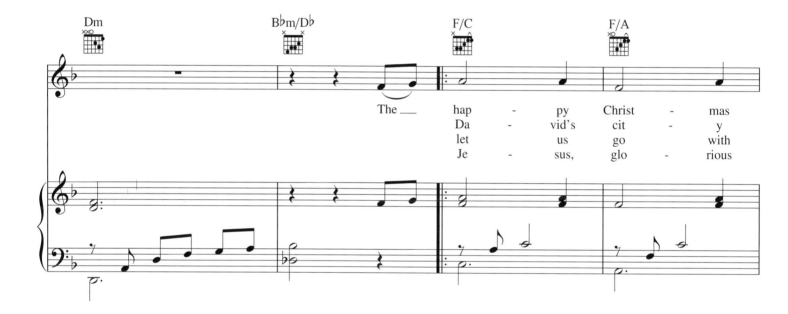

The ___ hap - py Christ - mas
Da - vid's cit - y
let us go with
Je - sus, glo - rious

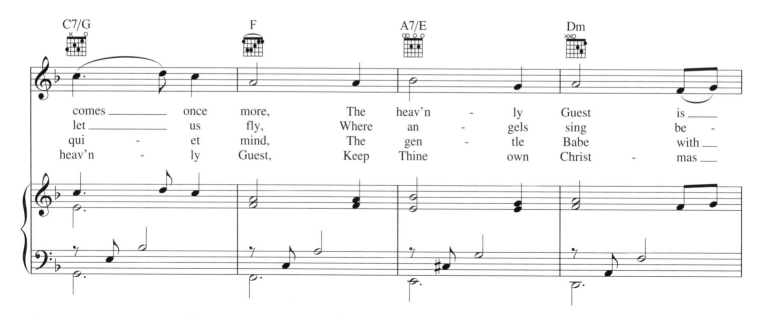

comes ___ once more, The heav'n - ly Guest is ___
let ___ us fly, Where an - gels sing be -
qui - et mind, The gen - tle Babe with ___
heav'n - ly Guest, Keep Thine own Christ - mas ___

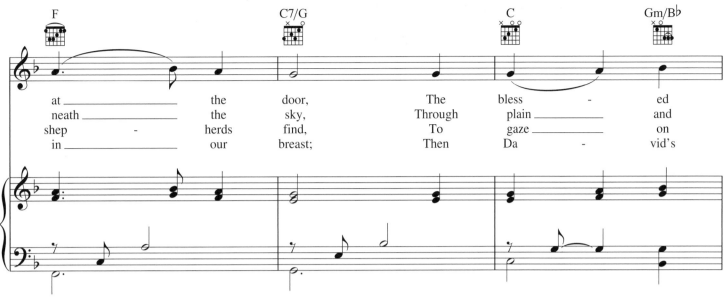

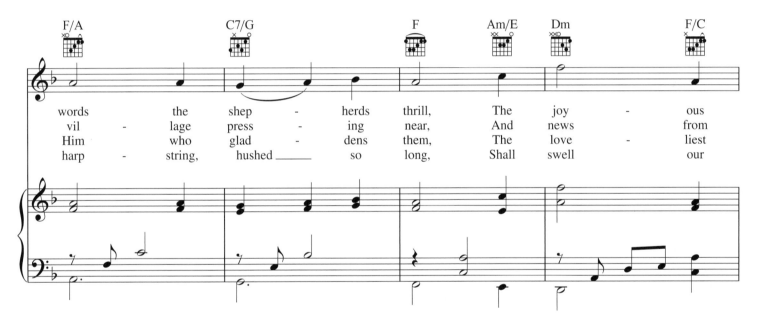

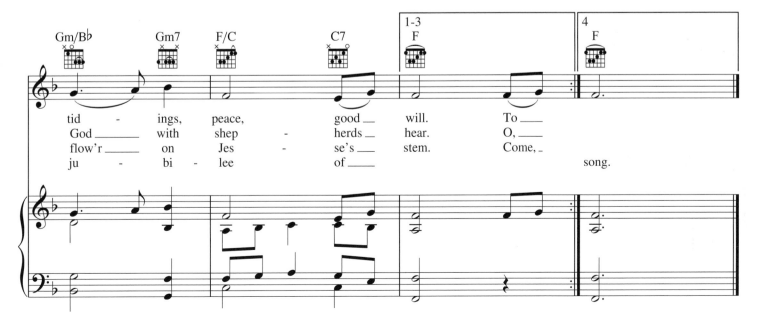

HARK! THE HERALD ANGELS SING

Words by CHARLES WESLEY
Altered by GEORGE WHITEFIELD
Music by FELIX MENDELSSOHN-BARTHOLDY
Arranged by WILLIAM H. CUMMINGS

Hark! The her- ald an- gels sing, _____
Christ, by high- est heav'n a- dored, _____
Hail, the heav'n- born Prince of Peace! _____

"Glo- ry to the new- born King!
Christ, the ev- er- last- ing Lord;
Hail, the Sun of Right- eous- ness!

Peace on earth, and
Late in time be-
Light and life to

mer- cy mild, _____
hold Him come, _____
all He brings, _____

God and sin- ners rec- on- ciled."
Off- spring of the vir- gin's womb.
Ris'n with heal- ing in His wings.

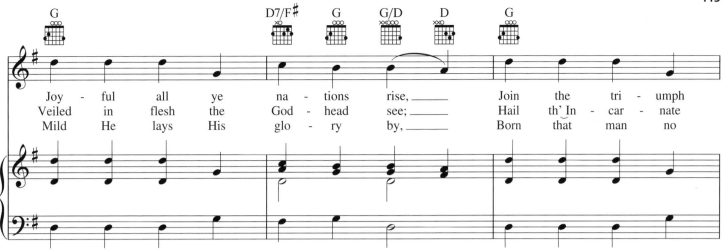

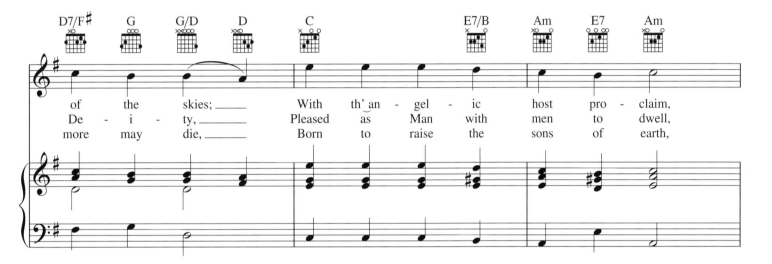

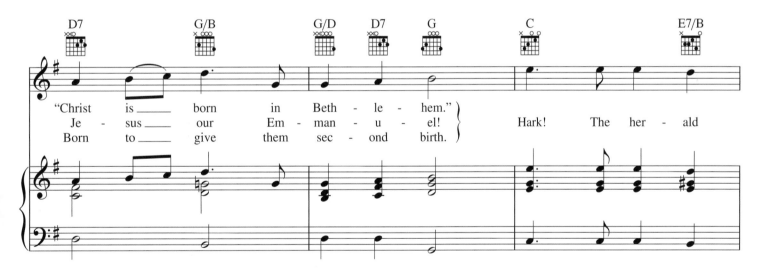

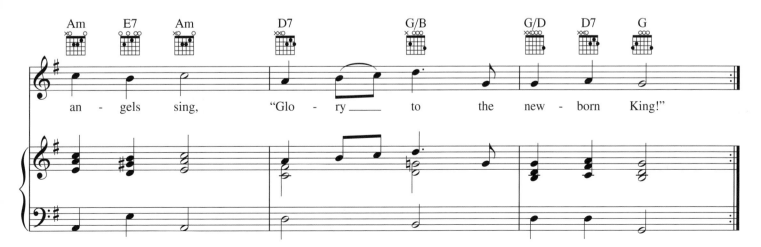

HE IS BORN
(Il est ne, le divin enfant)

Traditional French Carol

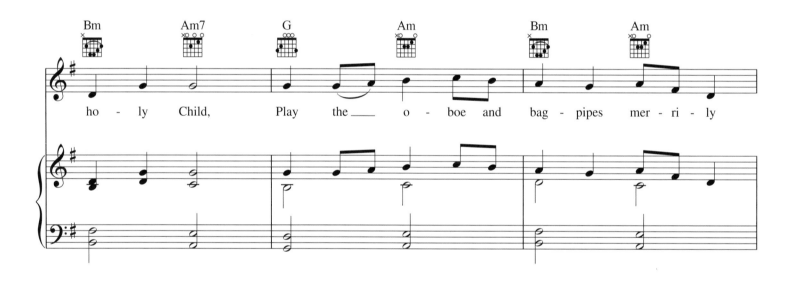

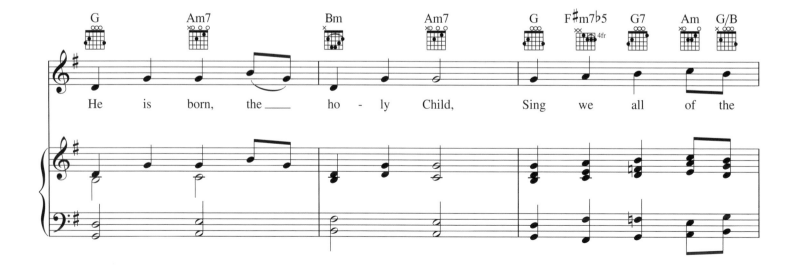

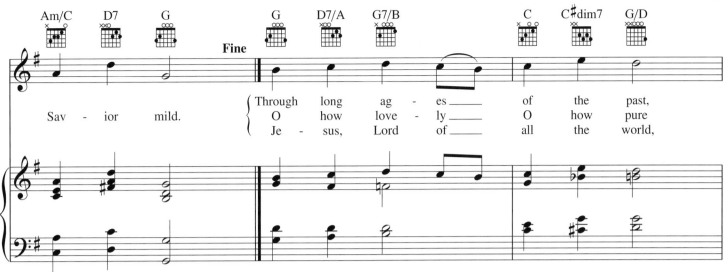

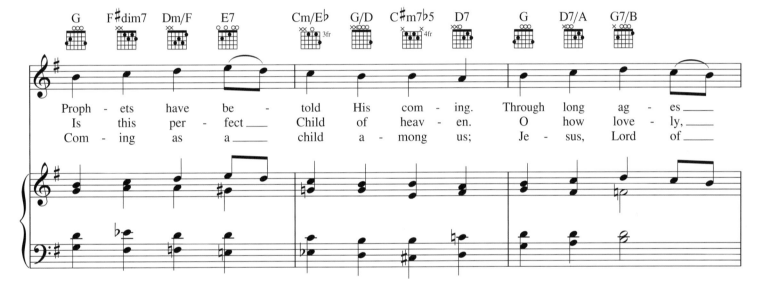

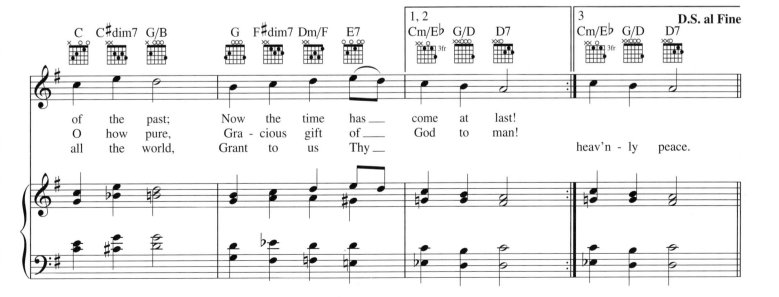

HEAR THEM BELLS

Words and Music by
D.S. McCOSH

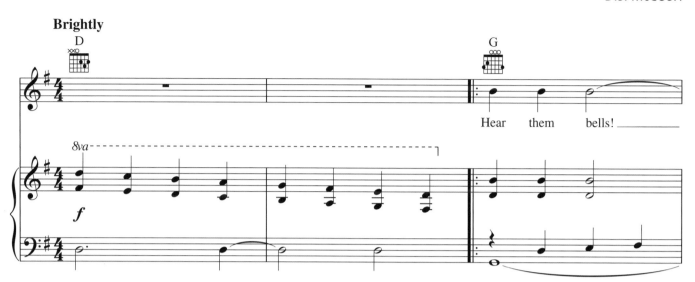

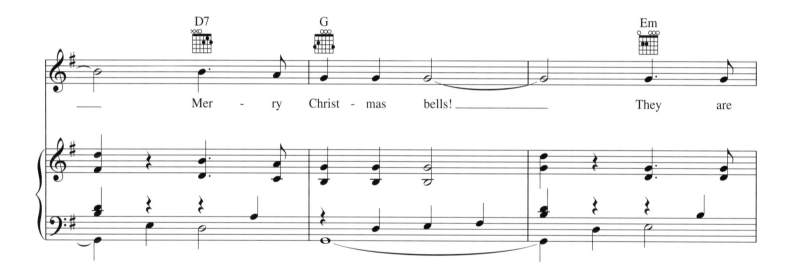

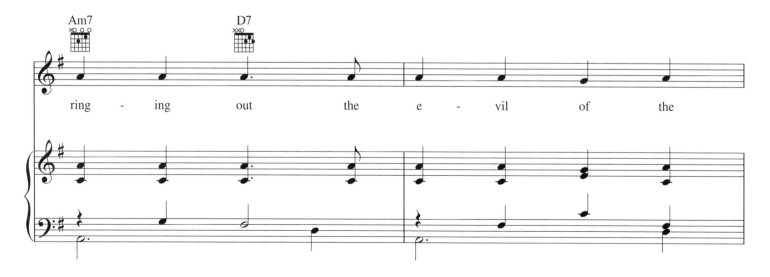

sword; _____ Hear them bells! _____

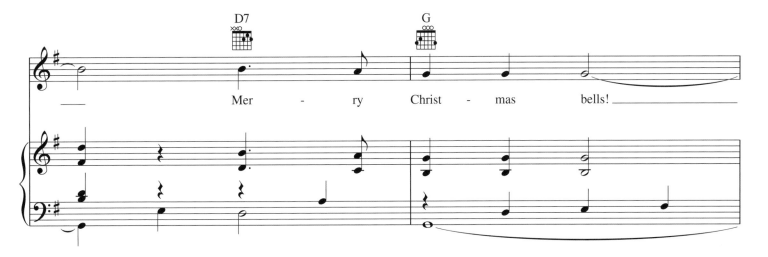

__ Mer - ry Christ - mas bells! _____

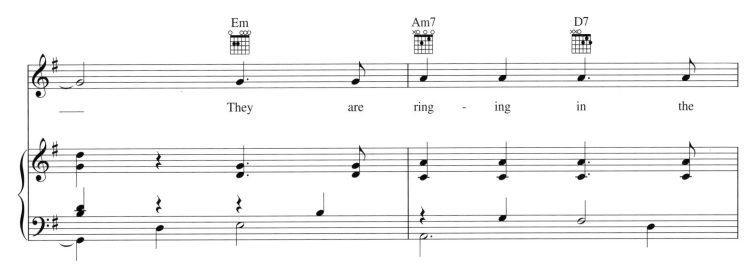

__ They are ring - ing in the

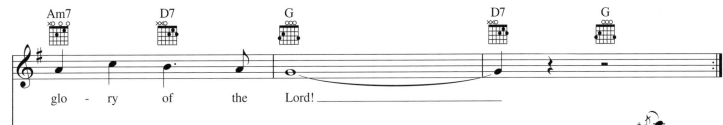

glo - ry of the Lord! _____

HERE WE COME A-WASSAILING

Traditional

Brightly

1. Here we come a-was-sail-ing A-mong the leaves so
2. We are not dai-ly beg-gars That beg from door to
3., 4. *(See additional lyrics)*

green; Here we come a-wan-d'ring, So fair to be
door, But we are neigh-bor chil-dren Whom you have seen be-

Refrain

seen:} Love and joy come to you, And to you your was-sail
fore:}

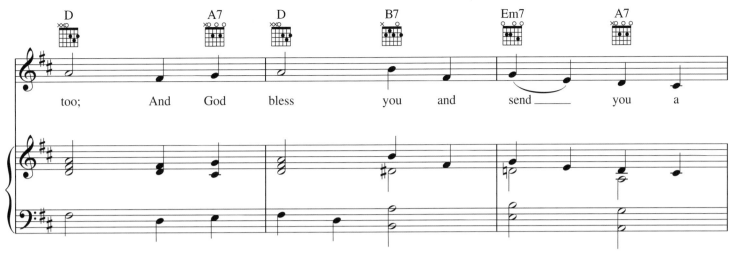

too; And God bless you and send ____ you a

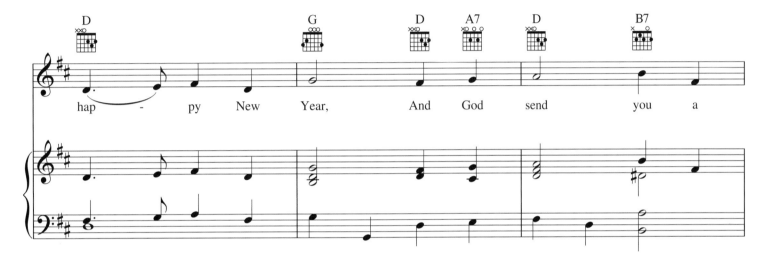

hap - py New Year, And God send you a

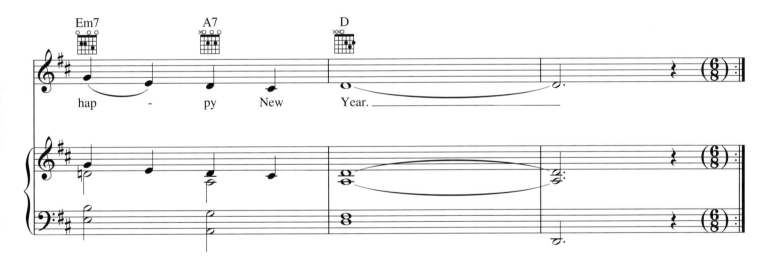

hap - py New Year. ____

Additional Lyrics

3. We have got a little purse
   Of stretching leather skin;
   We want a little money
   To line it well within:
   Refrain

4. God bless the master of this house,
   Likewise the mistress too;
   And all the little children
   That round the table go:
   Refrain

THE HOLLY AND THE IVY

18th Century English Carol

Moderately slow

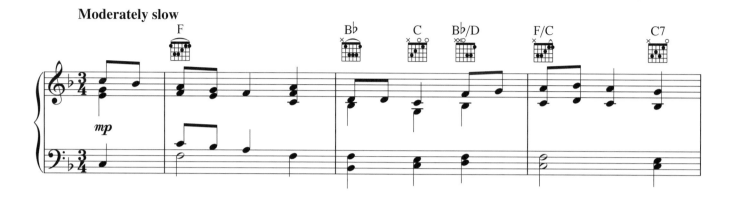

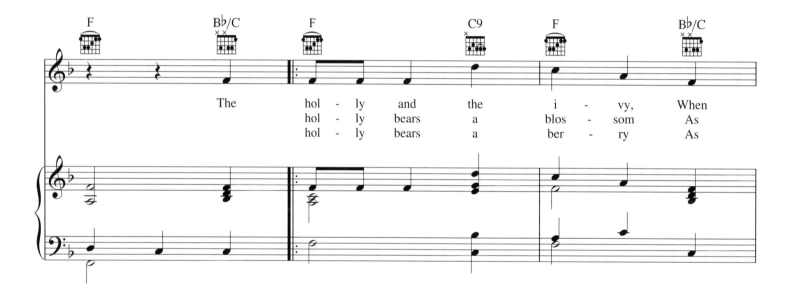

The hol - ly and the i - vy, When
hol - ly bears a blos - som As
hol - ly bears a ber - ry As

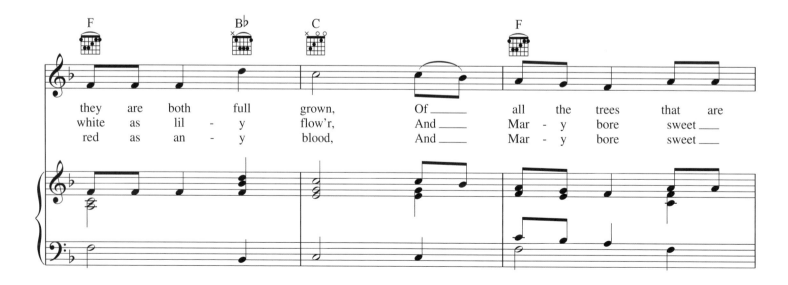

they are both full grown, Of ____ all the trees that are
white as lil - y flow'r, And ____ Mar - y bore sweet ____
red as an - y blood, And ____ Mar - y bore sweet ____

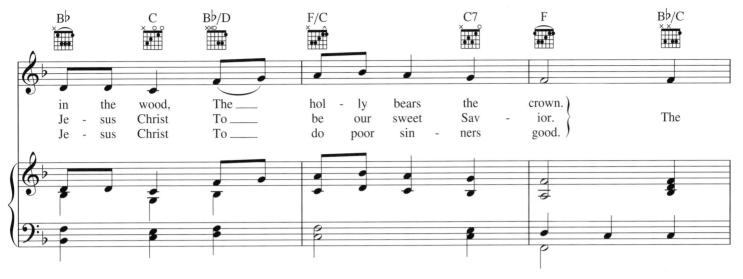

in the wood, The ___ hol - ly bears the crown.
Je - sus Christ To ___ be our sweet Sav - ior.
Je - sus Christ To ___ do poor sin - ners good.

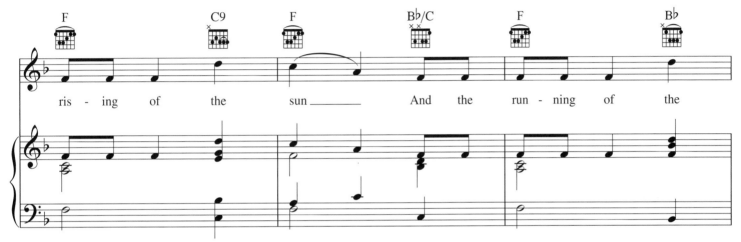

ris - ing of the sun ___ And the run - ning of the

deer, The ___ play - ing of the mer - ry or - gan, sweet

1, 2   3

sing - ing of the choir. The choir.

I HEARD THE BELLS ON CHRISTMAS DAY

Words by HENRY WADSWORTH LONGFELLOW
Music by JOHN BAPTISTE CALKIN

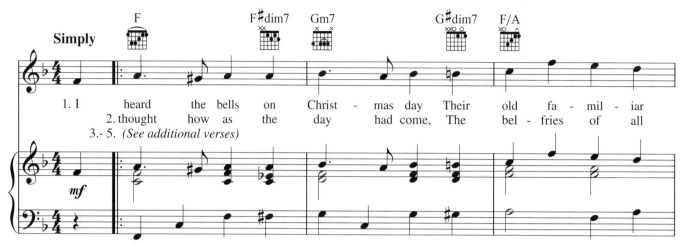

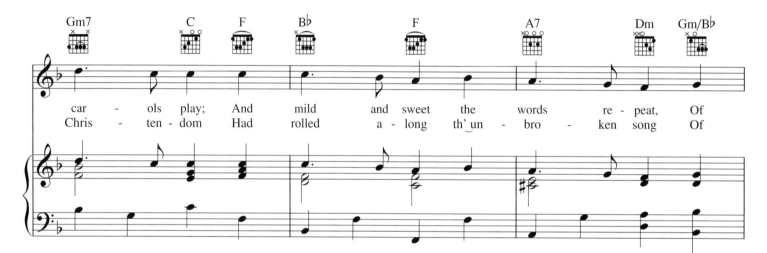

1. I heard the bells on Christ-mas day Their old fa-mil-iar
2. thought how as the day had come, The bel-fries of all
3.- 5. *(See additional verses)*

car-ols play; And mild and sweet the words re-peat, Of
Chris-ten-dom Had rolled a-long th' un-bro-ken song Of

peace on earth, good will to men. I will to men!
peace on earth, good will to men. And

Additional Verses

3. And in despair I bowed my head:
"There is no peace on earth," I said,
"For hate is strong, and mocks the song
Of peace on earth, good will to men."

4. Then pealed the bells more loud and deep:
"God is not dead, nor doth He sleep;
The wrong shall fail, the right prevail,
With peace on earth, good will to men."

5. Till, ringing, singing on its way,
The world revolved from night to day,
A voice, a chime, a chant sublime,
Of peace on earth, good will to men!

I SAW THREE SHIPS

Traditional English Carol

IN THE FIELD WITH THEIR FLOCKS ABIDING

Traditional

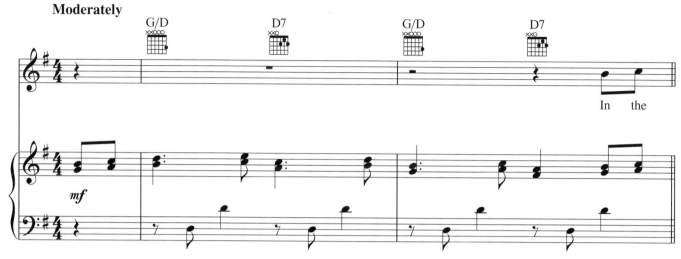

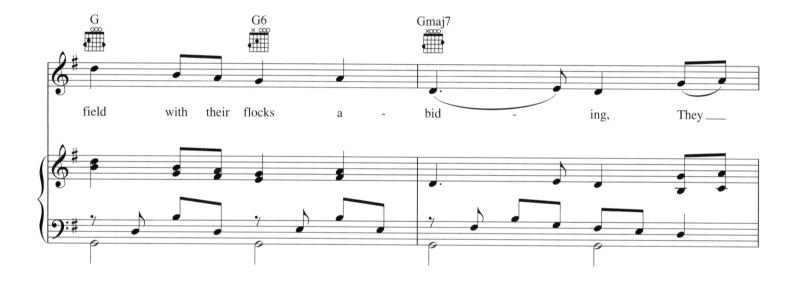

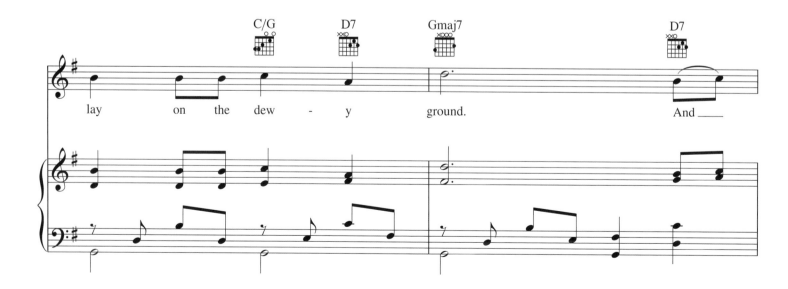

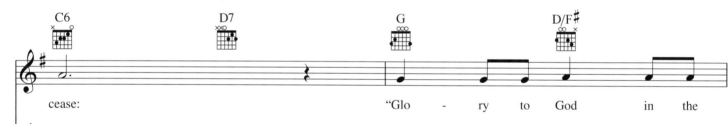

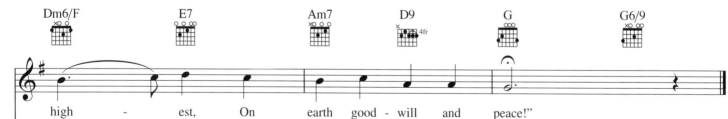

IN THE SILENCE OF THE NIGHT

Traditional Carol

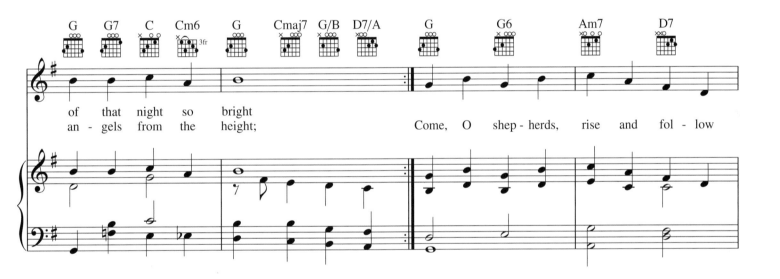

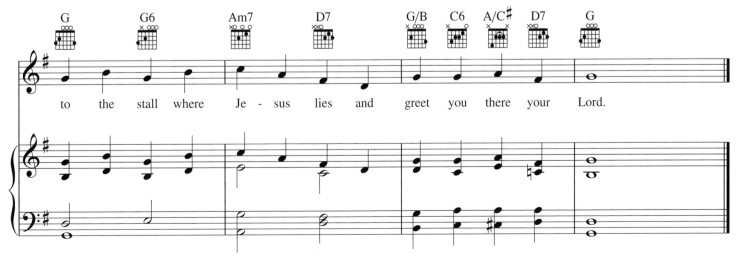

IN THE BLEAK MIDWINTER

Poem by CHRISTINA ROSSETTI
Music by GUSTAV HOLST

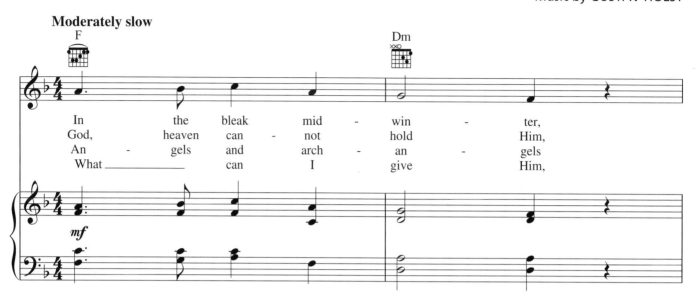

Moderately slow

In the bleak mid - win - ter,
God, heaven can - not hold Him,
An - gels and arch - an - gels

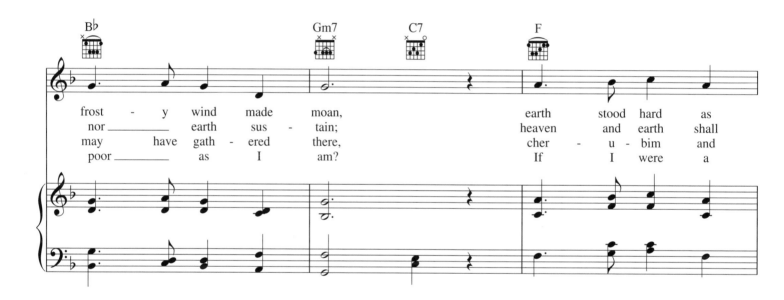

frost - y wind made moan, earth stood hard as
nor ___ earth sus - tain; heaven and earth shall
may have gath - ered there, cher - u - bim and
poor ___ as I am? If I were a

i - ron, wa - ter like a stone;
flee a - way when He comes to reign.
ser - a - phim throng - ed the air;
shep - herd, I would bring a lamb;

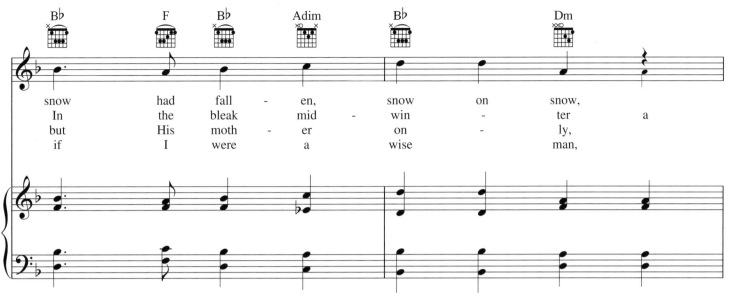

snow had fall - en, snow on snow,
In the bleak mid - win - ter a
but His moth - er on - ly,
if I were a wise man,

snow _____ on _____ snow, in the bleak mid -
sta - ble place suf - ficed the Lord _____ God Al -
in her maid - en bliss, wor - shiped the be -
I would do my part; yet what I can I

win - ter, long _____ a - go. Our
might - y, Je - sus Christ.
lov - ed with _____ a kiss.
give Him: give _____ my heart.

INFANT HOLY, INFANT LOWLY

Traditional Polish Carol

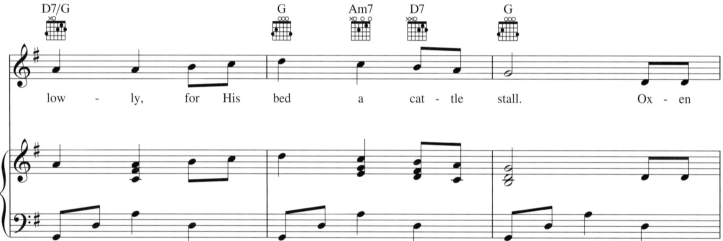

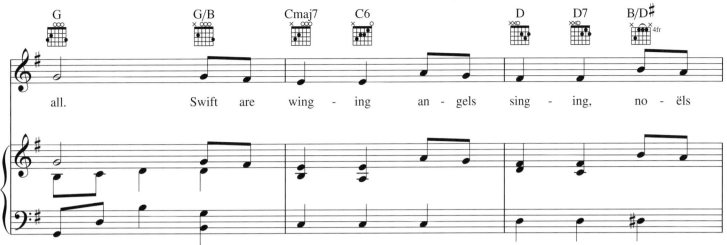

Swift are wing-ing an-gels sing-ing, no-ëls

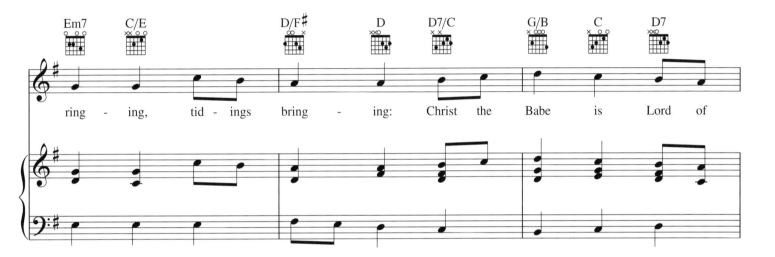

ring-ing, tid-ings bring-ing: Christ the Babe is Lord of

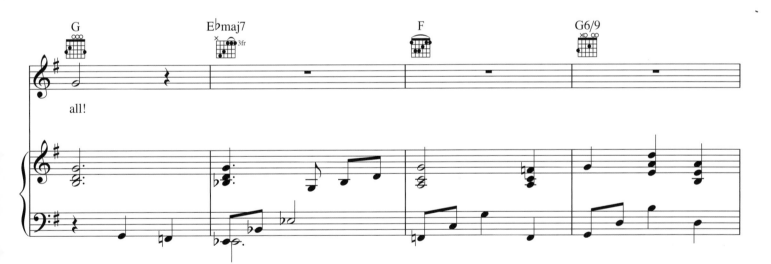

all!

Flocks are sleep-ing, shep-herds keep-ing vig-il

132

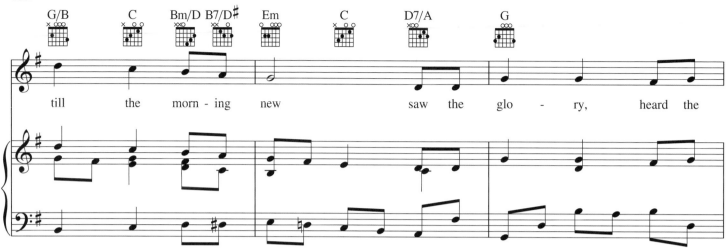

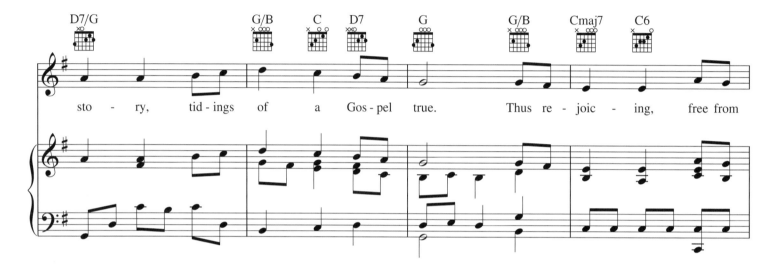

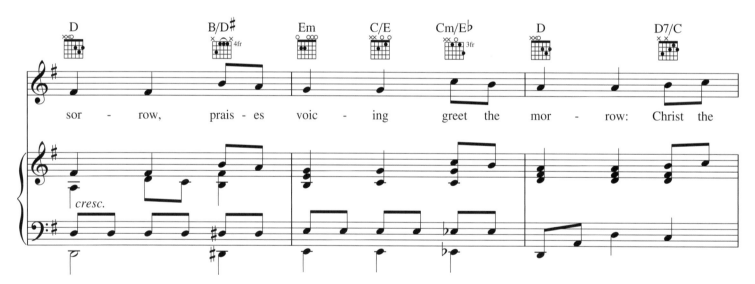

IT CAME UPON THE MIDNIGHT CLEAR

Words by EDMUND HAMILTON SEARS
Music by RICHARD STORRS WILLIS

earth To touch their harps _____ of gold: _____
floats O'er all the wea - ry world. _____
rolled Two thou - sand years _____ of wrong.

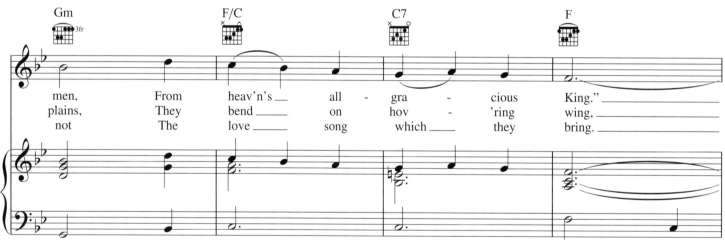

_____ "Peace on the earth, _____ good will to
_____ A - bove its sad _____ and low - ly
_____ And man, at war _____ with man, hears

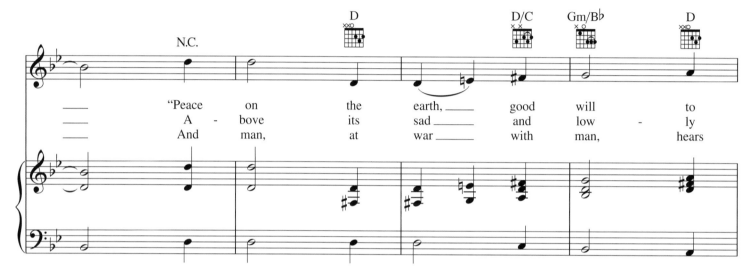

men, From heav'n's _____ all - gra - cious King." _____
plains, They bend _____ on hov - 'ring wing, _____
not The love _____ song which _____ they bring. _____

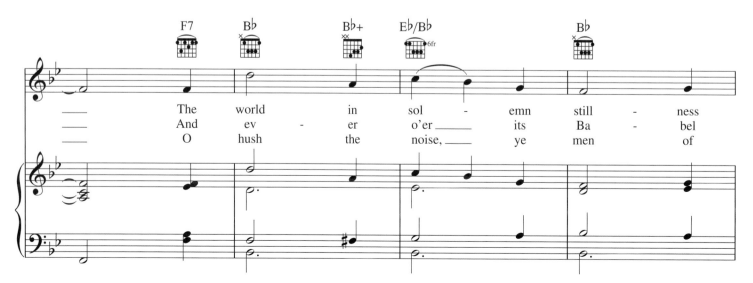

_____ The world in sol - emn still - ness
_____ And ev - er o'er its Ba - bel
_____ O hush the noise, _____ ye men of

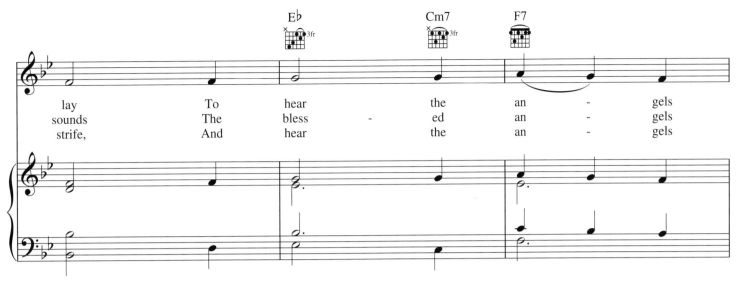

	Eb	Cm7	F7

lay · · · · To hear · · the an - gels
sounds · · The bless - ed an - gels
strife, · · And hear · · the an - gels

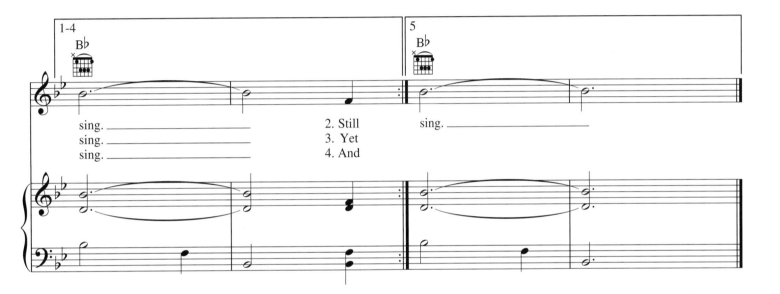

1-4 Bb

sing. _____ 2. Still
sing. _____ 3. Yet
sing. _____ 4. And

5 Bb

sing. _____

Additional Lyrics

4. And ye, beneath life's crushing load,
Whose forms are bending low,
Who toil along the climbing way
With painful steps and slow,
Look now! for glad and golden hours
Come swiftly on the wing.
O rest beside the weary road,
And hear the angels sing.

5. For lo! the days are hast'ning on,
By prophet-bards foretold.
When, with the ever-circling years,
Shall come the Age of Gold,
When peace shall over all the earth
Its heav'nly splendors fling,
And all the world give back the song
Which now the angels sing.

JESU, JOY OF MAN'S DESIRING
from CANTATA NO. 147

English Words by ROBERT BRIDGES
Music by JOHANN SEBASTIAN BACH

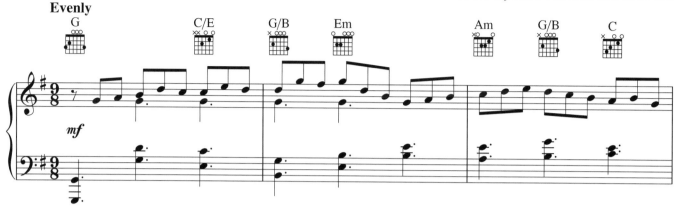

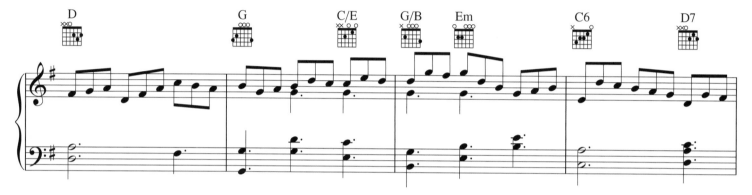

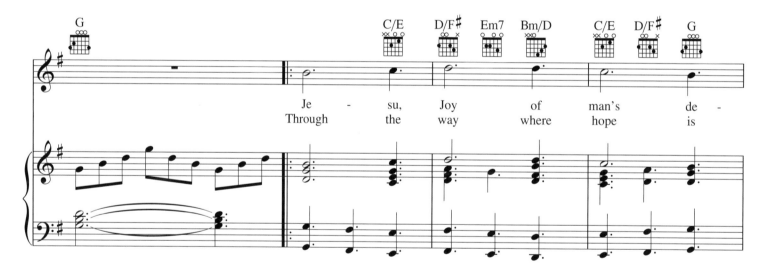

Je - su, Joy of man's de - si -
Through the way where hope is

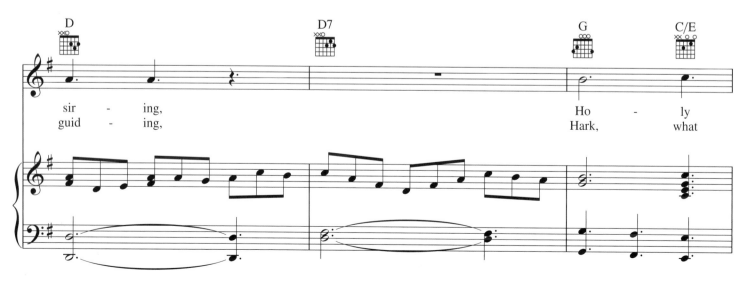

sir - ing, Ho - ly
guid - ing, Hark, what

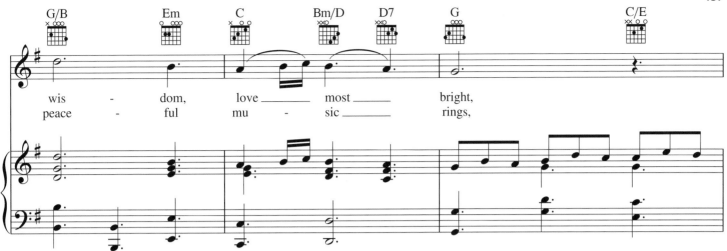

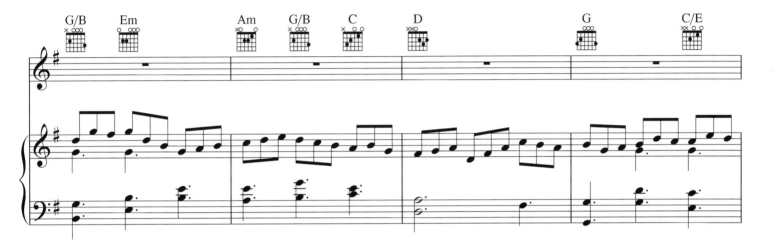

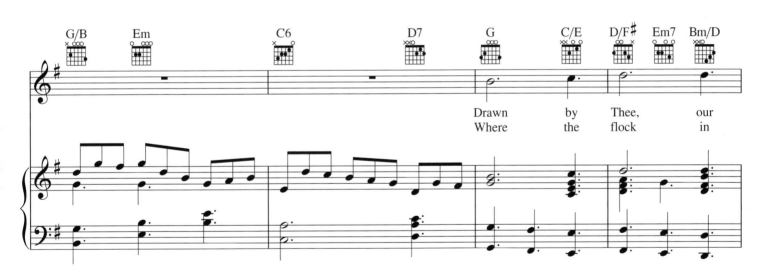

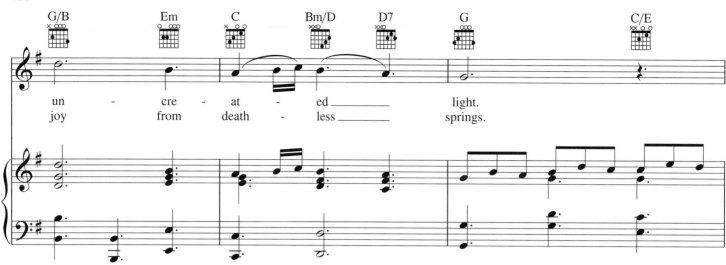

un - cre - at - ed _____ light.
joy from at death - less _____ springs.

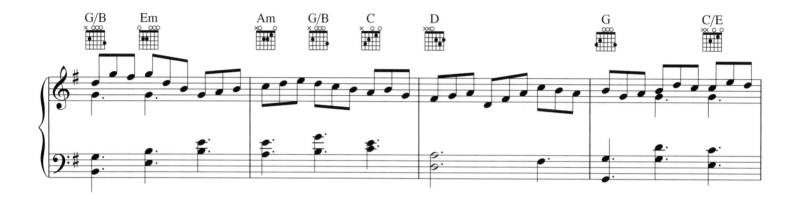

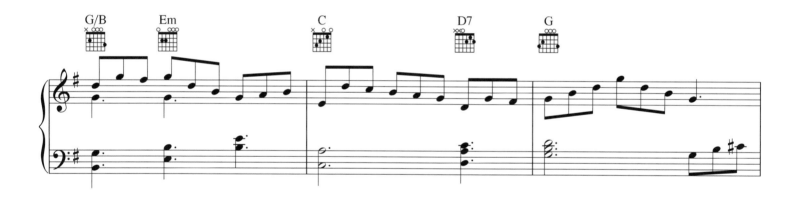

Word of God our flesh _____ that fash - ioned,
Theirs is beau - ty's fair - est pleas - ure,

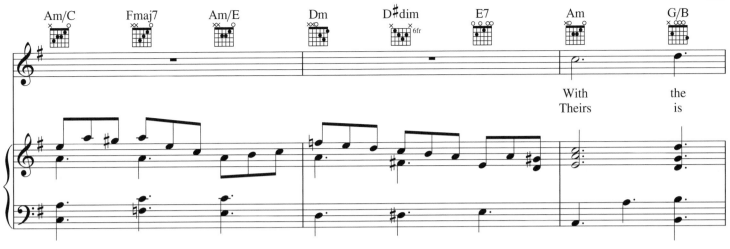

With the
Theirs is

fire of life ___ im - pas - sioned.
wis - dom's ho - liest treas - ure.

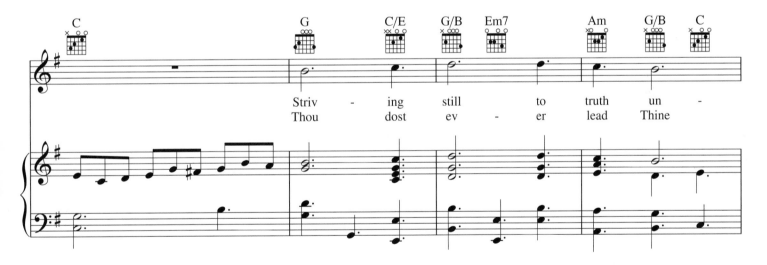

Striv - ing still to truth un -
Thou dost ev - er lead Thine

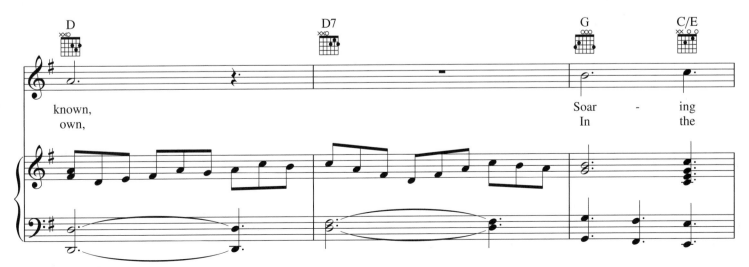

known, Soar - ing
own, In the

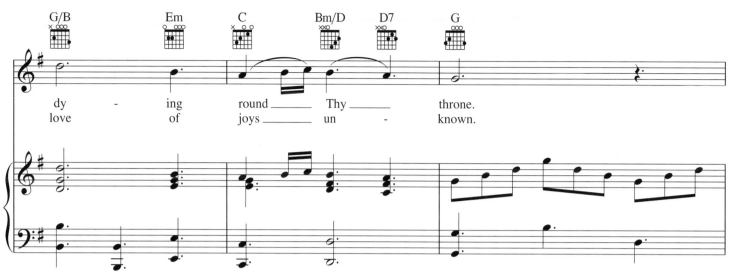

dy - ing round _____ Thy _____ throne.
love of joys _____ un - known.

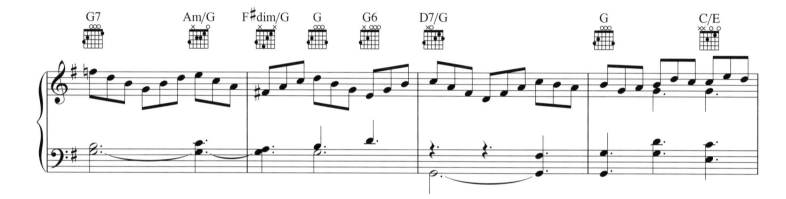

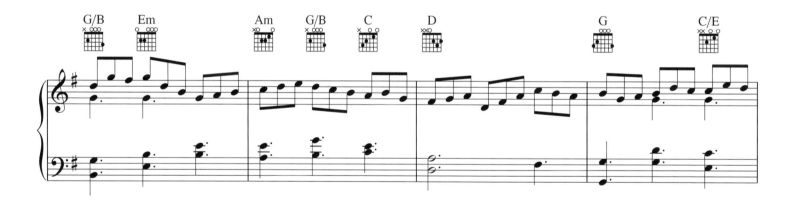

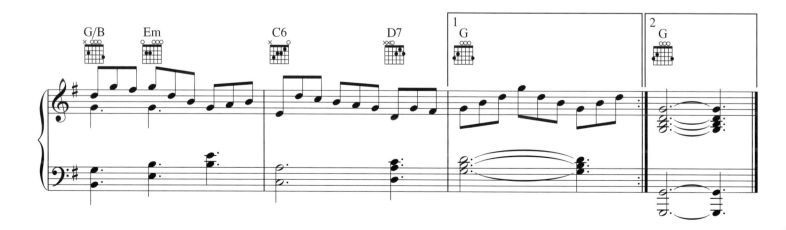

JINGLE BELLS

Words and Music by
J. PIERPONT

Bright 2

Dash - ing through the snow in a one - horse o - pen
day or two a - go I thought I'd take a
Now the ground is white; go it while you're

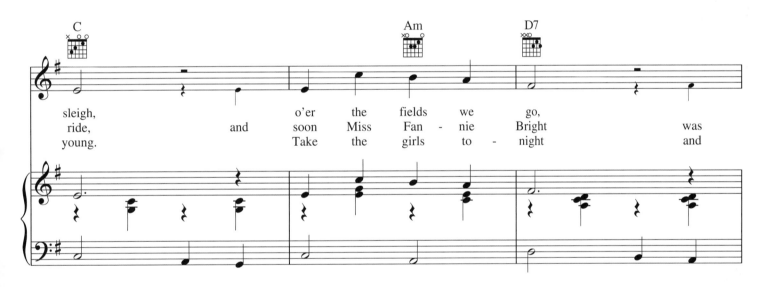

sleigh, o'er the fields we go,
ride, and soon Miss Fan - nie Bright was
young. Take the girls to - night and

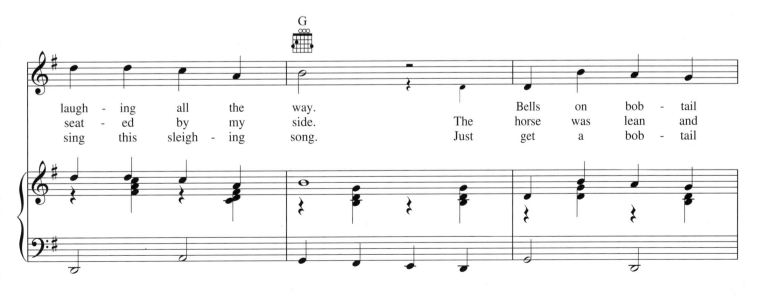

laugh - ing all the way. Bells on bob - tail
seat - ed all by my side. The horse was lean and
sing this sleigh - ing song. Just get a bob - tail

142

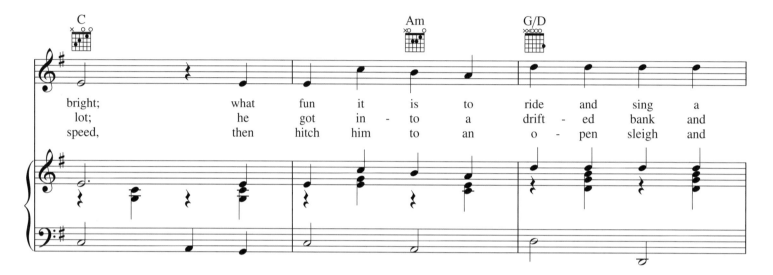

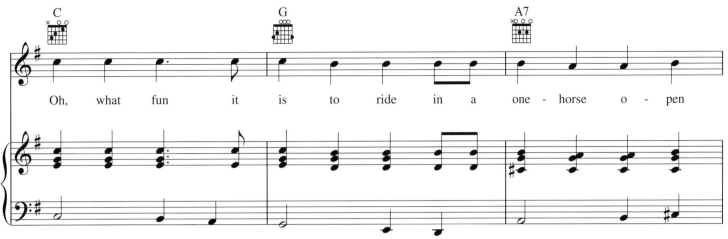

Oh, what fun it is to ride in a one-horse o-pen

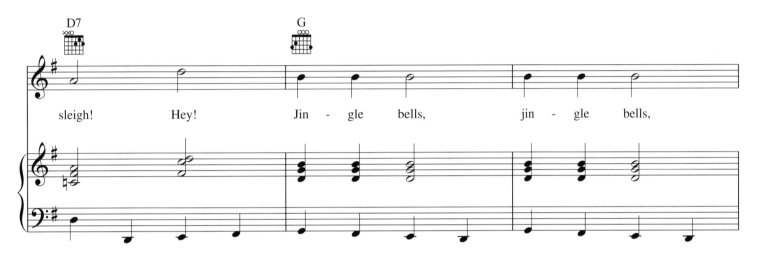

sleigh! Hey! Jin - gle bells, jin - gle bells,

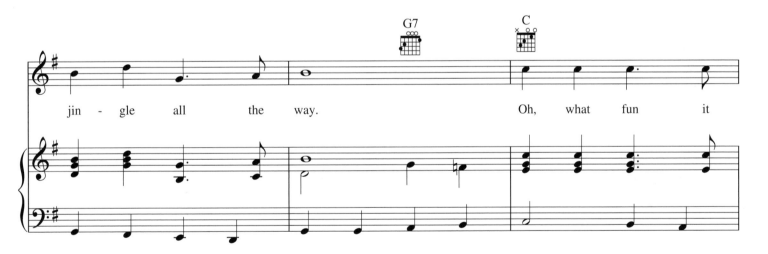

jin - gle all the way. Oh, what fun it

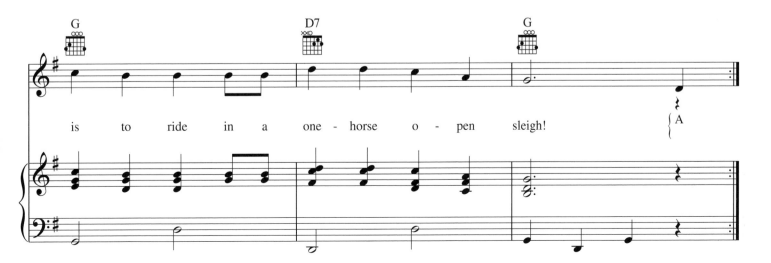

is to ride in a one-horse o-pen sleigh!

JOLLY OLD ST. NICHOLAS

Traditional 19th Century American Carol

Brightly

Jol - ly old Saint
When the clock is

Nich - o - las, lean your ear this way. Don't you tell a sin - gle soul
strik - ing twelve, when I'm fast a - sleep, down the chim - ney broad and black,

what I'm going to say. Christ - mas Eve is com - ing soon, now, you dear old
with your pack you'll creep. All the stock - ings you will find hang - ing in a

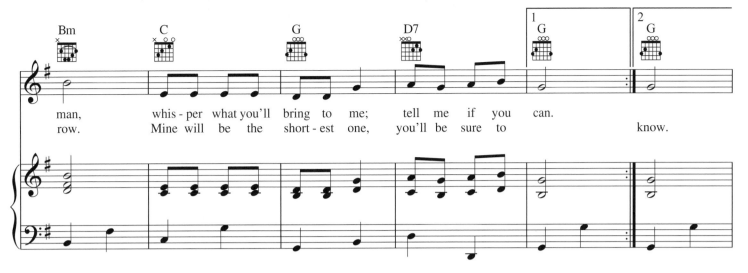

man, whis - per what you'll bring to me; tell me if you can.
row. Mine will be the short - est one, you'll be sure to know.

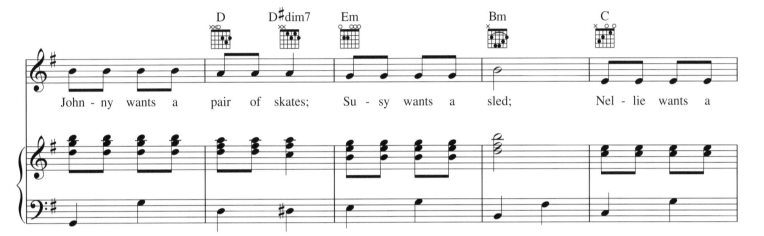

John - ny wants a pair of skates; Su - sy wants a sled; Nel - lie wants a

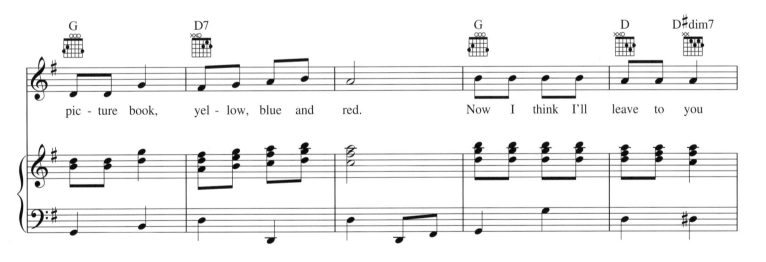

pic - ture book, yel - low, blue and red. Now I think I'll leave to you

what to give the rest. Choose for me, dear San - ta Claus. You will know the best.

JOSEPH DEAREST, JOSEPH MINE

Traditional German Carol

Moderately

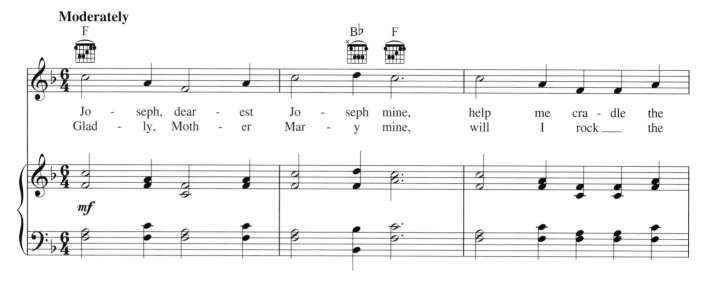

Jo - seph, dear - est Jo - seph mine, help me cra - dle the
Glad - ly, Moth - er Mar - y mine, will I rock ___ the

Babe di - vine. Sing to Him a lull - a - bye: "Now
Babe di - vine. While I sing a lull - a - bye: "O

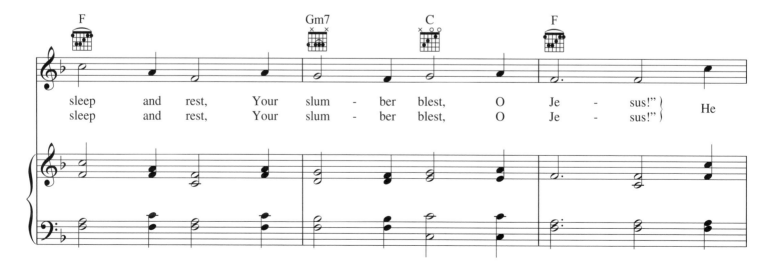

sleep and rest, Your slum - ber blest, O Je - sus!" } He
sleep and rest, Your slum - ber blest, O Je - sus!" }

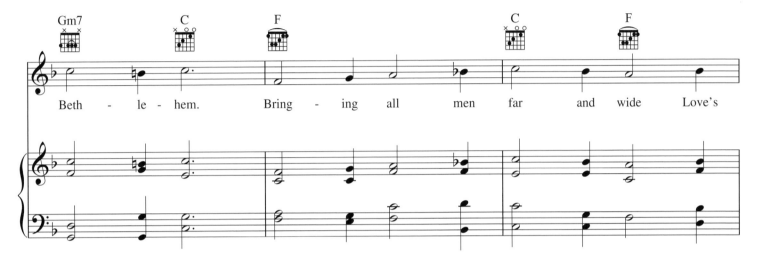

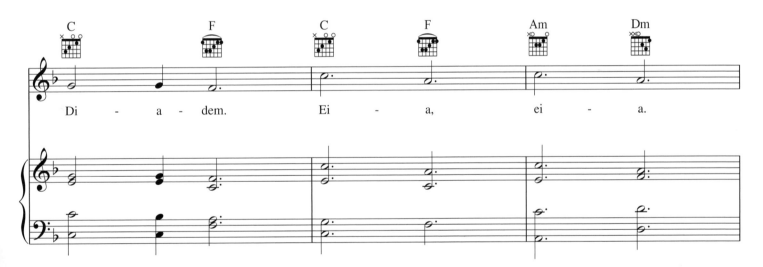

THE JOURNEY

Venezuelan Christmas Carol

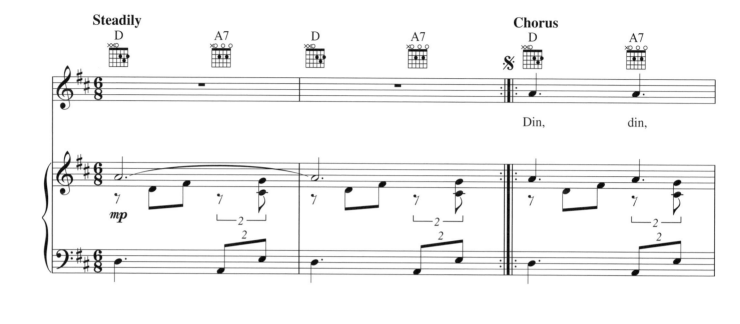

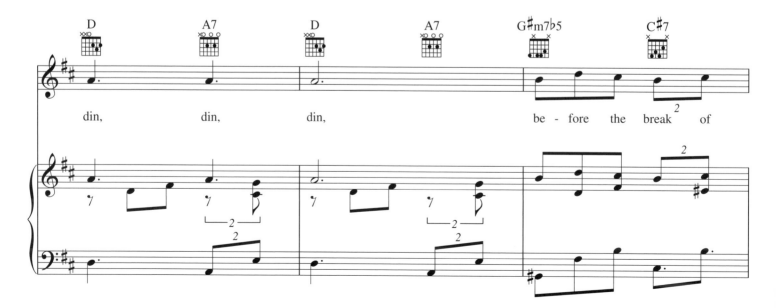

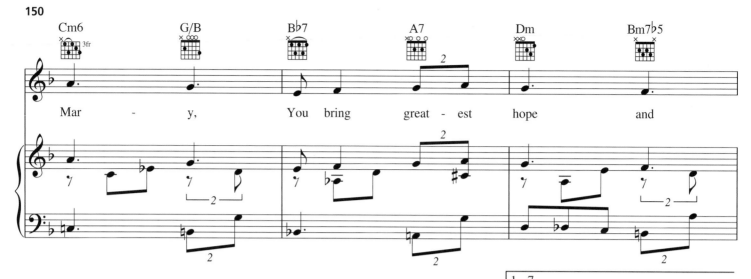

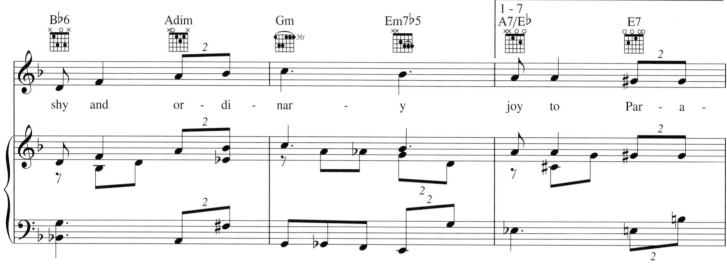

Additional Lyrics

2. Seated on a donkey,
   Mary now was ready;
   Joseph would be guiding,
   Walking all the way
   Chorus

3. Wishing God's protection,
   Friend were gathered 'round them,
   Clasping hands in blessing,
   Watching them depart.
   Chorus

4. O, how long the road was!
   And how hot the air was!
   But they both must bear it,
   For it was God's will.
   Chorus

5. Daylight's rays were dying
   Ere they were arriving,
   But they found no lodging
   In night's growing cold.
   Chorus

6. Joseph begged and pleaded,
   But he was not heeded;
   Not a door was open
   In all Bethlehem.
   Chorus

7. "Every road we travel,
   Crowded full of people!
   Where, O heavenly Father,
   Can we shelter find?
   Chorus

8. Trudging through a meadow,
   Stumbling on a grotto,
   Joseph led poor Mary
   Inside for the night.
   Chorus

MASTERS IN THIS HALL

Traditional English

No - ël! No - ël! No - ël! No - ël! sing we
No - ël! No - ël! No - ël! No - ël! sing we

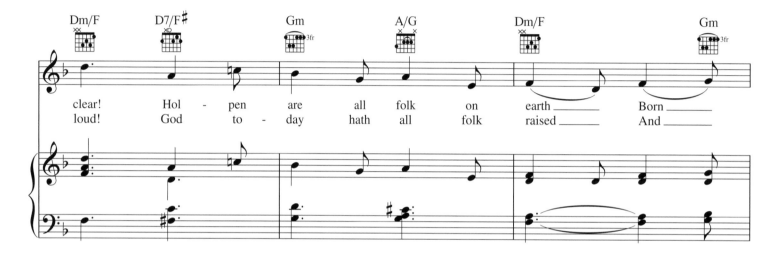

clear! Hol - pen are all folk on earth _____ Born _____
loud! God to - day hath all on folk raised _____ And _____

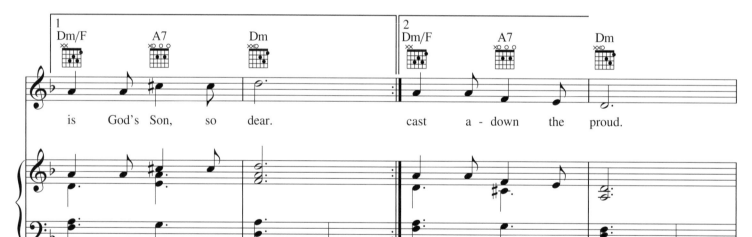

1
is God's Son, so dear.
2
cast a - down the proud.

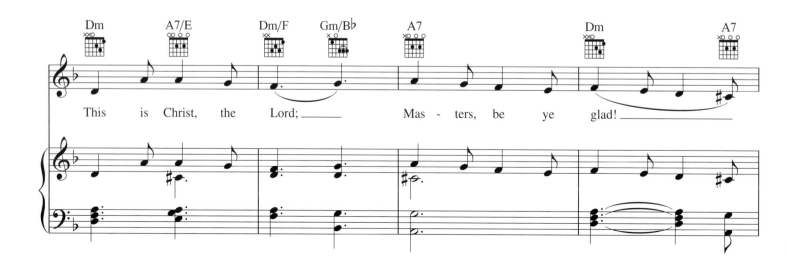

This is Christ, the Lord; _____ Mas - ters, be ye glad! _____

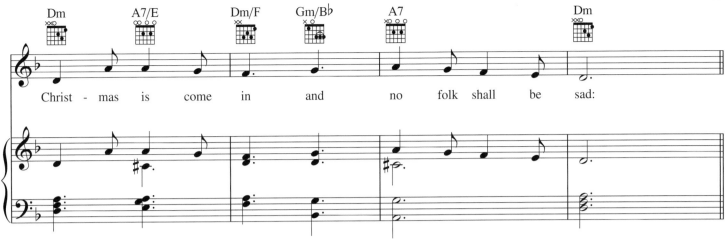

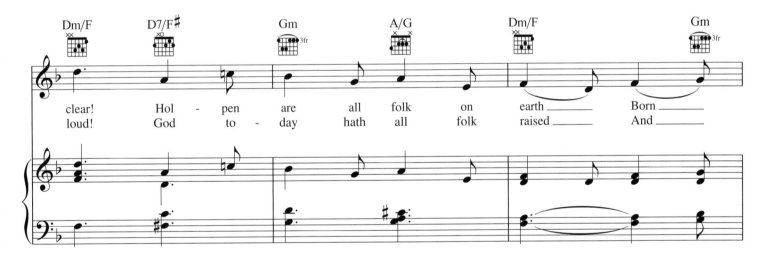

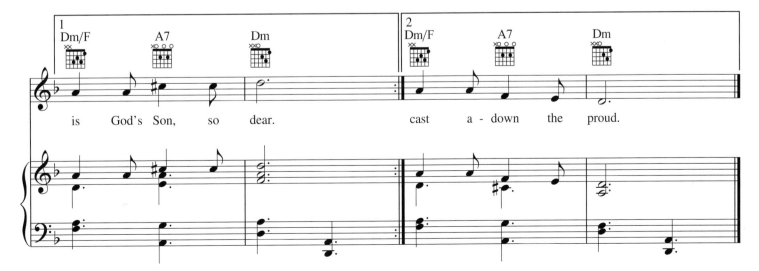

JOY TO THE WORLD

Words by ISAAC WATTS
Music by GEORGE FRIDERIC HANDEL
Arranged by LOWELL MASON

With spirit

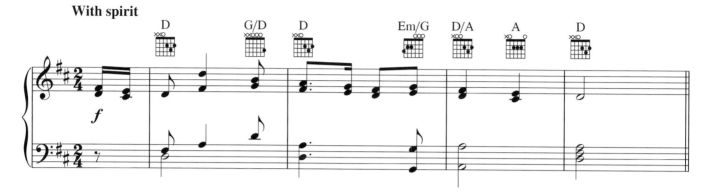

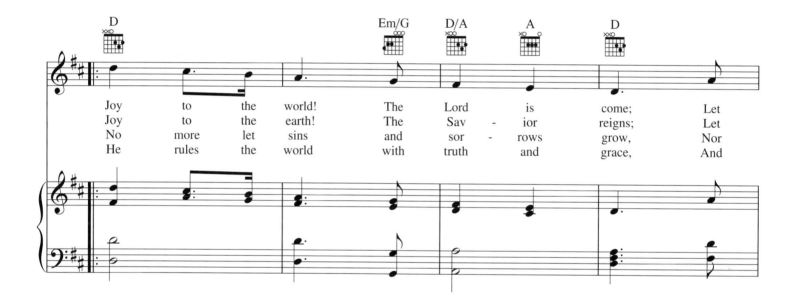

Joy to the world! The Lord is come; Let
Joy to the earth! The Sav - ior reigns; Let
No more let sins and sor - rows grow, Nor
He rules the world with truth and grace, And

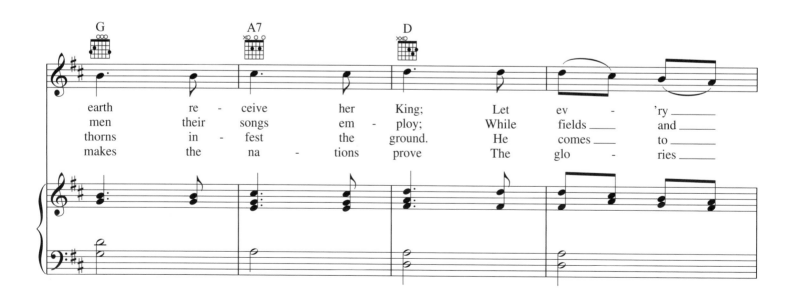

earth re - ceive her King; Let ev - 'ry
men their songs em - ploy; While fields and
thorns in - fest the ground. He comes to
makes the na - tions prove The glo - ries

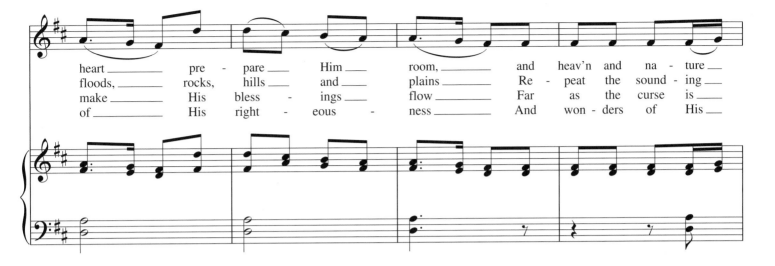

heart ___ pre - pare ___ Him ___ room, ___ and heav'n and na - ture ___
floods, ___ rocks, hills ___ and ___ plains ___ Re - peat the sound - ing ___
make ___ His bless - ings ___ flow ___ Far as the curse is ___
of ___ His right - eous - ness ___ And won - ders of His ___

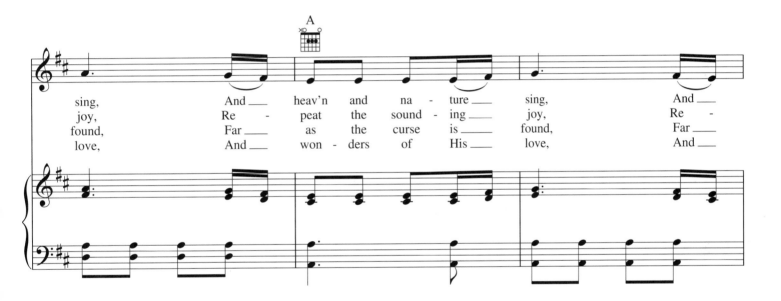

A

sing, And ___ heav'n and na - ture ___ sing, And ___
joy, Re - peat the sound - ing ___ joy, Re -
found, Far ___ as the curse is ___ found, Far ___
love, And ___ won - ders of His ___ love, And ___

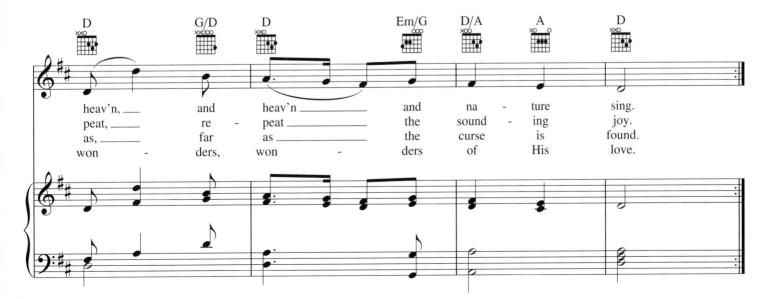

D   G/D   D   Em/G   D/A   A   D

heav'n, ___ and heav'n ___ and na - ture sing.
peat, ___ re - peat ___ the sound - ing joy.
as, ___ far as ___ the curse is found.
won - ders, won - ders of His love.

LITTLE CHILDREN, WAKE AND LISTEN

Traditional French Carol

Lit - tle chil - dren, wake and lis - ten! Songs are
this that they are tell - ing sing - ing
left His throne of glo - ry, and a

break - ing o'er the earth. While the stars in heav - en
in the qui - et street? While their voic - es high are
low - ly cra - dle found. Well might an - gels tell the

LO, HOW A ROSE E'ER BLOOMING

15th Century German Carol
Translated by THEODORE BAKER
Music from *Alte Catholische Geistliche Kirchengesäng*

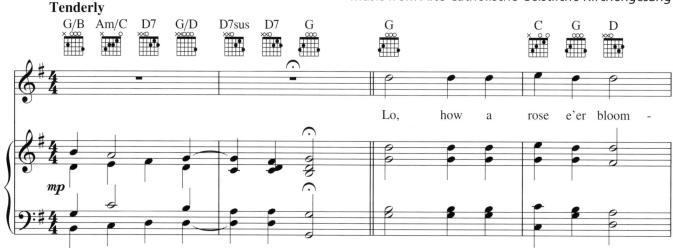

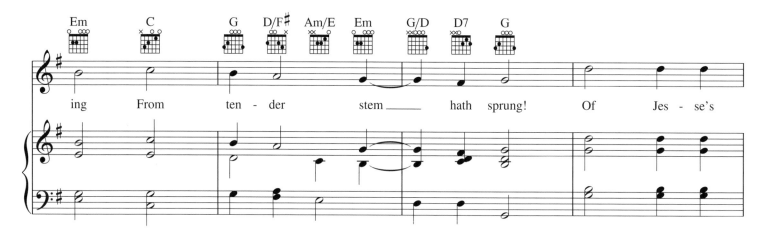

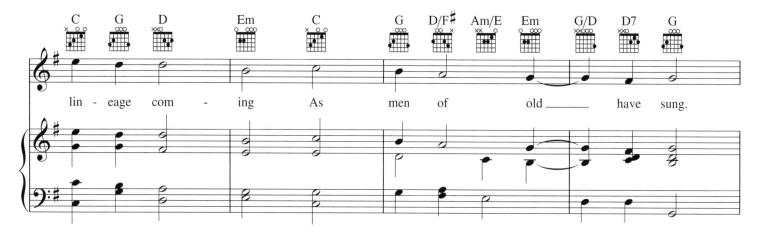

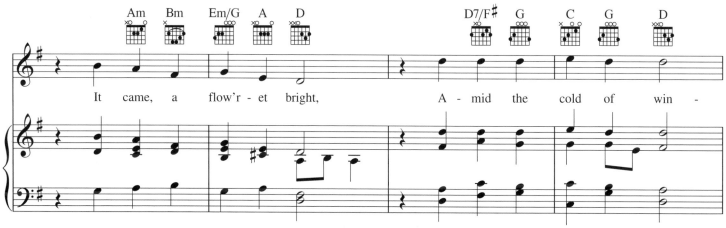

MARCH OF THE THREE KINGS

Words by M.L. HOHMAN
Traditional French Melody

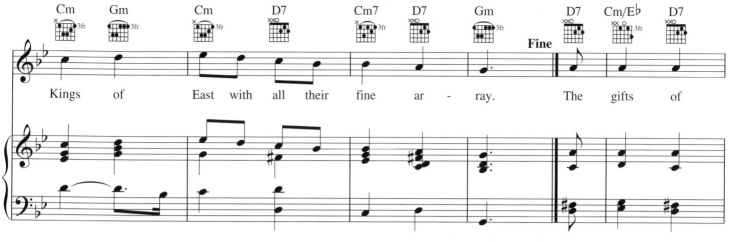

Kings of East with all their fine ar - ray. The gifts of

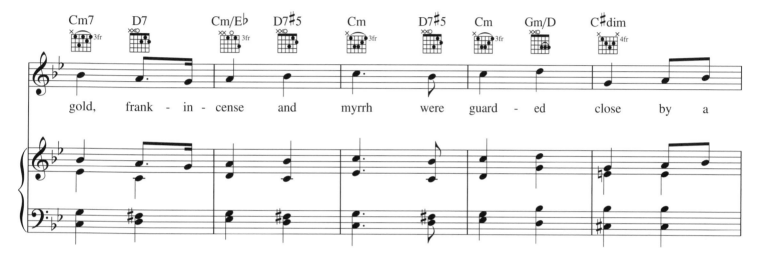

gold, frank - in - cense and myrrh were guard - ed close by a

band of stur - dy war - riors, their swords, their shields, and their buck - lers

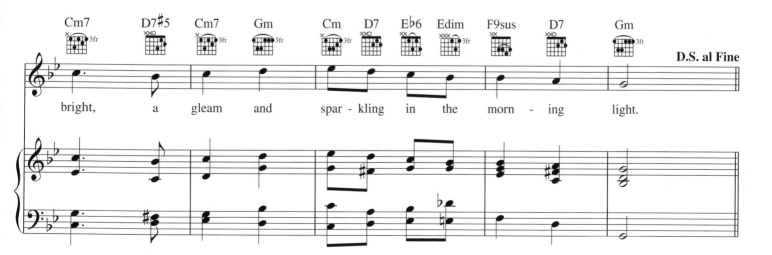

bright, a gleam and spar - kling in the morn - ing light.

MARCH OF THE TOYS

from BABES IN TOYLAND

By VICTOR HERBERT

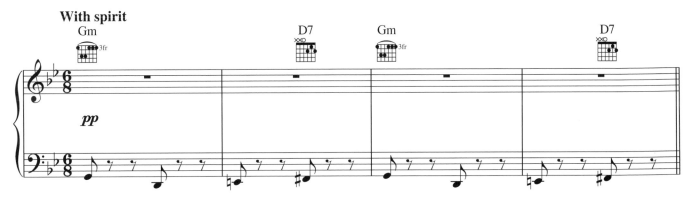

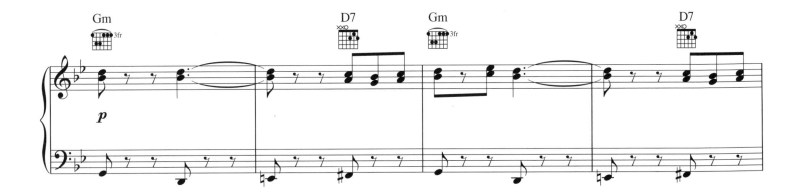

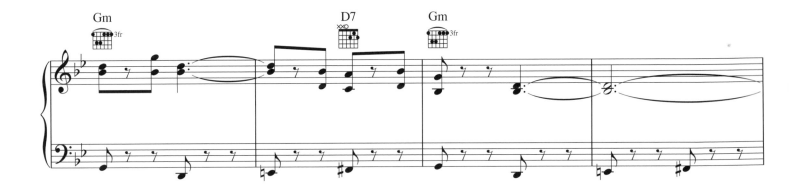

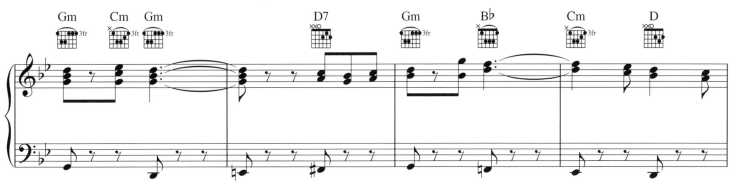

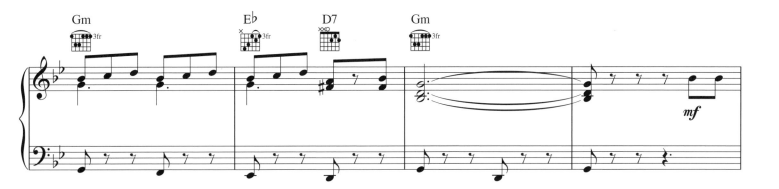

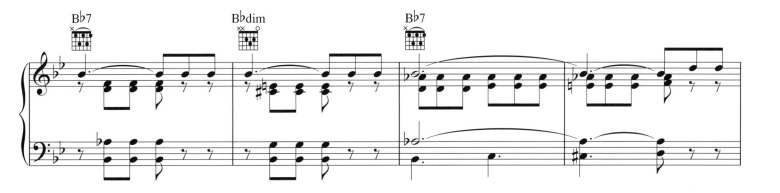

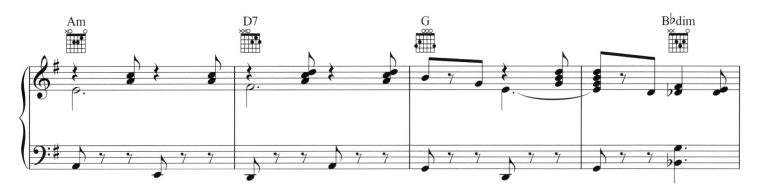

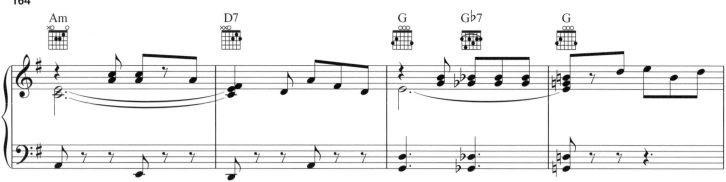
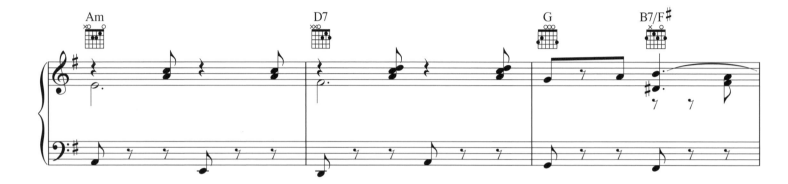
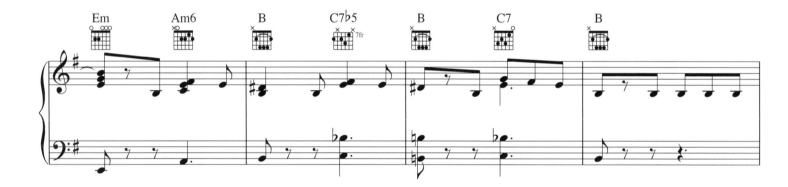
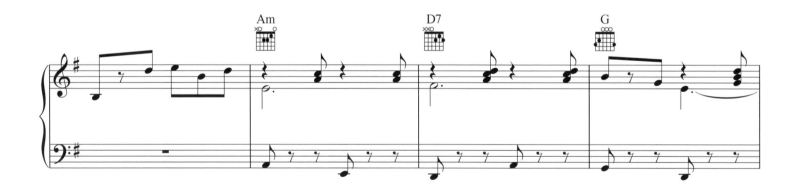

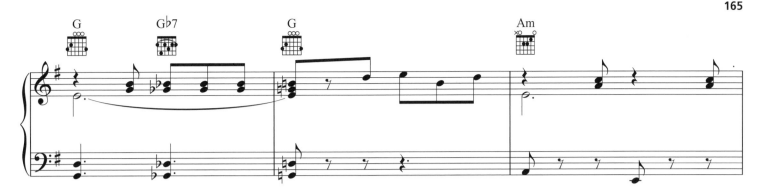

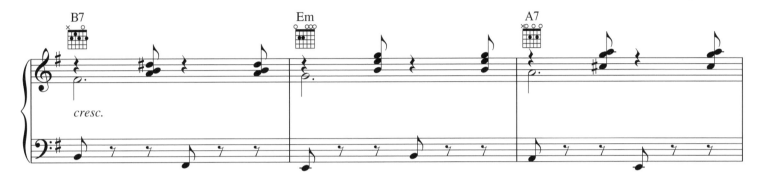

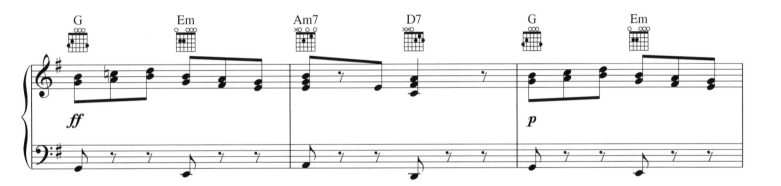

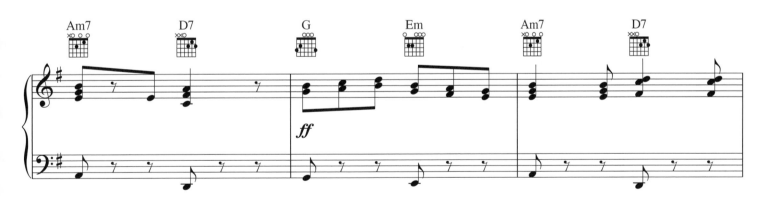

MARY HAD A BABY

African-American Spiritual

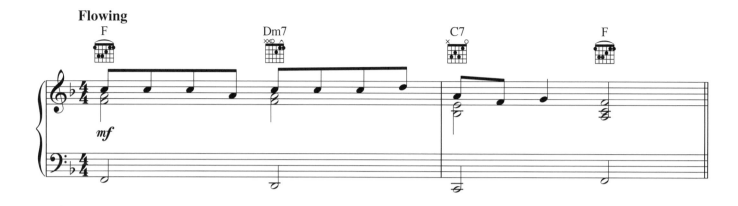

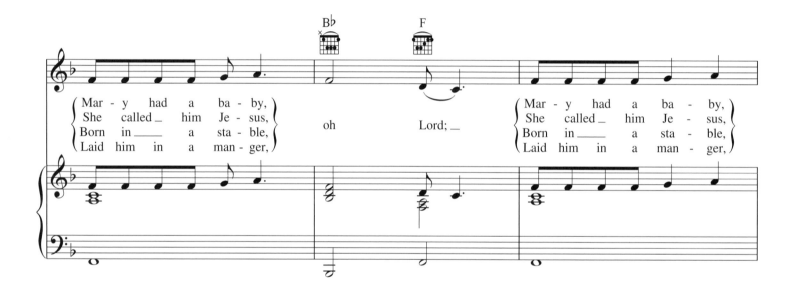

Mar - y had a ba - by,
She called __ him Je - sus,
Born in ____ a sta - ble,
Laid him in a man - ger,

oh Lord; __

Mar - y had a ba - by,
She called __ him Je - sus,
Born in ____ a sta - ble,
Laid him in a man - ger,

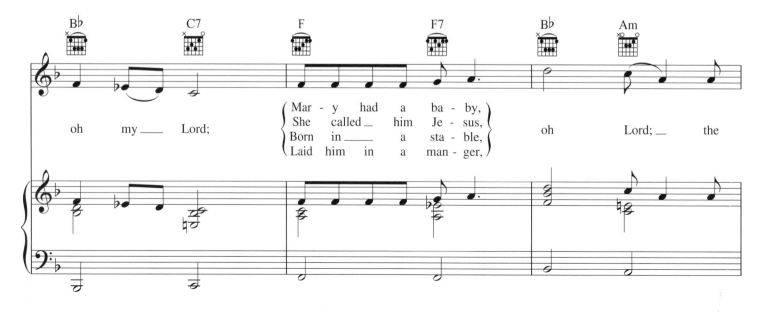

oh my __ Lord;

Mar - y had a ba - by,
She called __ him Je - sus,
Born in ____ a sta - ble,
Laid him in a man - ger,

oh Lord; __ the

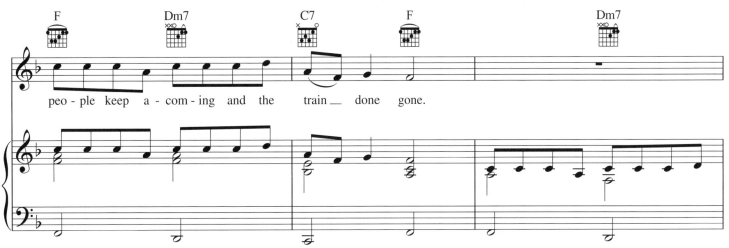

peo - ple keep a - com - ing and the train __ done gone.

{ What did she name Him?
Where was He born? __
Where did they lay Him?
Mar - y had a ba - by. }

Oh Lord; __

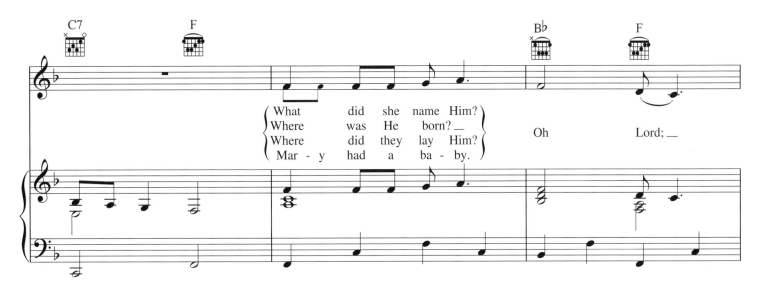

{ What did she name Him?
Where was He born? __
Where did they lay Him?
Mar - y had a ba - by. }

Oh my __ Lord;

{ What did she name Him?
Where was He born? __
Where did they lay Him?
Mar - y had a ba - by. }

Oh Lord; __ the peo - ple keep a - com - ing and the train __ done gone.

NEIGHBOR, WHAT HAS YOU SO EXCITED?

Traditional French

"Neigh - bor, what has you so ex -
"It would be pleas - ant to go

cit - ed? Do tell me, please."
with you. Like - ly I'll go.

"Have - n't you heard? A Boy is
But can't we take our time to

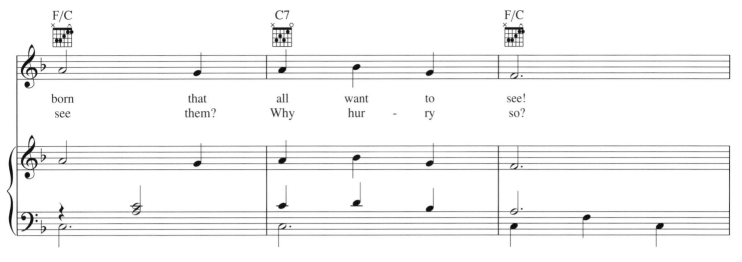

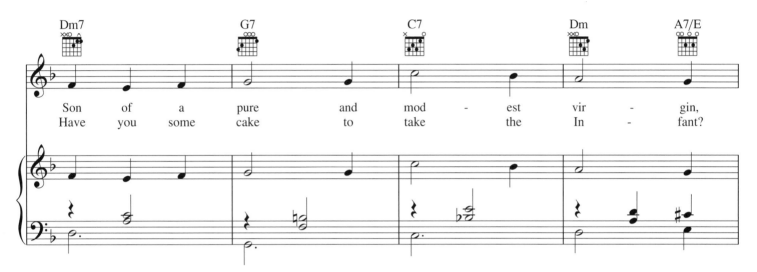

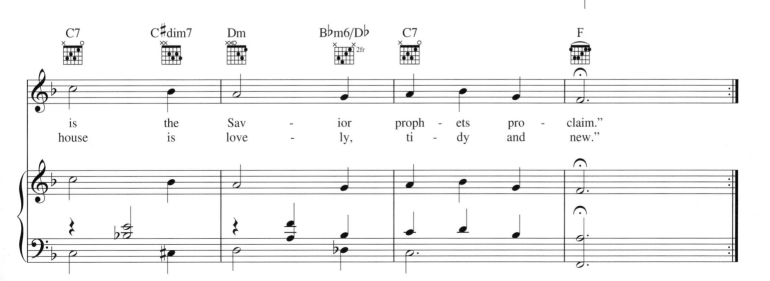

NOËL! NOËL!

French-English Carol

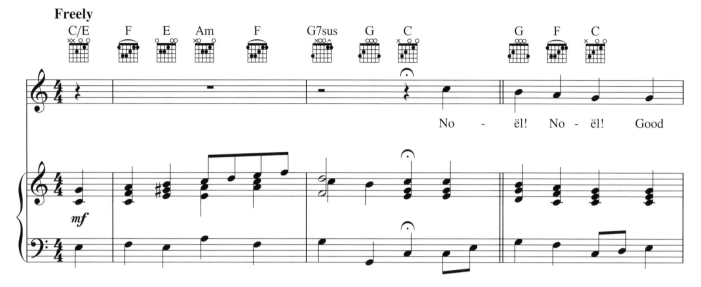

Freely

No - ël! No - ël! Good

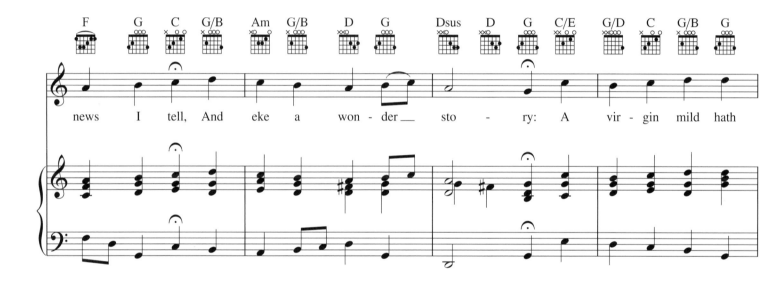

news I tell, And eke a won - der sto - ry: A vir - gin mild hath

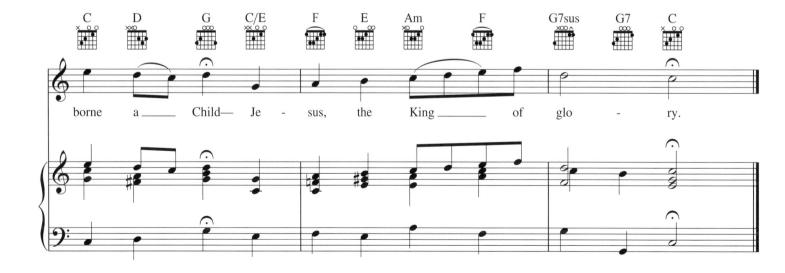

borne a Child— Je - sus, the King of glo - ry.

O COME, O COME IMMANUEL

Plainsong, 13th Century
Words translated by JOHN M. NEALE
and HENRY S. COFFIN

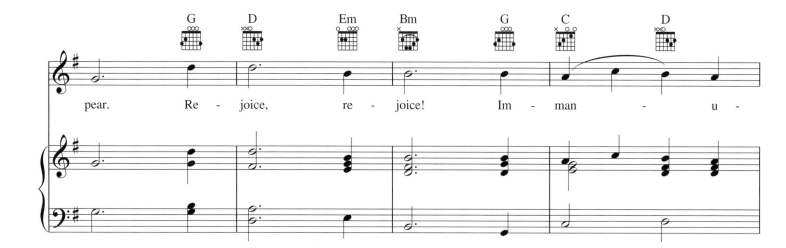

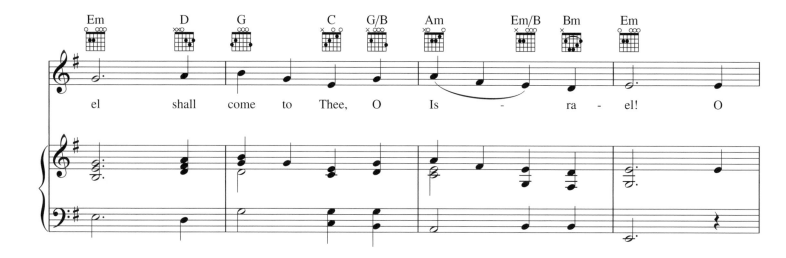

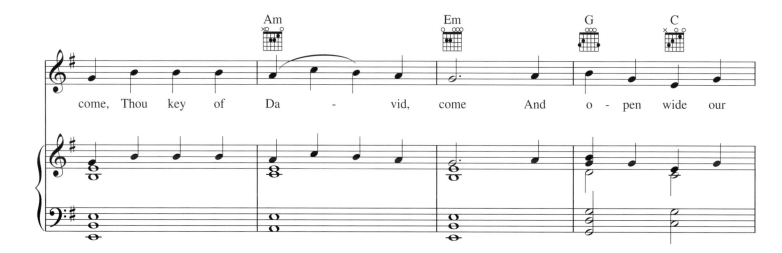

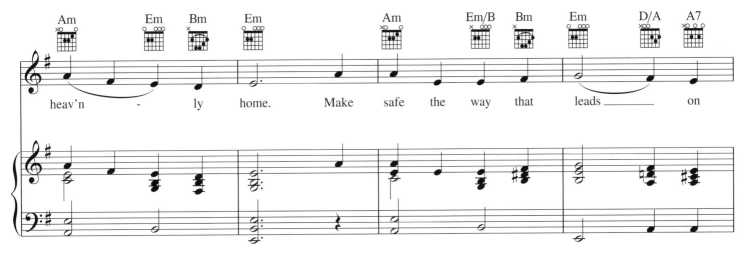

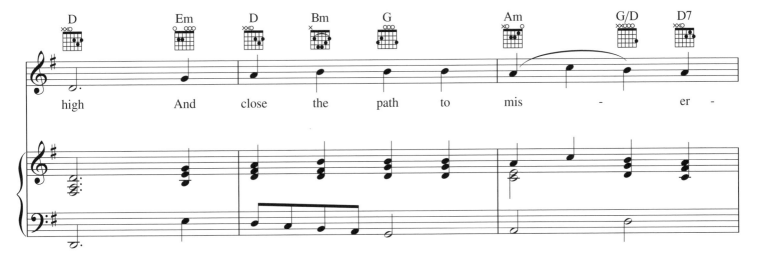

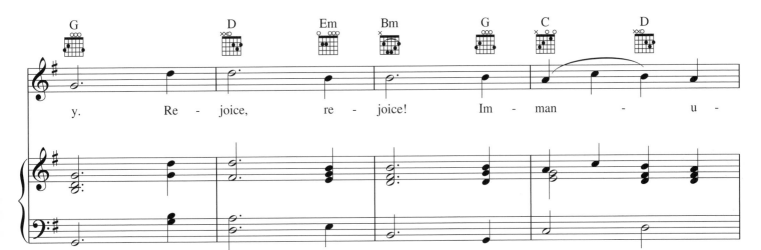

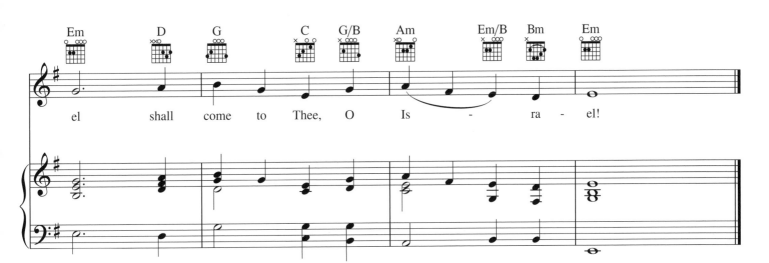

O BETHLEHEM

Traditional Spanish

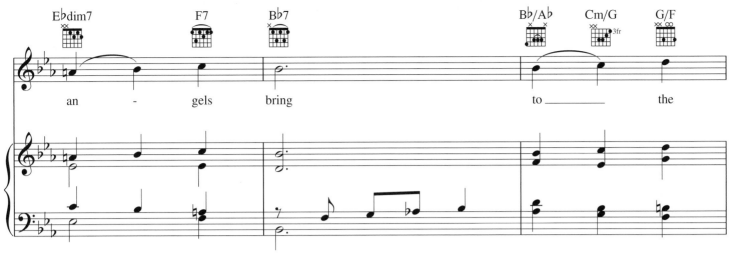

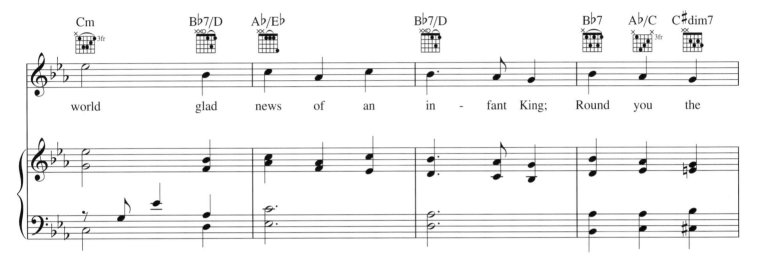

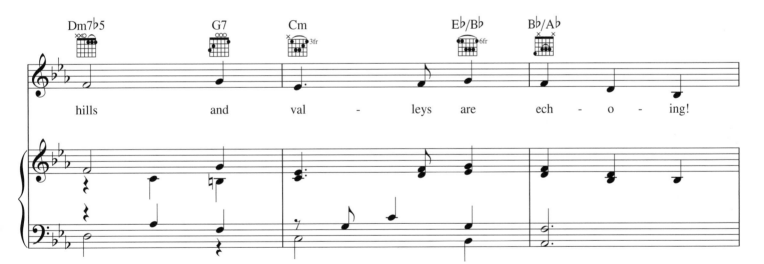

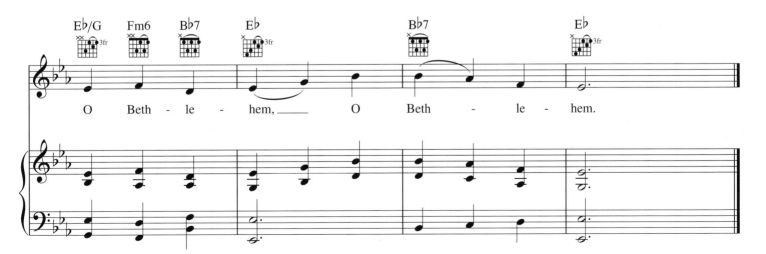

O CHRISTMAS TREE

Traditional German Carol

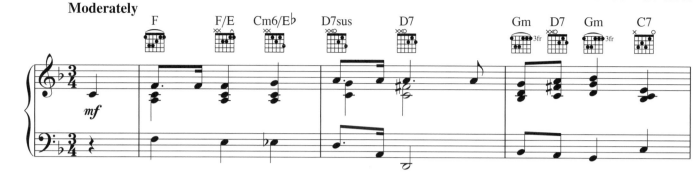

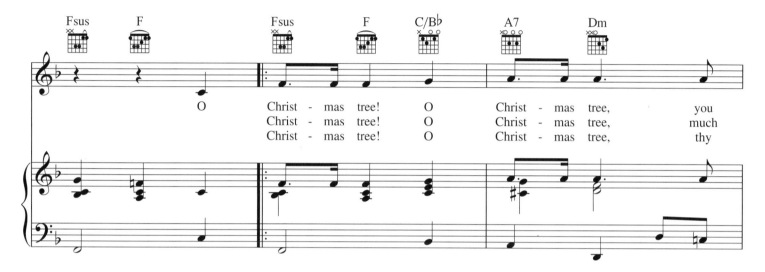

O Christ - mas tree! O Christ - mas tree, you
Christ - mas tree! O Christ - mas tree, much
Christ - mas tree! O Christ - mas tree, thy

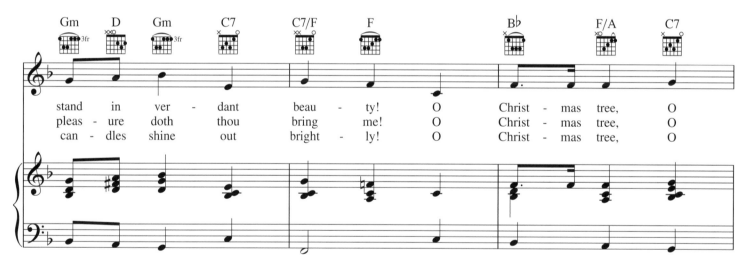

stand in ver - dant beau - ty! O Christ - mas tree, O
pleas - ure doth thou bring me! O Christ - mas tree, O
can - dles shine out bright - ly! O Christ - mas tree, O

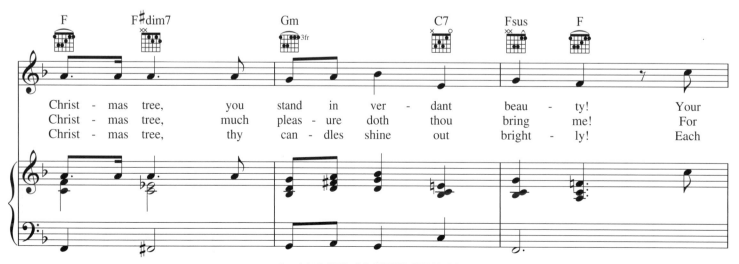

Christ - mas tree, you stand in ver - dant beau - ty! Your
Christ - mas tree, much pleas - ure doth thou bring me! For
Christ - mas tree, thy can - dles shine out bright - ly! Each

O COME, ALL YE FAITHFUL
(Adeste fideles)

Music by JOHN FRANCIS WADE
Latin Words translated by FREDERICK OAKELEY

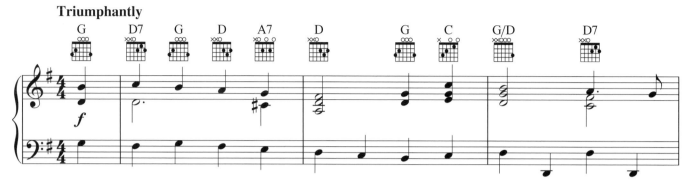

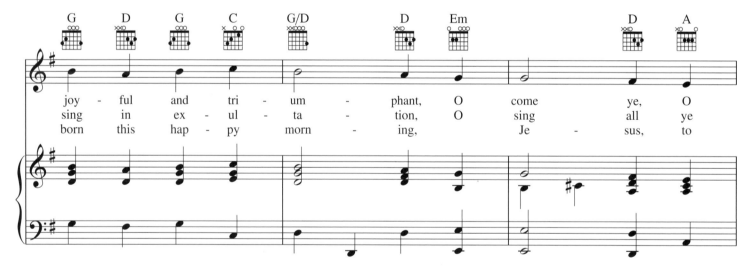

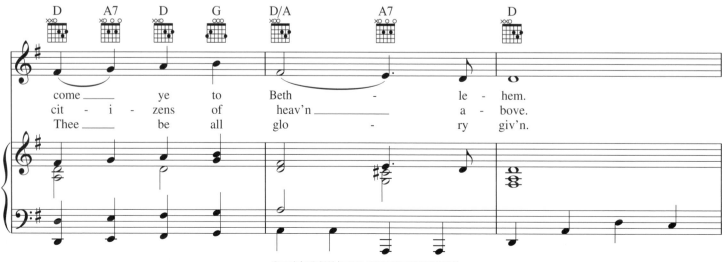

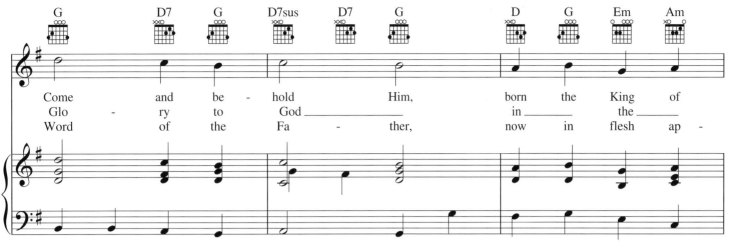

Come and be - hold Him, born the King of
Glo - ry to God _____ in _____ the _____
Word of the Fa - ther, now in flesh ap -

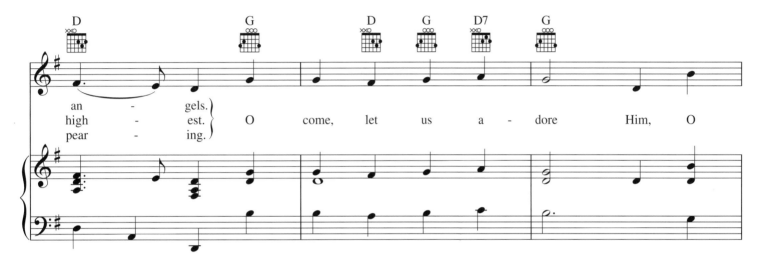

an - gels. }
high - est. } O come, let us a - dore Him, O
pear - ing. }

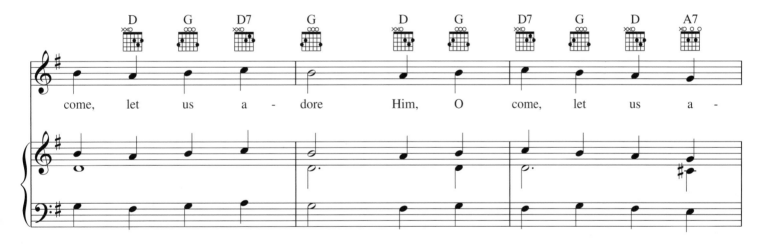

come, let us a - dore Him, O come, let us a -

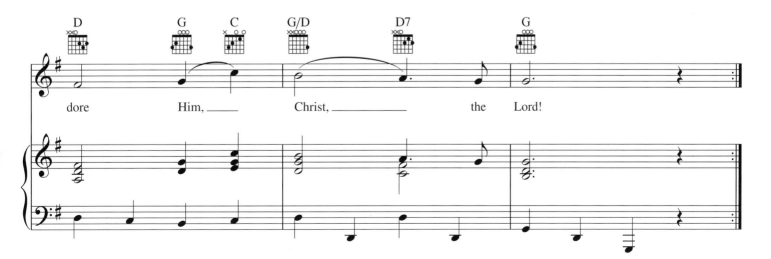

dore Him, _____ Christ, _____ the Lord!

O COME AWAY, YE SHEPHERDS

18th Century French Text
Tune from Air, "Nanon Dormait"

O COME, LITTLE CHILDREN

Words by C. VON SCHMIDT
Music by J.P.A. SCHULZ

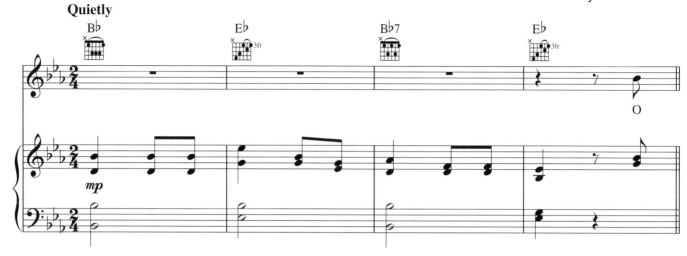

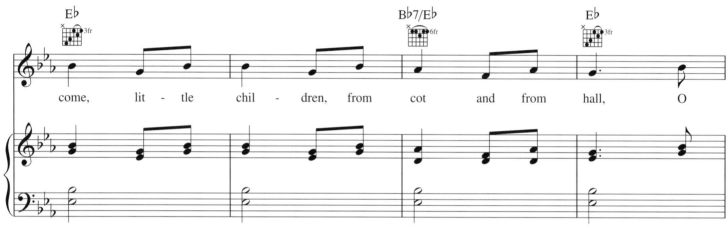

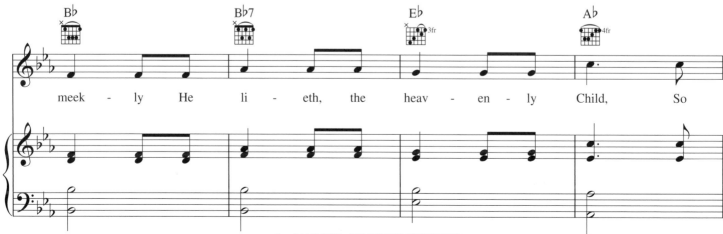

poor and so hum - ble, so sweet and so mild. Now "Glo - ry to

God!" sing the an - gels on high, And "Peace up - on earth!" heav'n - ly

voic - es re - ply. Then come, lit - tle chil - dren, and join in the

day That glad - dened the world on that first Christ - mas Day.

O COME REJOICING

Traditional Polish Carol

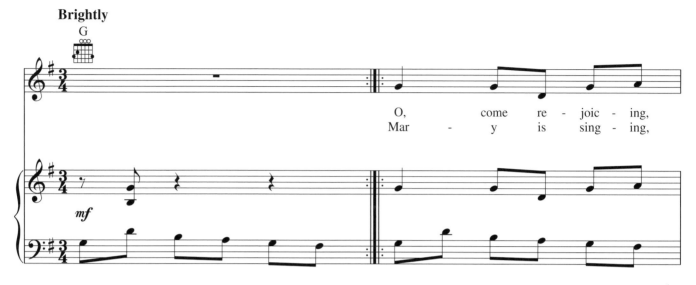

to thee! }
glo - rious. }
Tru - ly He com - eth, Christ, our sal - va - tion.

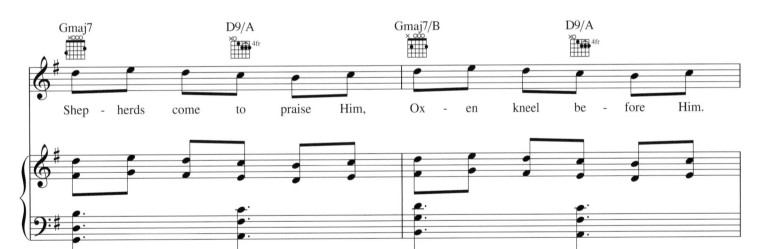

An - gels are voic - ing their ju - bi - la - tion.

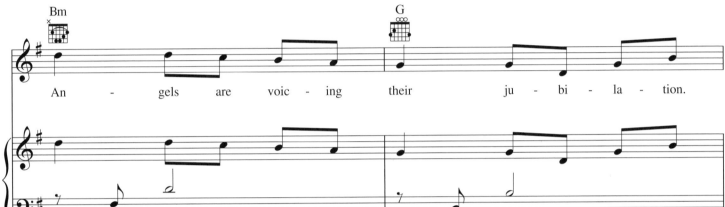

Shep - herds come to praise Him, Ox - en kneel be - fore Him.

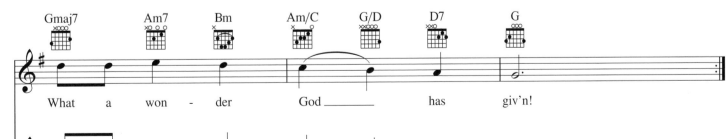

What a won - der God _____ has giv'n!

O HOLY NIGHT

French Words by PLACIDE CAPPEAU
English Words by JOHN S. DWIGHT
Music by ADOLPHE ADAM

Slow and flowing

O ho- ly night, _____ the
Tru- ly He taught us to

stars are bright- ly shin - ing; it is the night of the
love one an- oth - er; His law is love, and His

dear Sav- ior's birth. _____ Long lay the
gos - pel is peace. _____ Chains shall He

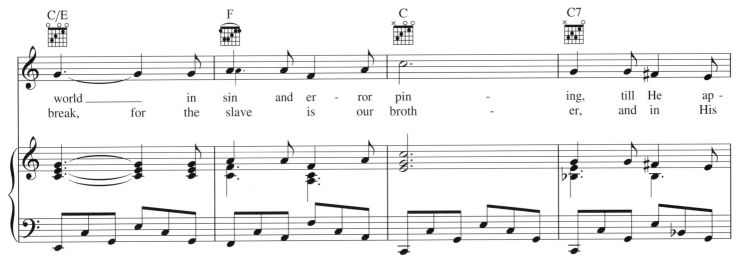

world _____ in sin and er - ror pin - ing, till He ap -
break, for the slave is our broth - er, and in His

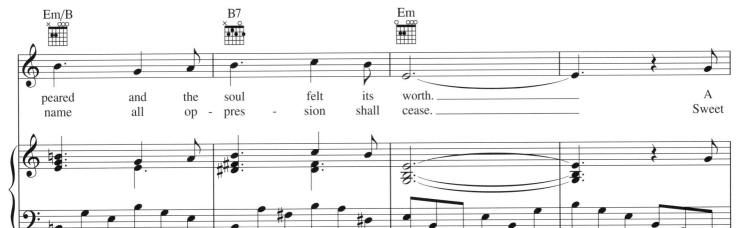

peared and the soul felt its worth. _____ A
name all op - pres - sion shall cease. _____ Sweet

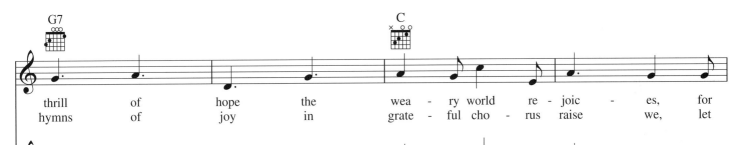

thrill of hope the wea - ry world re - joic - es, for
hymns of joy in grate - ful cho - rus raise we, let

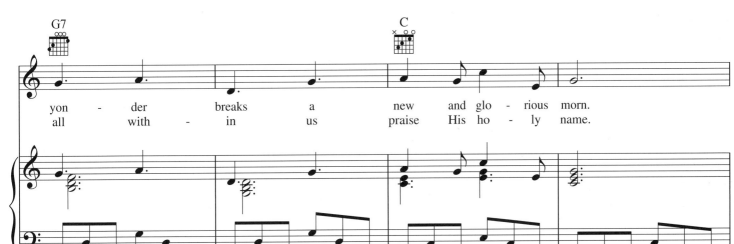

yon - der breaks a new and glo - rious morn.
all with - in us praise His ho - ly name.

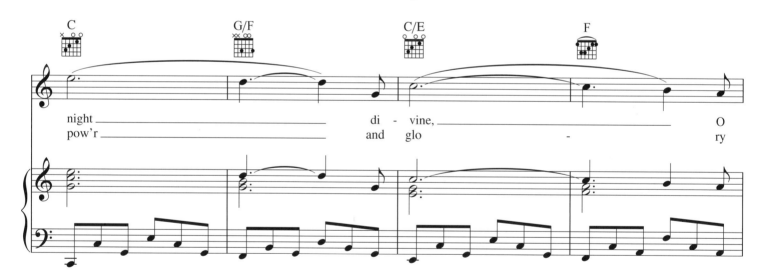

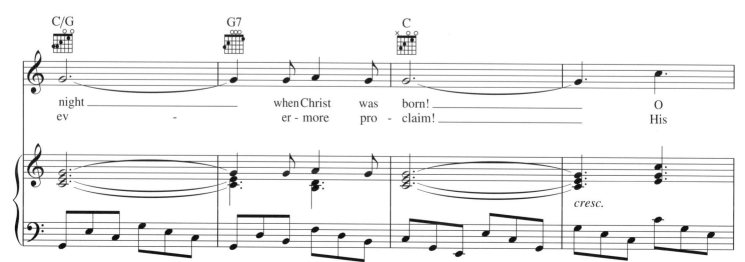

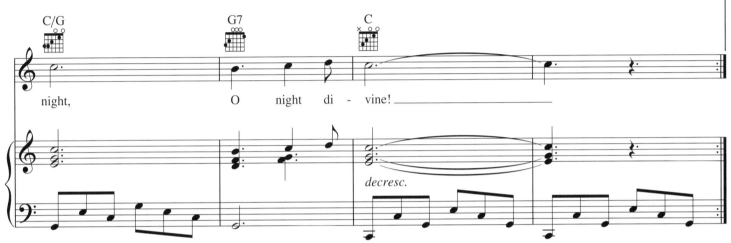

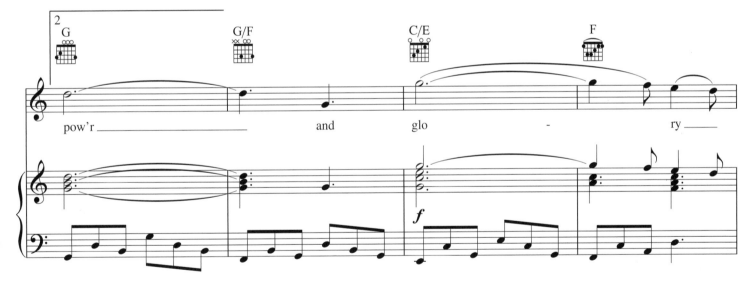

O LET US ALL BE GLAD TODAY

Words by MARTIN LUTHER
Music from *Geistliche Lieder*, 1539

1. O let us all be glad to-day, And
2. wake, my soul, from sad-ness rise. Come,
3.- 6. *(See additional lyrics)*

with the shep-herds hom-age pay. Come, see what God to
see what in the man-ger lies. Who is this smil - ing

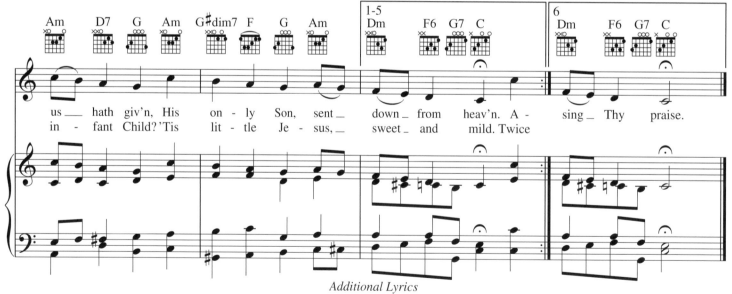

us hath giv'n, His on - ly Son, sent down from heav'n. A - sing Thy praise.
in - fant Child? 'Tis lit - tle Je - sus, sweet and mild. Twice

Additional Lyrics

3. Twice welcome, O Thou heavenly guest,
   To save a world with sin distressed;
   Com'st Thou in lowly guise for me?
   What homage shall I give to Thee?

4. Ah! Lord eternal, heavenly King,
   Hast Thou become so mean a thing?
   And hast Thou left Thy blissful seat,
   To rest where colts and oxen eat?

5. Jesus, my Savior, come to me,
   Make here a little crib for Thee;
   A bed make in this heart of mine,
   That I may ay remember Thine.

6. Then from my soul glad songs shall ring;
   Of Thee each day I'll gladly sing;
   Then glad hosannas will I raise,
   From heart that loves to sing Thy praise.

RISE UP, SHEPHERD, AND FOLLOW

African-American Spiritual

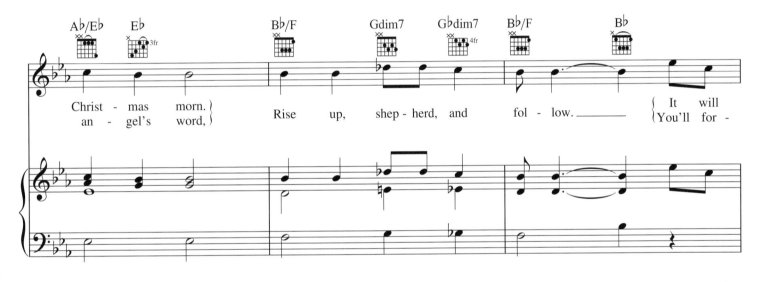

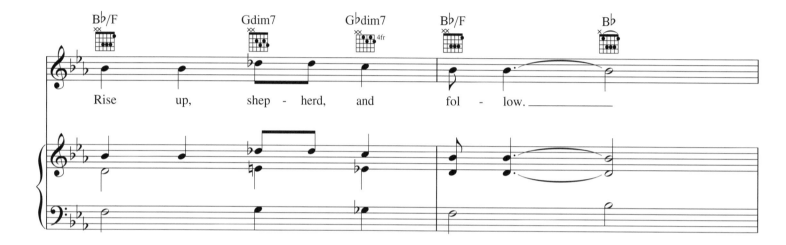

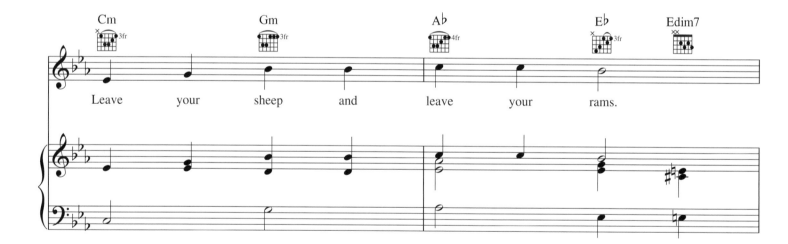

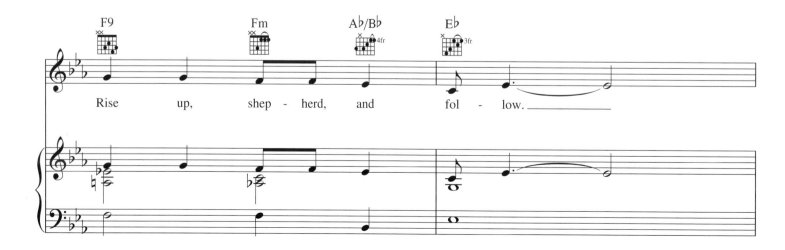

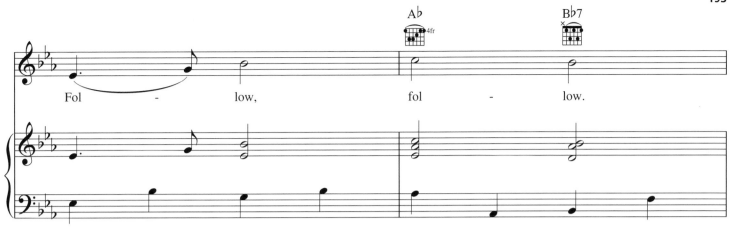

Fol - low, fol - low.

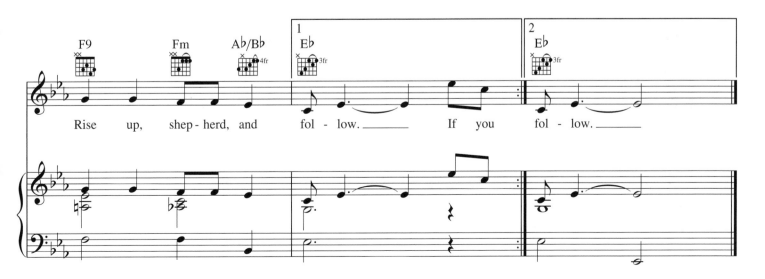

Rise up, shep - herd, and fol - low. _____

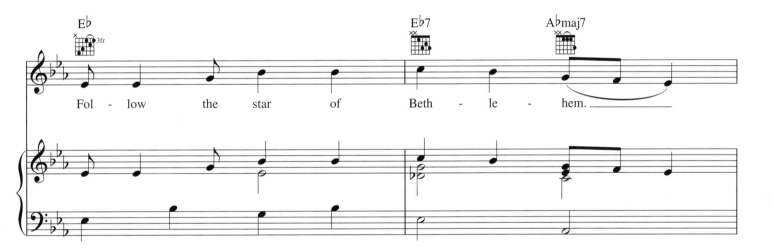

Fol - low the star of Beth - le - hem. _____

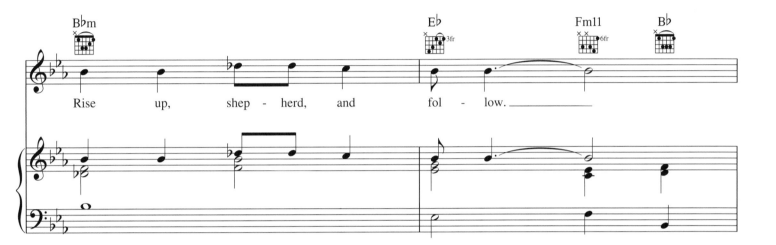

Rise up, shep-herd, and fol - low. _____ If you fol - low. _____

O LITTLE TOWN OF BETHLEHEM

Words by PHILLIPS BROOKS
Music by LEWIS H. REDNER

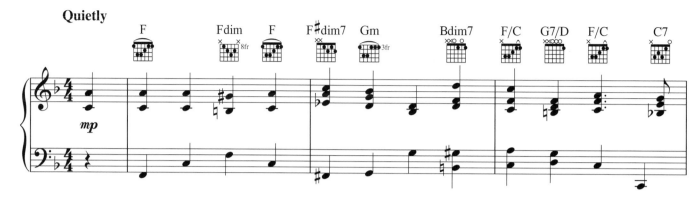

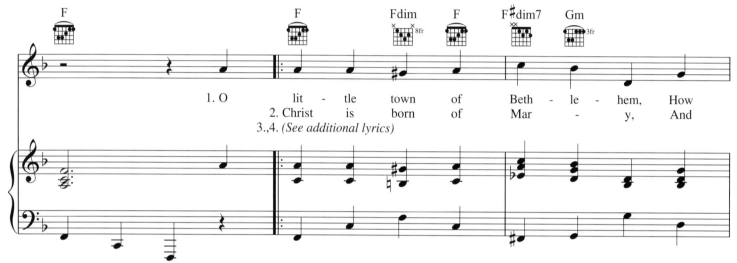

1. O lit - tle town of Beth - le - hem, How
2. Christ is born of Mar - y, And
3.,4. *(See additional lyrics)*

still we ___ see thee lie! A - bove thy deep and
gath - ered ___ all a - bove, While mor - tals deep sleep and the

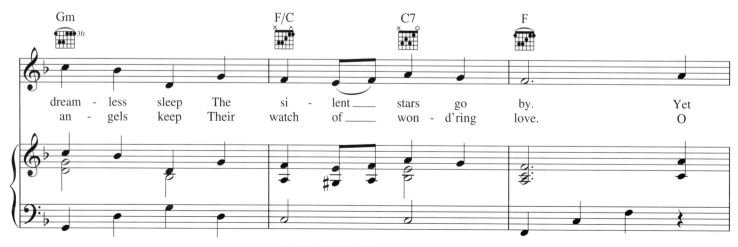

dream - less sleep The si - lent ___ stars go by. Yet
an - gels keep Their watch of ___ won - d'ring love. O

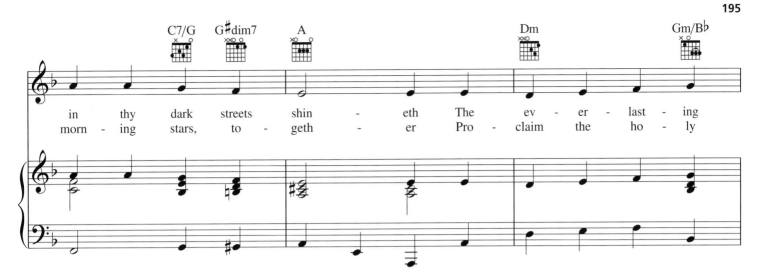

in thy dark streets shin - eth The ev - er - last - ing
morn - ing stars, to - geth - er Pro - claim the ho - ly

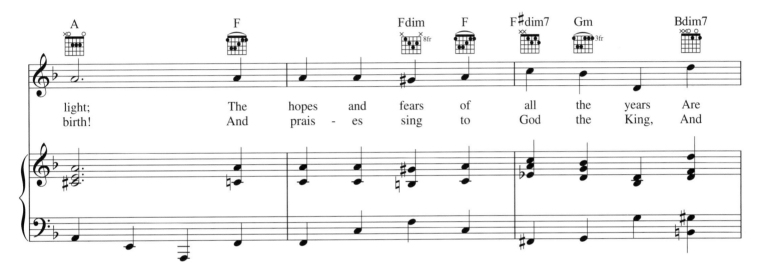

light; The hopes and fears of all the years Are
birth! And prais - es sing to God the King, And

met in thee to - night. 2. For el!
peace to men on earth. 3. How

Additional Lyrics

3. How silently, how silently
   The wondrous Gift is giv'n!
   So God imparts to human hearts
   The blessings of His heav'n.
   No ear may hear His coming,
   But in this world of sin,
   Where meek souls will receive Him still,
   The dear Christ enters in.

4. O Holy Child of Bethlehem,
   Descend to us, we pray.
   Cast out our sin, and enter in,
   Be born in us today.
   We hear the Christmas angels
   The great glad tidings tell.
   O come to us, abide with us,
   Our Lord Immanuel!

O SANCTISSIMA

Sicilian Carol

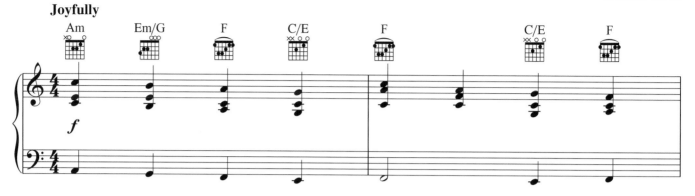

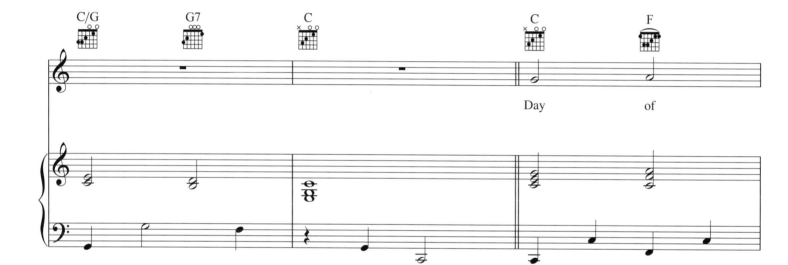

Day of

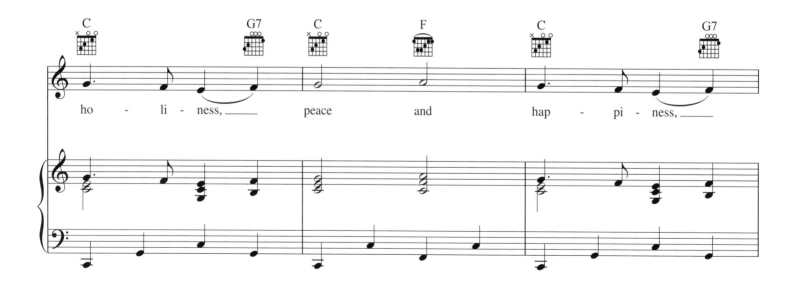

ho - li - ness, ___ peace and hap - pi - ness, ___

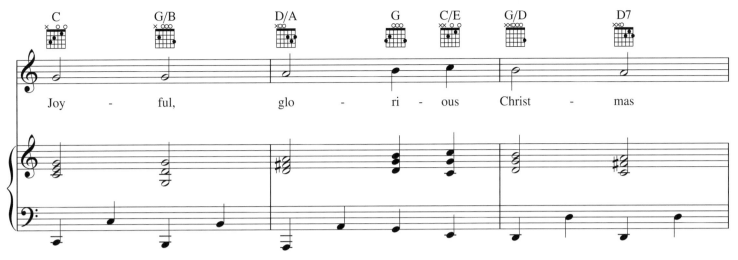

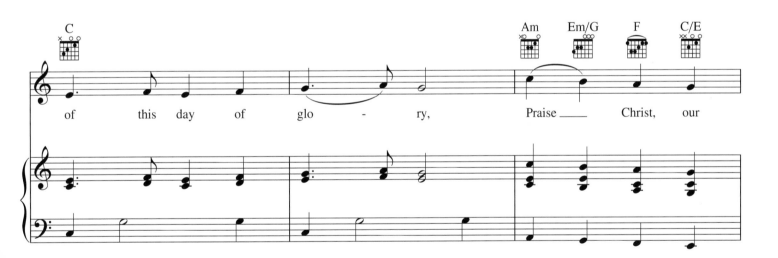

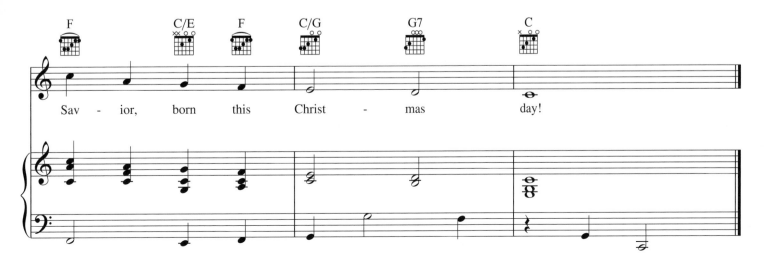

ON CHRISTMAS NIGHT

Sussex Carol

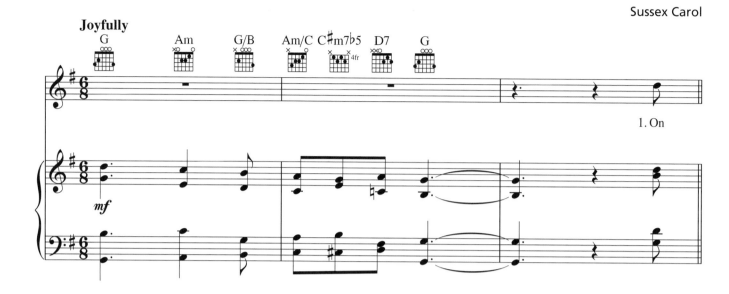

1. On

Christ - mas night true Chris - tians sing, To hear the news ___ the
2. King of kings to us ___ is giv'n, The Lord of earth ___ and
3.,4. (See additional lyrics)

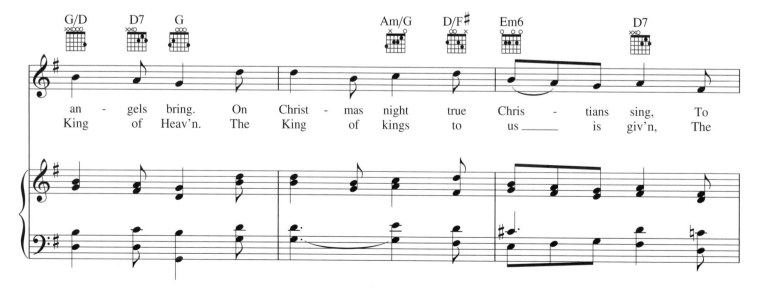

an - gels bring. On Christ - mas night true Chris - tians sing, To
King of Heav'n. The King of kings to us ___ is giv'n, The

hear the news ___ the an - gels bring. News of great
Lord of earth ___ and King of Heav'n. An - gels great and

joy ___ and of ___ great mirth, Tid - ings
men ___ with joy ___ may sing Of blest

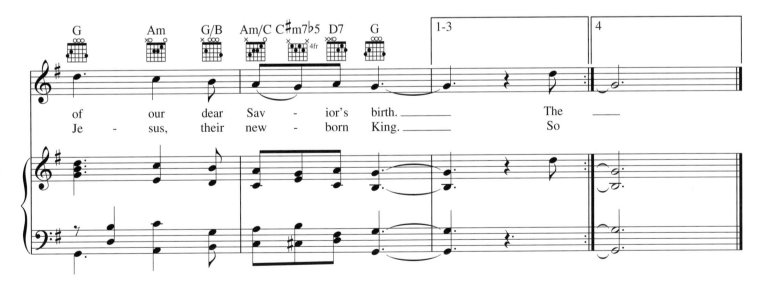

of our dear Sav - ior's birth. ___ The ___
Je - sus, their new - born King. ___ So

Additional Lyrics

3. So how on earth can men be sad,
   When Jesus comes to make us glad?
   So how on earth can men be sad,
   When Jesus comes to make us glad?
   From all our sins to set us free,
   Buying for us our liberty.

4. From out the darkness have we light,
   Which makes the angels sing this night.
   From out the darkness have we light,
   Which makes the angels sing this night:
   "Glory to God, His peace to men,
   And good will, evermore! Amen."

ONCE IN ROYAL DAVID'S CITY

Words by CECIL F. ALEXANDER
Music by HENRY J. GAUNTLETT

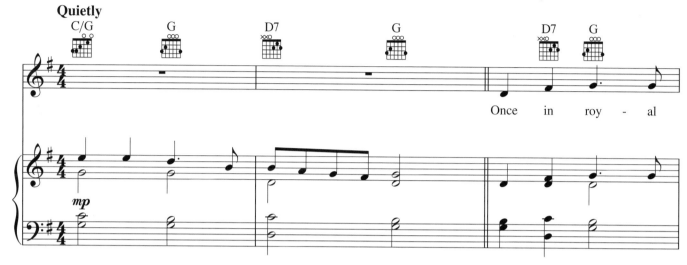

Once in roy - al

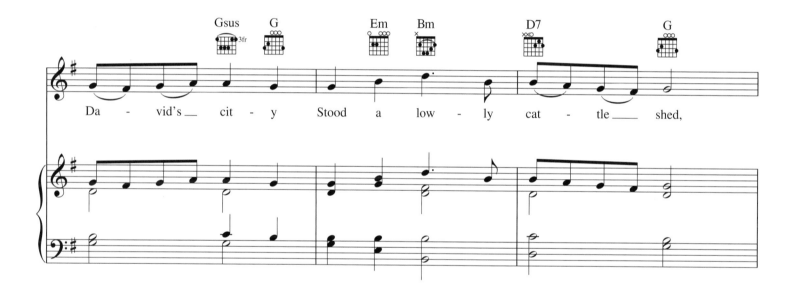

Da - vid's __ cit - y Stood a low - ly cat - tle __ shed,

Where a moth - er laid __ her __ Ba - by In a man - ger for __ His __ bed.

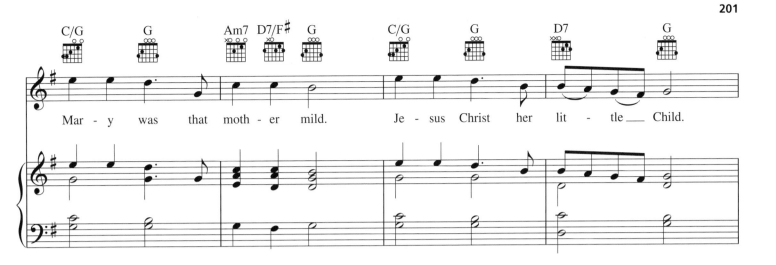

Mar - y was that moth - er mild. Je - sus Christ her lit - tle __ Child.

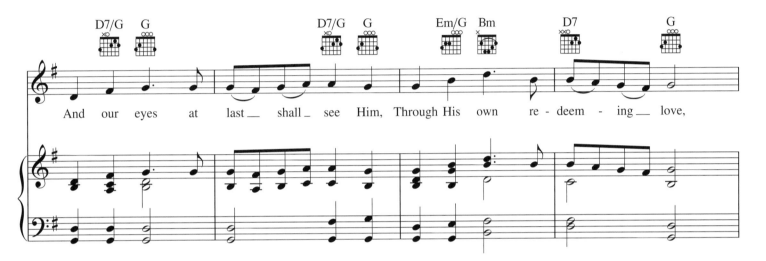

And our eyes at last __ shall __ see Him, Through His own re - deem - ing __ love,

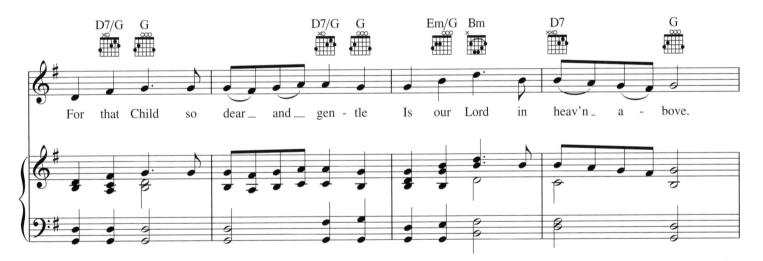

For that Child so dear __ and __ gen - tle Is our Lord in heav'n __ a - bove.

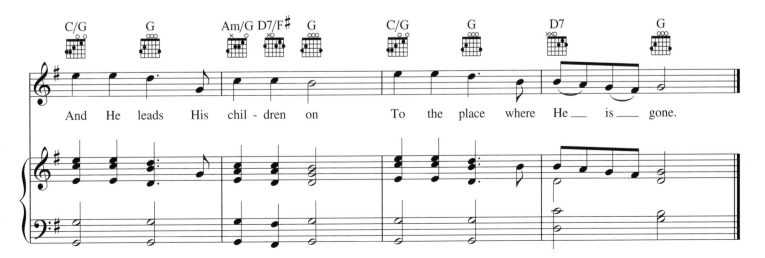

And He leads His chil - dren on To the place where He __ is __ gone.

PAT-A-PAN
(Willie, Take Your Little Drum)

Words and Music by
BERNARD de la MONNOYE

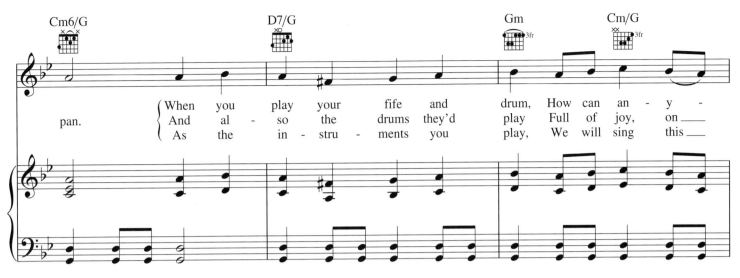

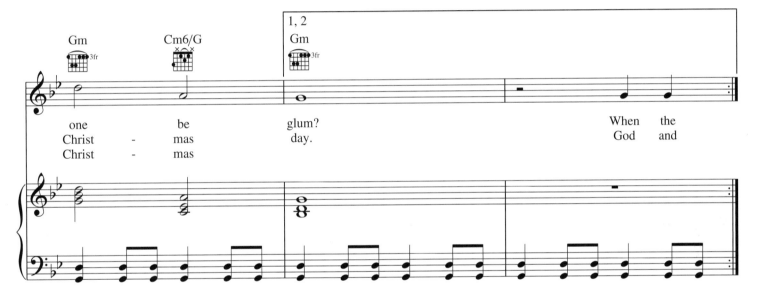

REJOICE AND BE MERRY

Traditional English Carol

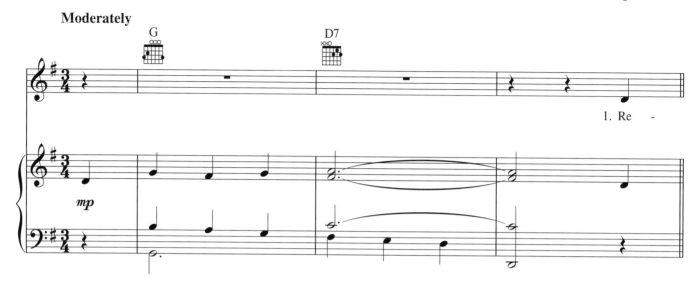

1. Re -

joice and be mer - ry in songs and in
2. heav - en - ly vi - sion ap - peared in the
3.,4. (See additional lyrics)

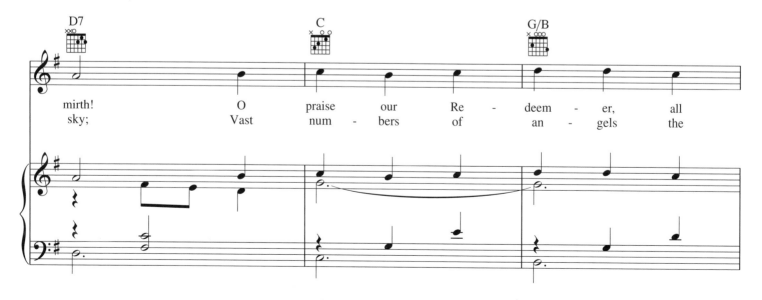

mirth! O praise our Re - deem - er, all
sky; Vast num - bers of an - gels all the

mor - tals on earth! For this is the
shep - herds did spy, Pro - claim - ing the

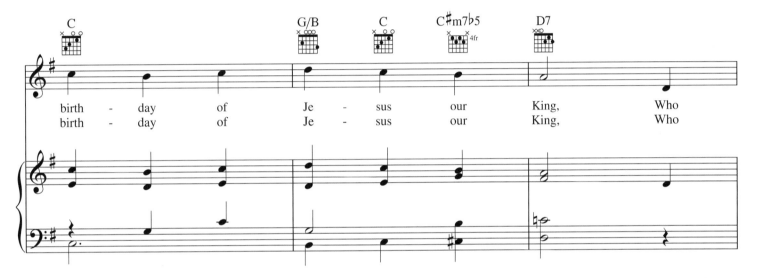

birth - day of Je - sus our King, Who
birth - day of Je - sus our King, Who

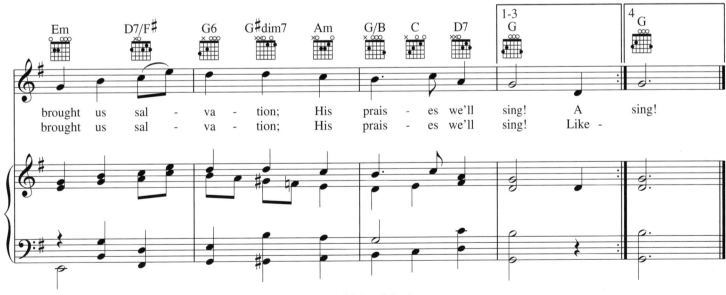

brought us sal - va - tion; His prais - es we'll sing! A sing!
brought us sal - va - tion; His prais - es we'll sing! Like -

Additional Lyrics

3. Likewise a bright star in the sky did appear,
Which led the wise men from the east to draw near.
They found the Messiah, sweet Jesus our King,
Who brought us salvation; His praises we'll sing!

4. And when they were come, they their treasures unfold,
And unto Him offered myrrh, incense and gold.
So blessed forever be Jesus our King,
Who brought us salvation; His praises we'll sing!

RING OUT, YE WILD AND MERRY BELLS

Words and Music by
C. MAITLAND

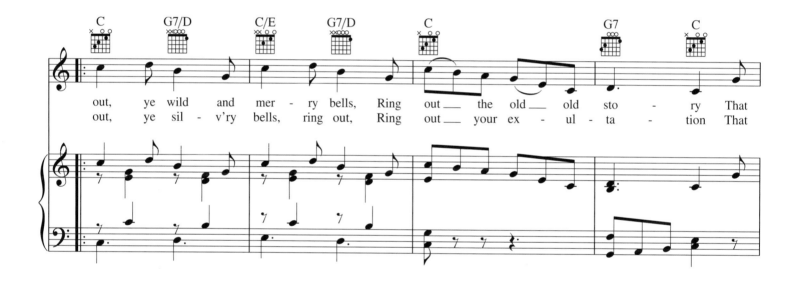

out, ye wild and mer - ry bells, Ring out __ the old __ old sto - - ry That
out, ye sil - v'ry bells, ring out, Ring out __ your ex - ul - ta - - tion That

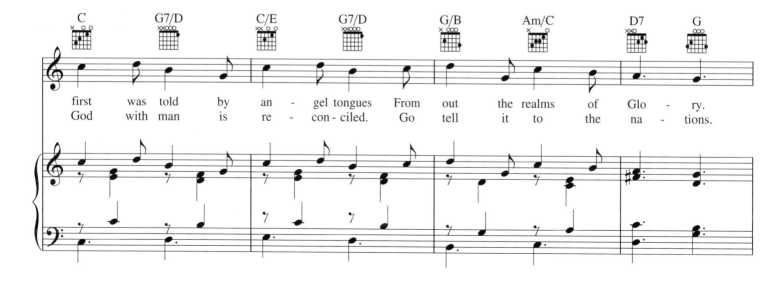

first was told by an - gel tongues From out the realms of Glo - - ry.
God with man is re - con - ciled. Go tell it to the na - - tions.

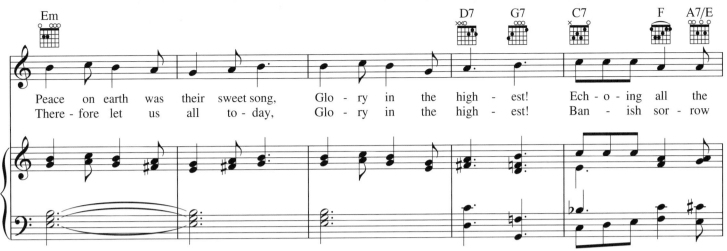

Peace on earth was their sweet song, Glo - ry in the high - est! Ech - o - ing all the
There - fore let us all to - day, Glo - ry in the high - est! Ban - ish sor - row

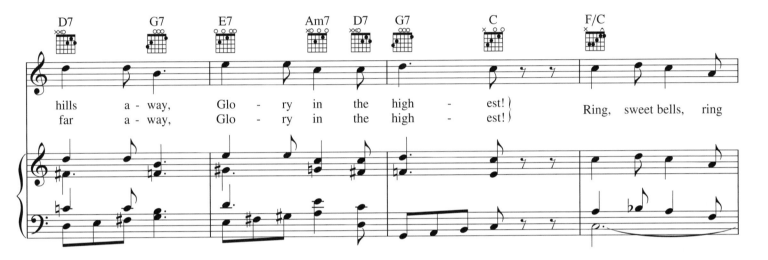

hills a - way, Glo - ry in the high - est! }
far a - way, Glo - ry in the high - est! } Ring, sweet bells, ring

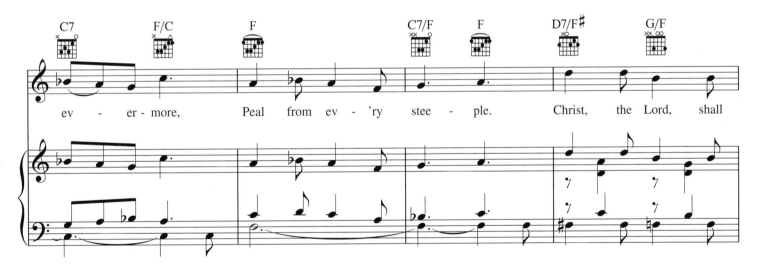

ev - er - more, Peal from ev - 'ry stee - ple. Christ, the Lord, shall

be our God And we ___ shall be His peo - ple! Ring peo - ple!

SHEPHERDS, SHAKE OFF YOUR DROWSY SLEEP

Traditional French Carol

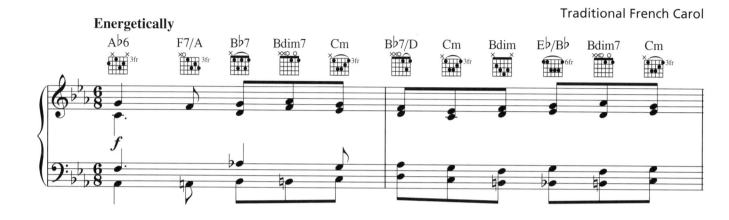

Shep - herd! shake off your drows - y sleep; Rise and
flow'rs all burst a - new, Think - ing
up and quick a - way! Seek the

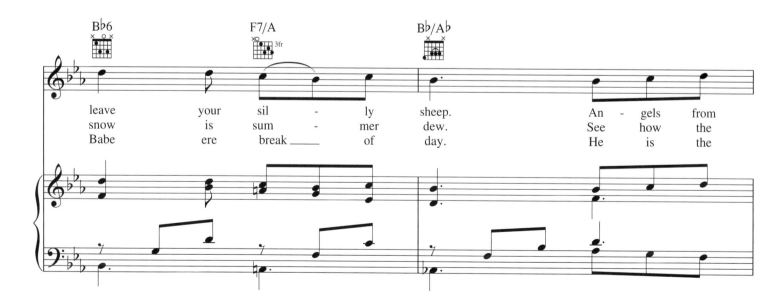

leave your sil - ly sheep. An - gels from
snow is sum - mer dew. See how the
Babe ere break of day. He is the

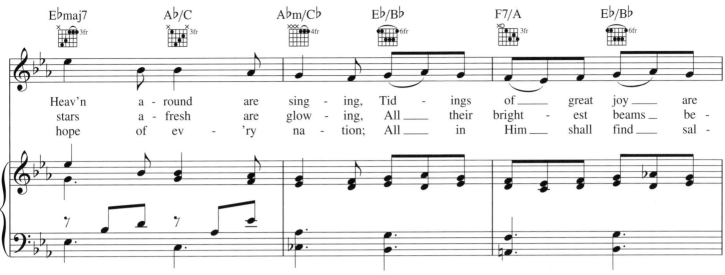

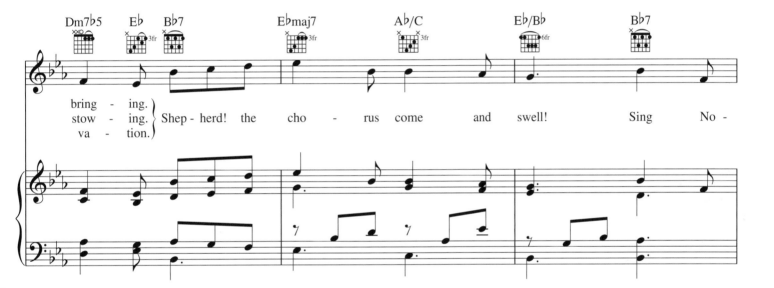

SHEPHERDS' CRADLE SONG

Words and Music by
C.D. SCHUBERT

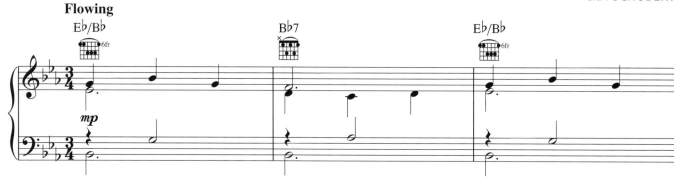

Flowing

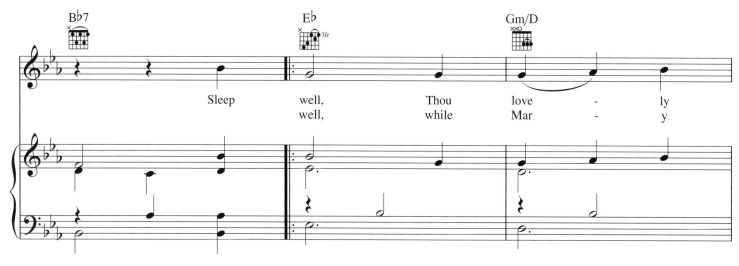

Sleep well, Thou love - ly
well, while Mar - y

heav'n - ly Babe. Sleep well, Thou
holds Thee close. Sleep well up -

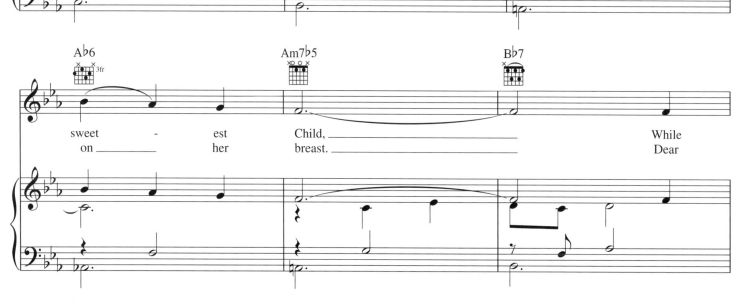

sweet - est Child, _____ While
on _____ her breast. _____ Dear

an - gels with _____ their soft white
Jo - seph scarce - ly dares to

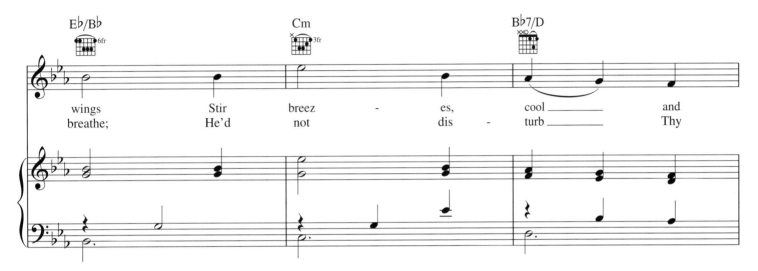

wings Stir breez - es, cool _____ and
breathe; He'd not dis - turb _____ Thy

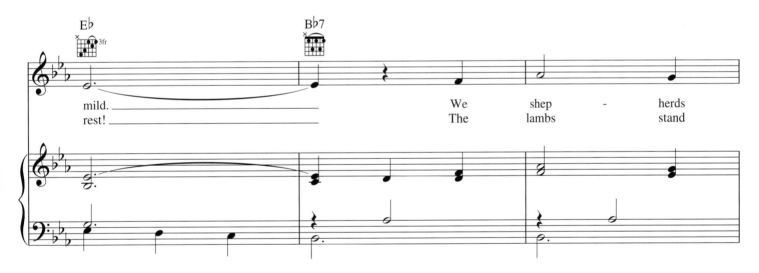

mild. _____ We shep - herds
rest! _____ The lambs stand

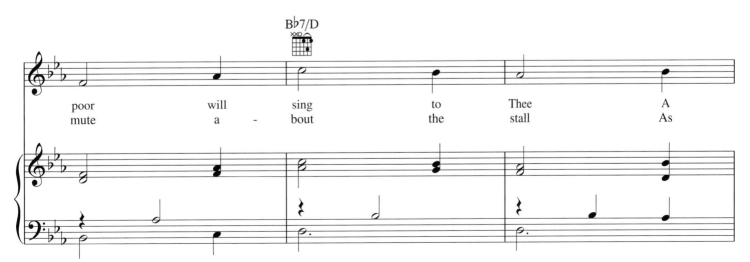

poor will sing to Thee A
mute a - bout the stall As

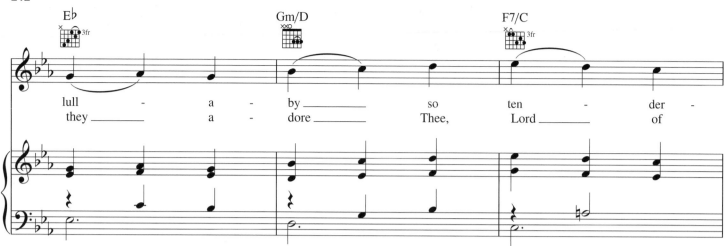

lull - a - by _____ so ten - der -
they _____ a - dore _____ Thee, Lord _____ of

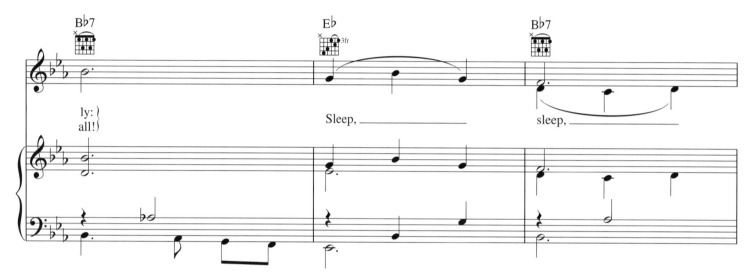

ly: }
all!})
Sleep, _____ sleep, _____

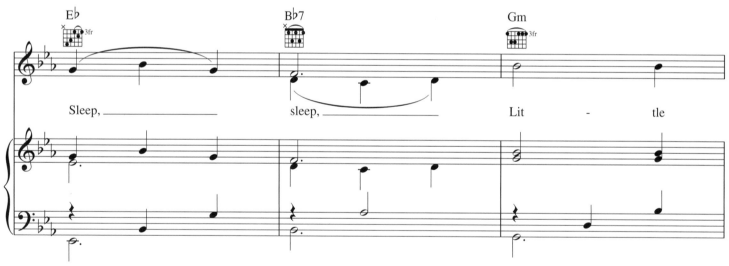

Sleep, _____ sleep, _____ Lit - tle

Son _____ of Heav - en, sleep! Sleep sleep!

SING WE NOW OF CHRISTMAS
(Noël nouvelet)

Traditional French Carol

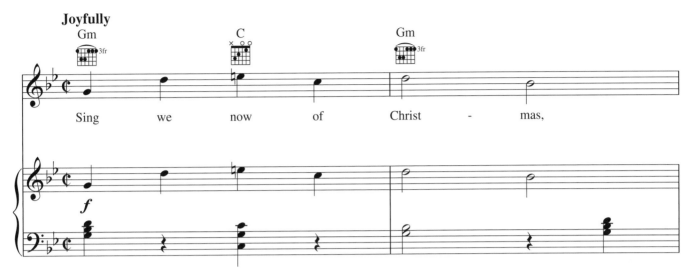

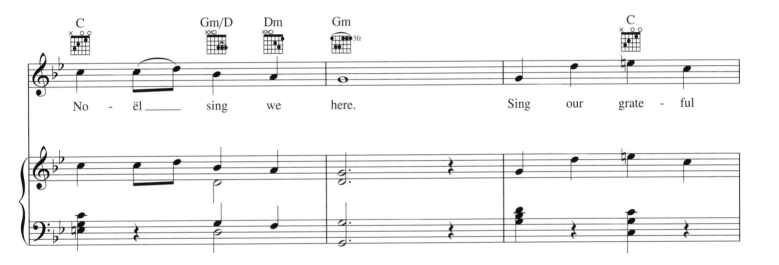

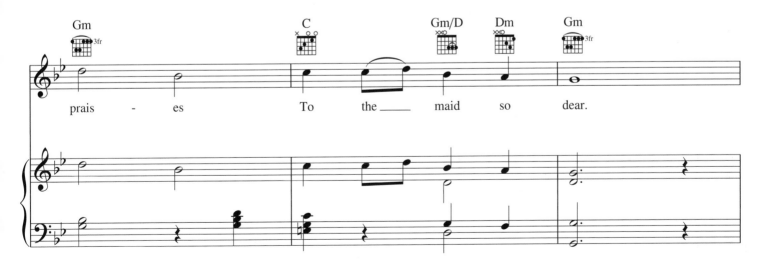

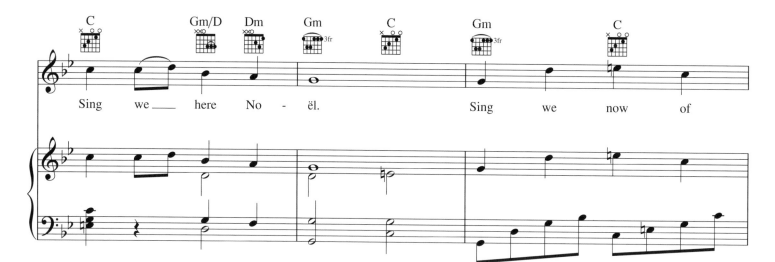

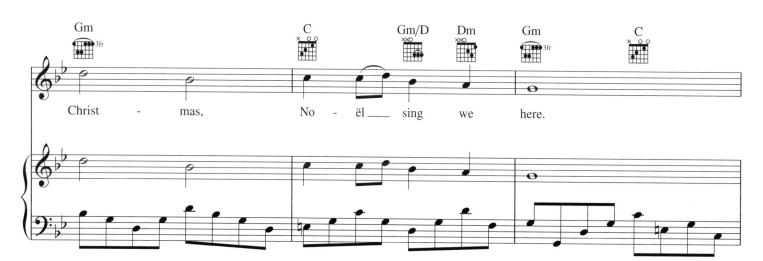

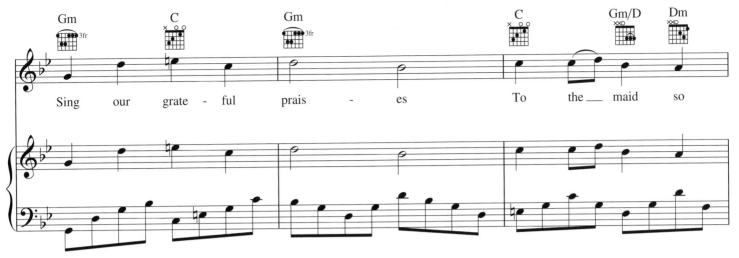

Sing our grate - ful prais - es To the ___ maid so

dear. Sing we No - ël! The

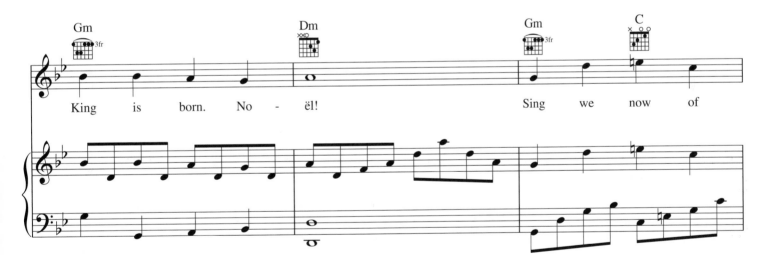

King is born. No - ël! Sing we now of

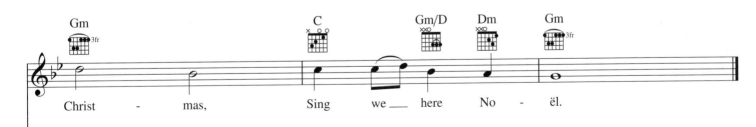

Christ - mas, Sing we ___ here No - ël.

SHOUT THE GLAD TIDINGS

Words by WILLIAM MÜHLENBERG
Music by CHARLES AVISON

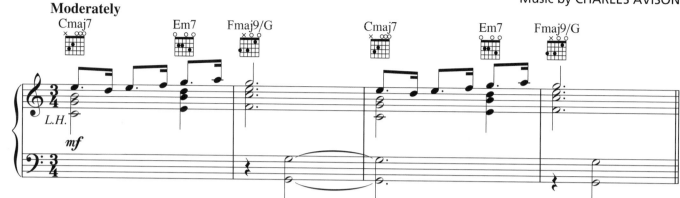

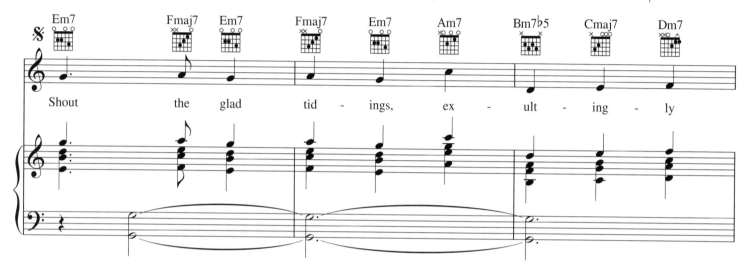

Shout the glad tid - ings, ex - ult - ing - ly

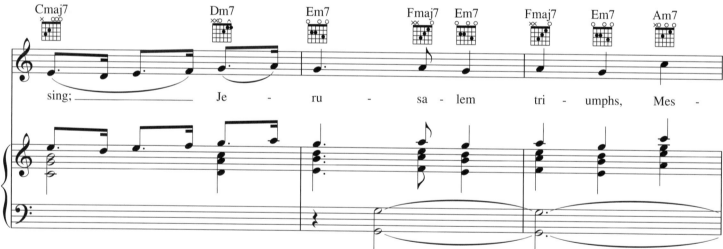

sing; _____ Je - ru - sa - lem tri - umphs, Mes -

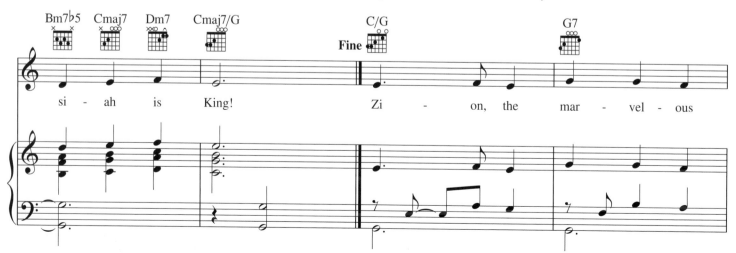

si - ah is King! Zi - on, the mar - vel - ous

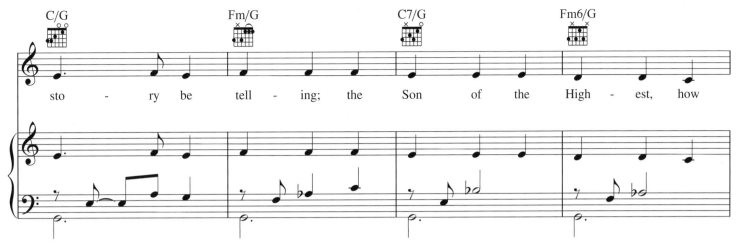

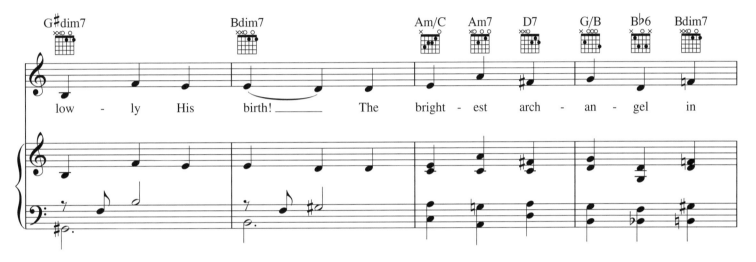

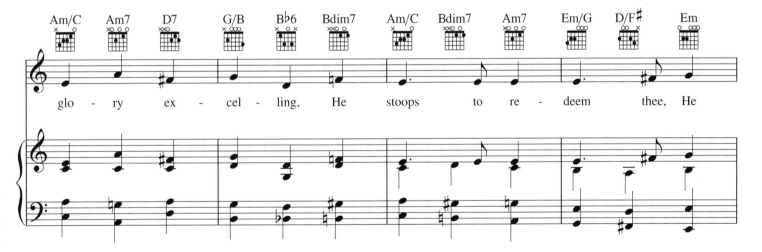

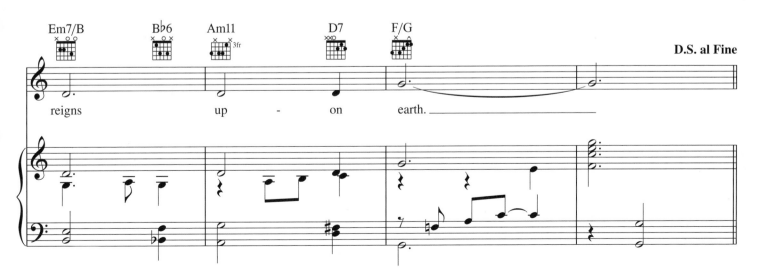

SILENT NIGHT

Words by JOSEPH MOHR
Translated by JOHN F. YOUNG
Music by FRANZ X. GRUBER

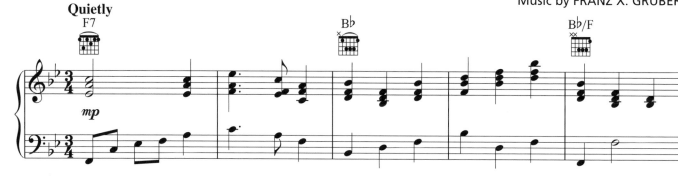

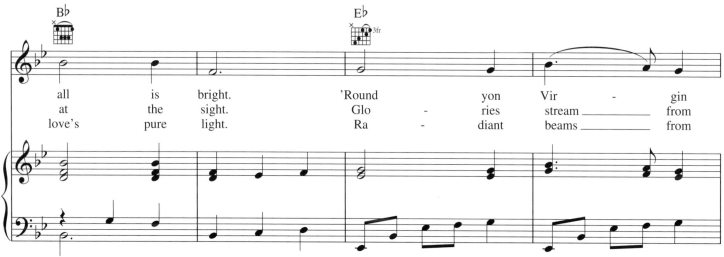

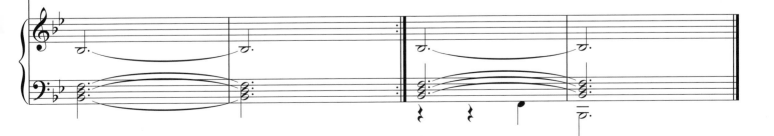

THE SIMPLE BIRTH

Traditional Flemish Carol

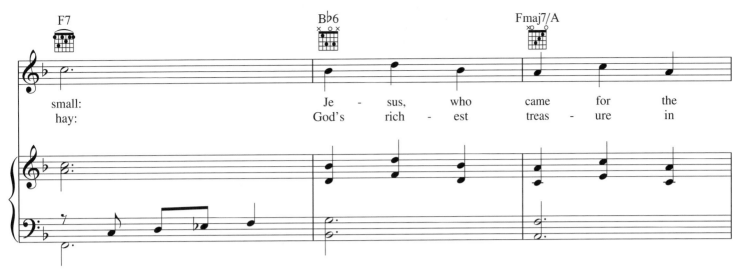

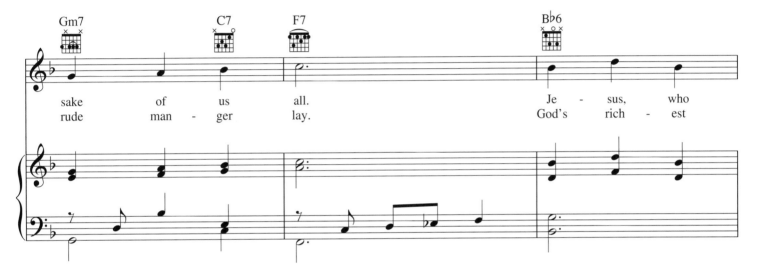

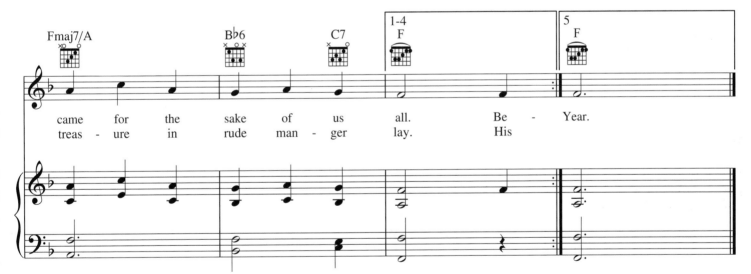

Additional Lyrics

3. His eyes of blackest jet were sparkling with light, *(Repeat)*
   Rosy cheeks bloomed on His face fair and bright. *(Repeat)*

4. And from His lovely mouth, the laughter did swell, *(Repeat)*
   When He saw Mary, whom He loved so well. *(Repeat)*

5. He came to weary earth, so dark and so drear, *(Repeat)*
   To wish mankind a blessed New Year. *(Repeat)*

SING, O SING, THIS BLESSED MORN

Words by CHRISTOPHER WORDSWORTH
Traditional German Tune

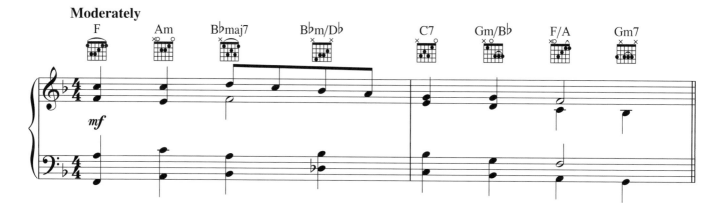

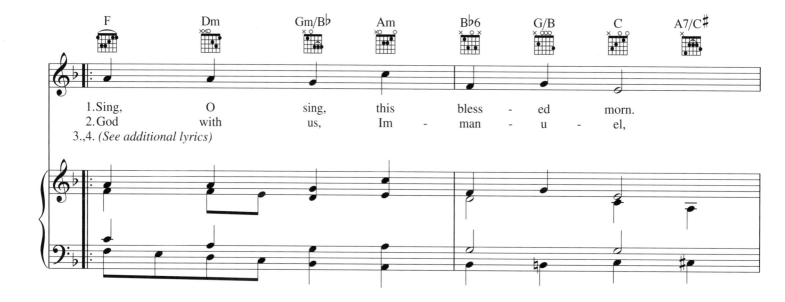

1. Sing, O sing, this bless - ed morn.
2. God with us, Im - man - u - el,
3., 4. *(See additional lyrics)*

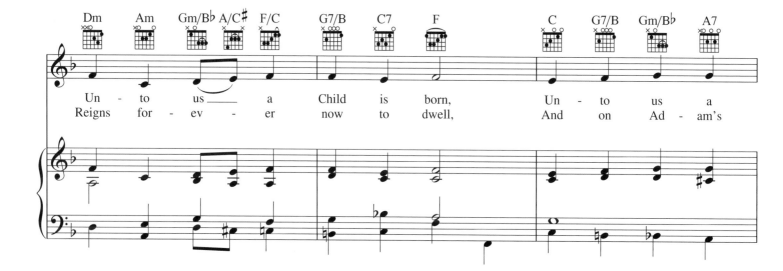

Un - to us ___ a Child is born, Un - to us a
Reigns for - ev - er now to dwell, And on Ad - am's

223

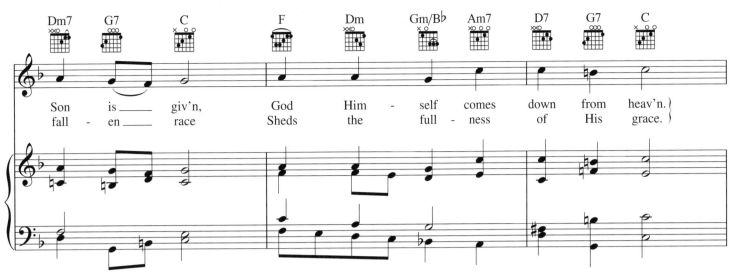

Son is _____ giv'n, God Him-self comes down from heav'n.
fall-en _____ race Sheds the full-ness of His grace.

Refrain

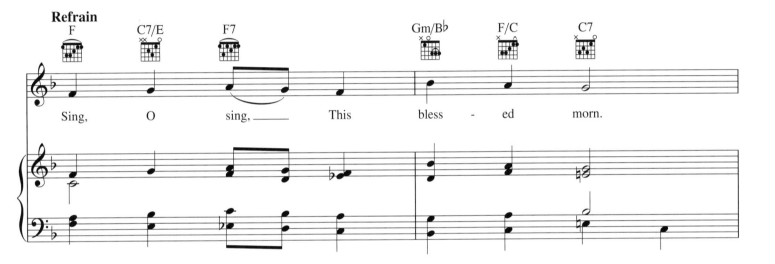

Sing, O sing, _____ This bless-ed morn.

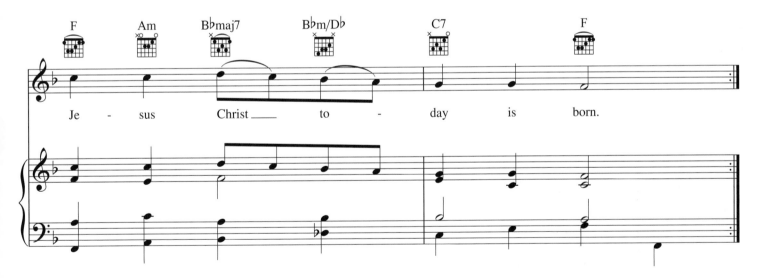

Je-sus Christ _____ to-day is born.

Additional Lyrics

3. God comes down that man may rise,
Lifted by Him to the skies;
Christ is Son of Man that we
Son of God in Him may be:
Refrain

4. O renew us, Lord, we pray,
With Thy spirit day by day;
That we ever one may be
With the Father and with Thee:
Refrain

SLEEP, HOLY BABE

Words by EDWARD CASWELL
Music by J.B. DYKES

Sleep, Ho - ly Babe, Up -

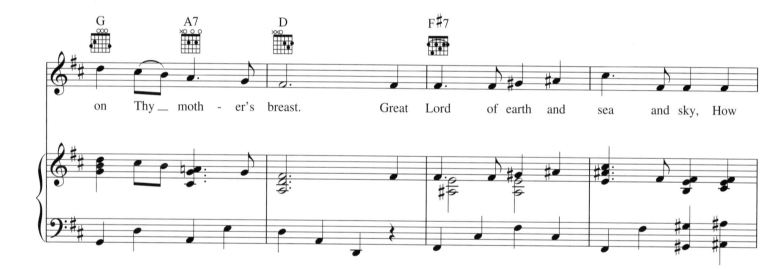

on Thy __ moth - er's breast. Great Lord of earth and sea and sky, How

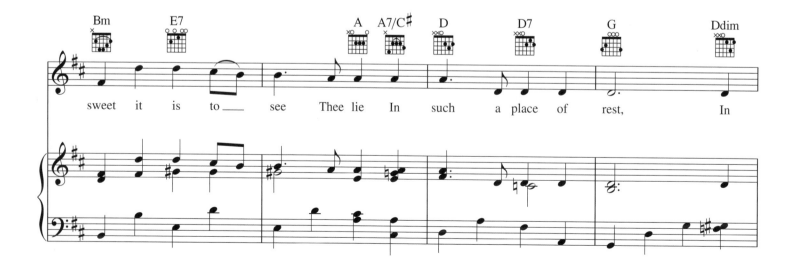

sweet it is to __ see Thee lie In such a place of rest, In

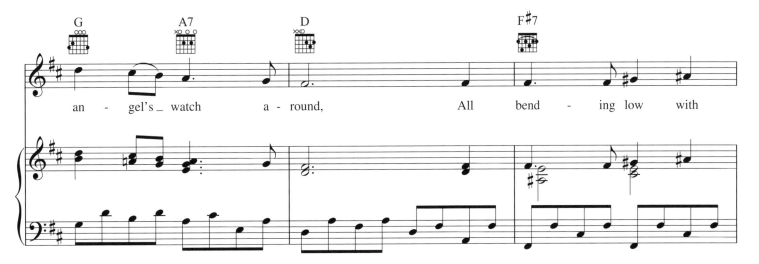

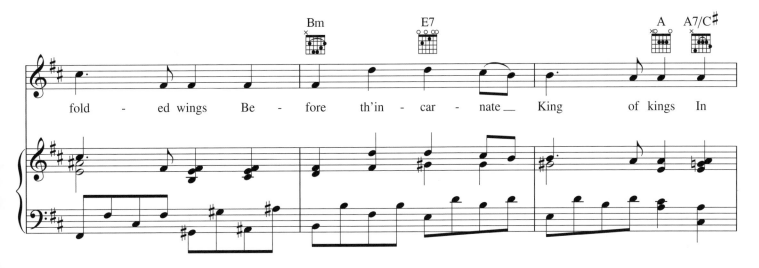

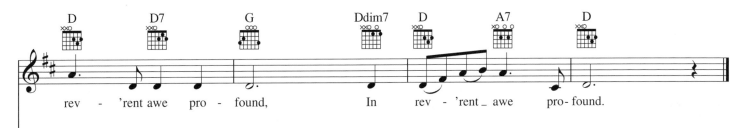

SLEEP, O SLEEP, MY PRECIOUS CHILD

Traditional Italian Carol

Slowly, with expression

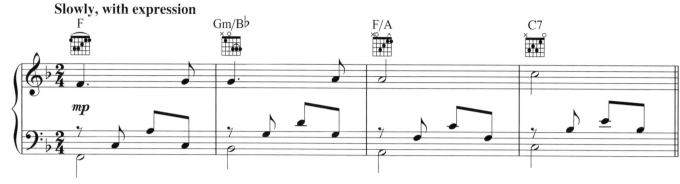

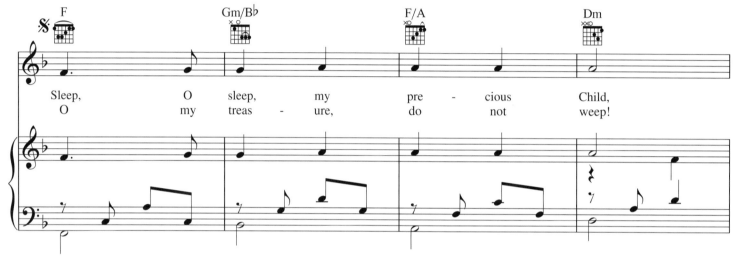

Sleep, O sleep, my pre - cious Child,
O my treas - ure, do not weep!

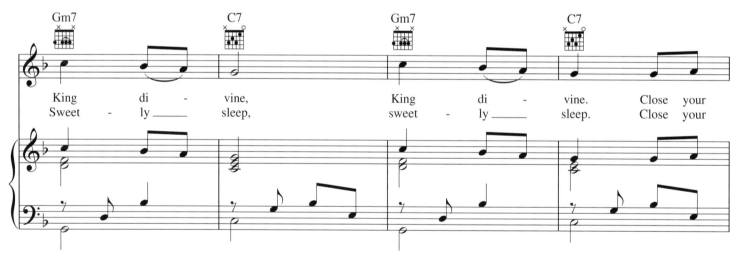

King di - vine, King di - vine. Close your
Sweet - ly ___ sleep, sweet - ly ___ sleep. Close your

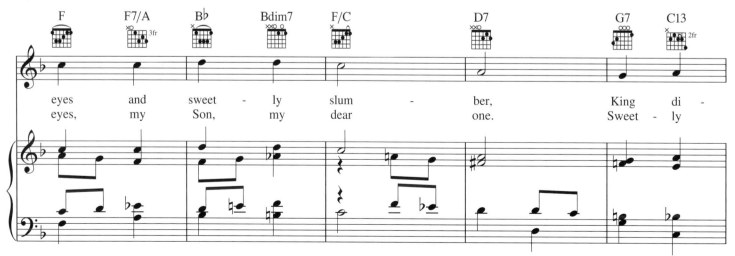

eyes, and sweet - ly slum - ber, King di -
eyes, my sweet Son, my dear one. Sweet - ly

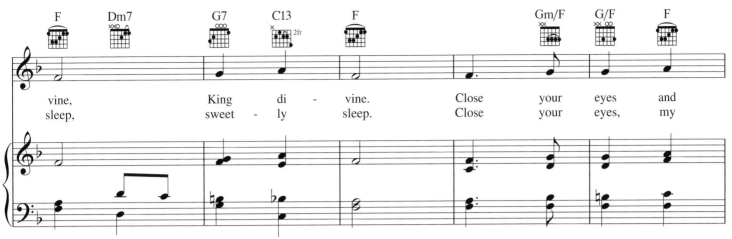

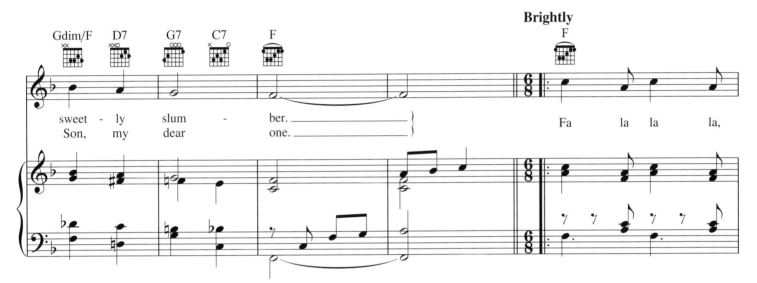

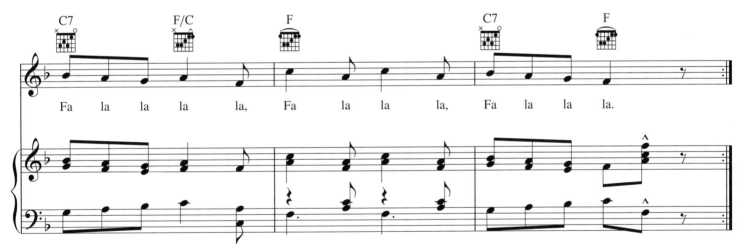

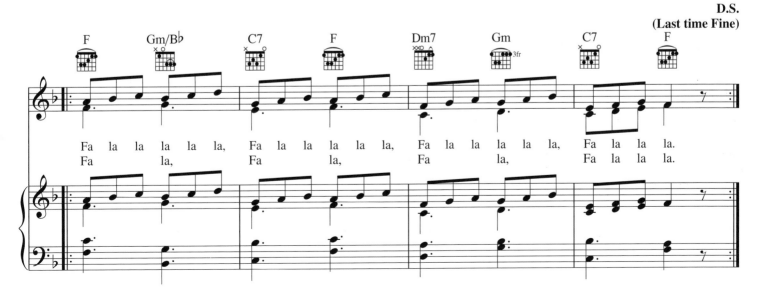

THE SNOW LAY ON THE GROUND

Traditional Irish Carol

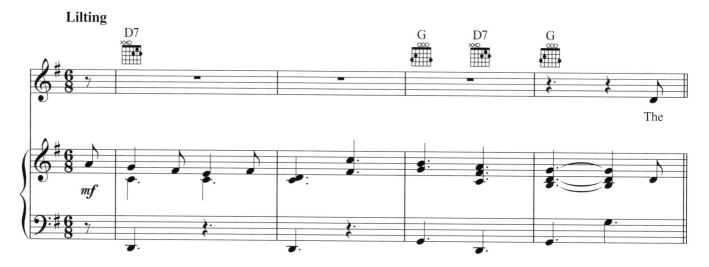

Lilting

The

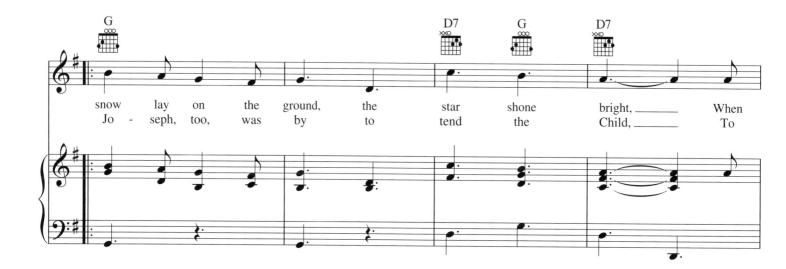

snow lay on the ground, the star shone bright, When
Jo- seph, too, was by to tend the star shone the Child, To

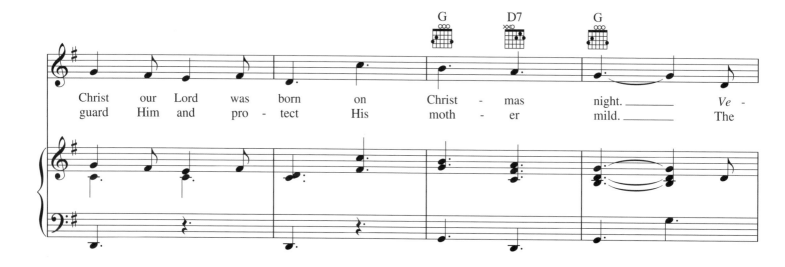

Christ our Lord was born on Christ - mas night. Ve -
guard Him and pro - tect on His moth - er mild. The

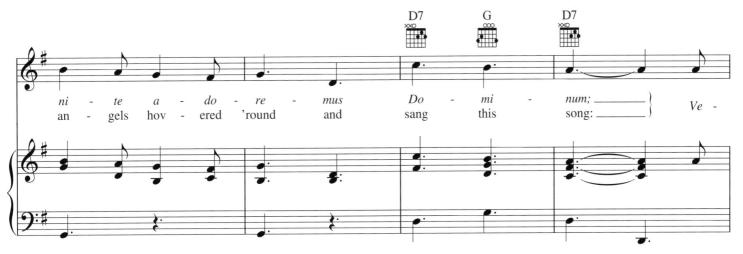

ni - te a - do - re - mus Do - mi - num; ____ } Ve -
an - gels hov - ered 'round and sang this song: ____

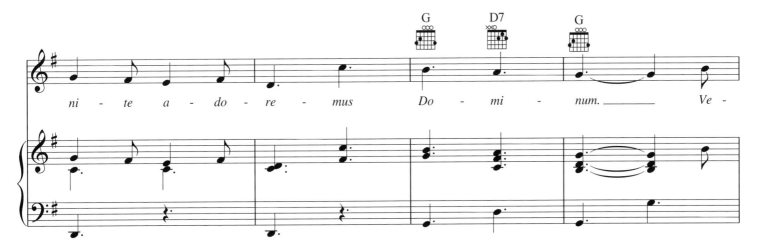

ni - te a - do - re - mus Do - mi - num. ____ Ve -

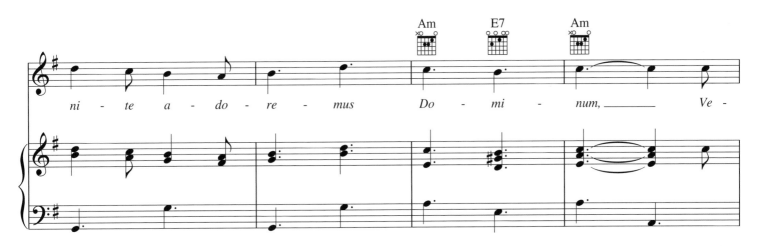

ni - te a - do - re - mus Do - mi - num, ____ Ve -

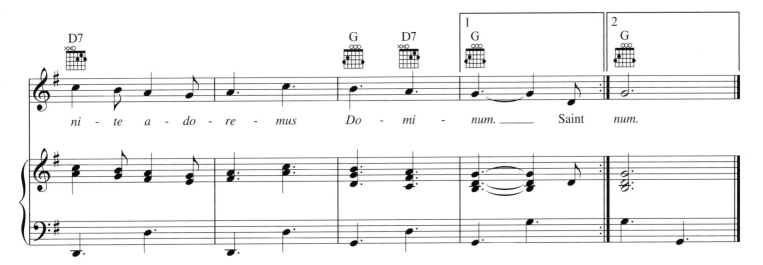

ni - te a - do - re - mus Do - mi - num. ____ Saint num.

THE STAR OF CHRISTMAS MORNING

Traditional

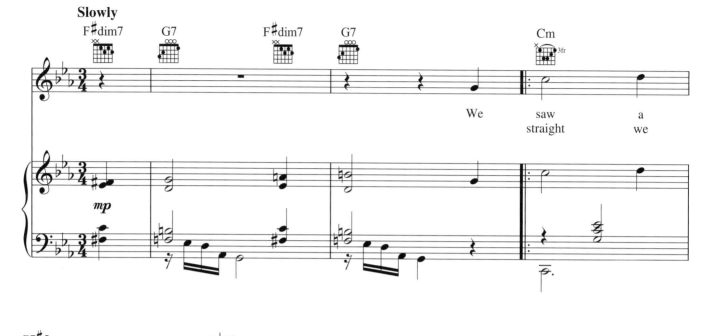

We saw a
straight we

light shine out a - far, On Christ - mas
knew it was Christ's star, Bright beam - ing

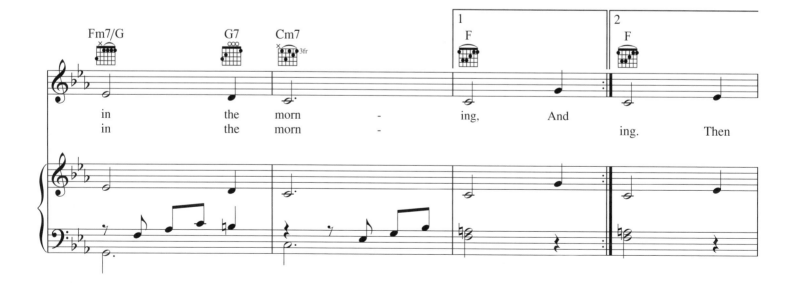

in the morn - ing, And
in the morn - ing. Then

STAR OF THE EAST

Words by GEORGE COOPER
Music by AMANDA KENNEDY

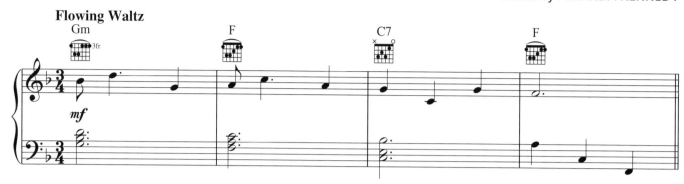

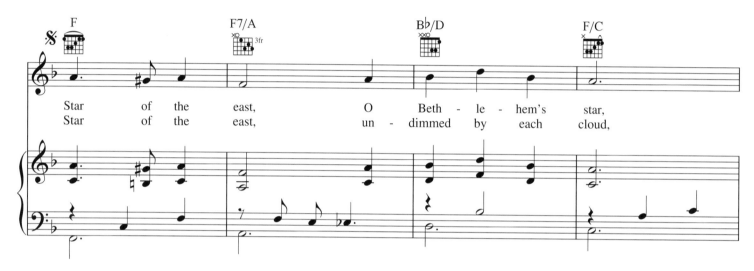

Star of the east, O Beth-le-hem's star,
Star of the east, un-dimmed by each cloud,

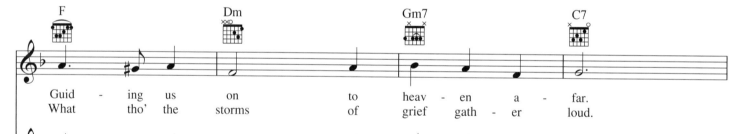

Guid-ing us on to heav-en a- far.
What tho' the storms of grief gath-er loud.

Sor- row and grief are lulled by thy light, Thou
Faith- ful and pure, thy rays' beam to save, Still

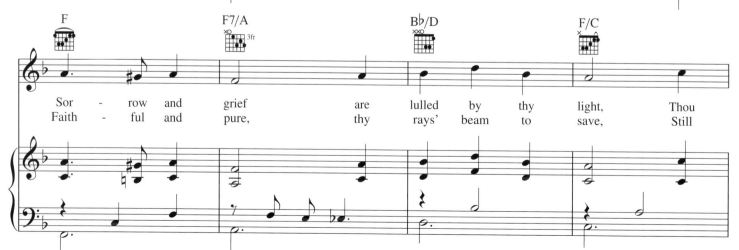

233

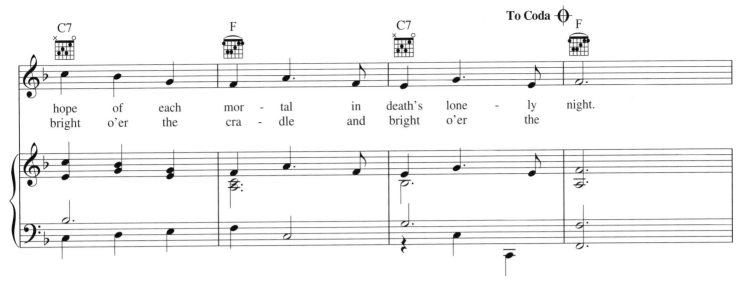

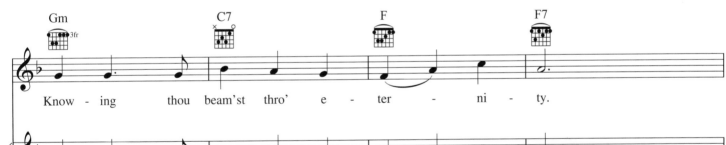

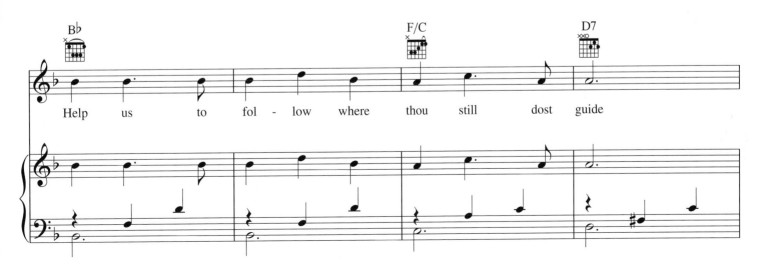

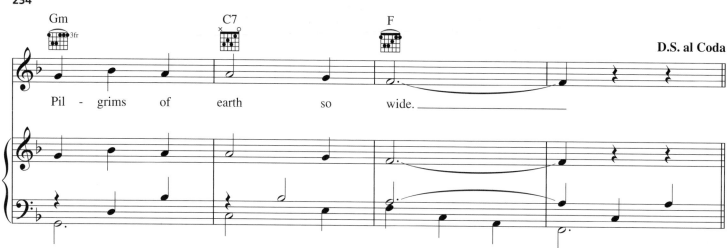

D.S. al Coda

Pil - grims of earth so wide. _____

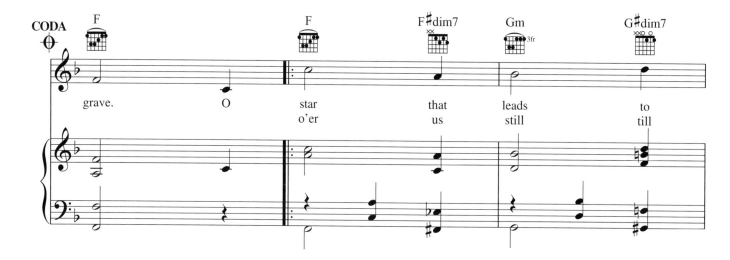

CODA

grave. O star that leads to
o'er us still till

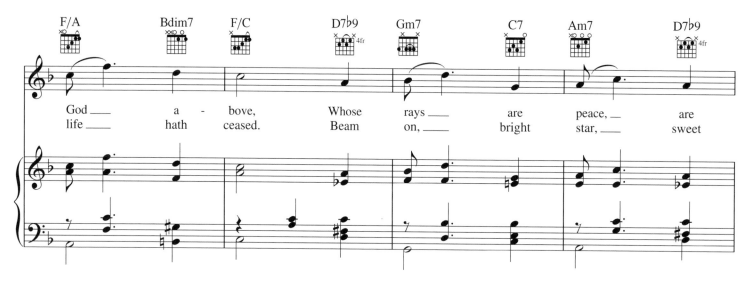

God ___ a - bove, Whose rays ___ are peace, ___ are
life ___ a hath ceased. Beam on, ___ bright star, ___ sweet

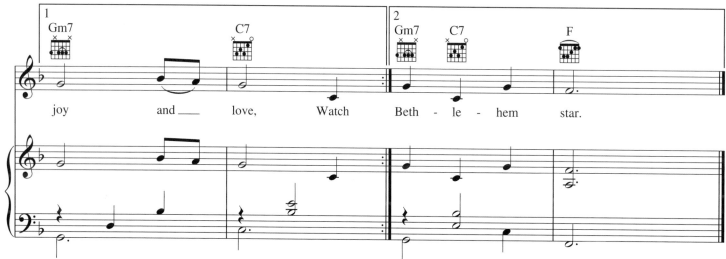

joy and ___ love, Watch Beth - le - hem star.

THE THREE KINGS SONG

Traditional Carol

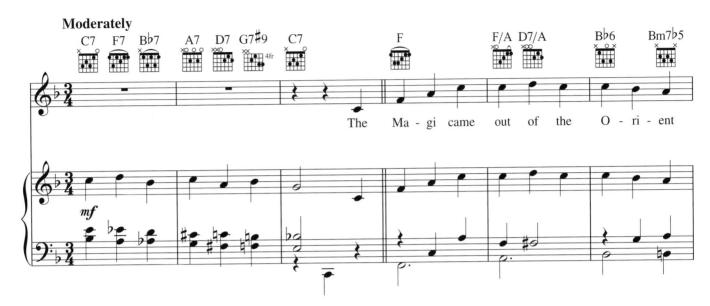

The Ma - gi came out of the O - ri - ent

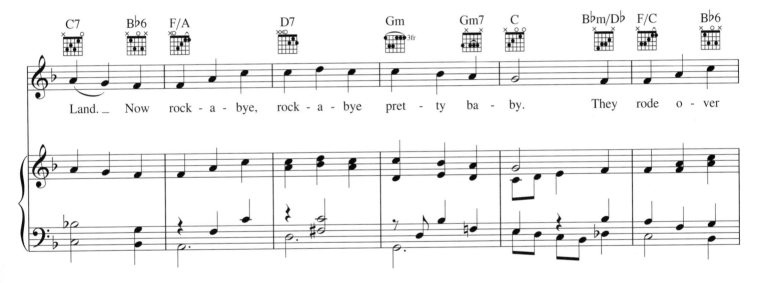

Land.__ Now rock - a - bye, rock - a - bye pret - ty ba - by. They rode o - ver

rock and they rode o - ver sand. Right __ glad, then, were those three.

STILL, STILL, STILL

Salzburg Melody, c.1819
Traditional Austrian Text

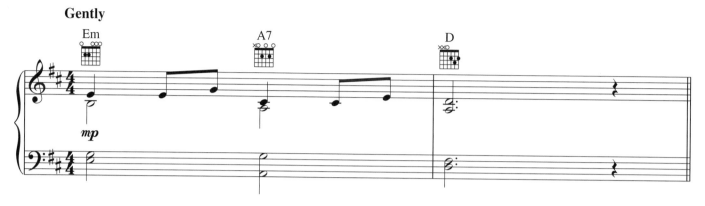

Still, _____ still, _____ still; to _____ sleep is _____ now His _____
Sleep, _____ sleep, _____ sleep, while _____ we Thy _____ vig - il _____

will. On Mar - y's _____ breast He rests in _____ slum - ber
keep. And an - gels _____ come from Heav - en _____ sing - ing

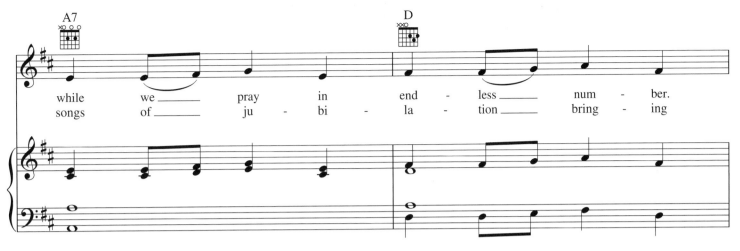

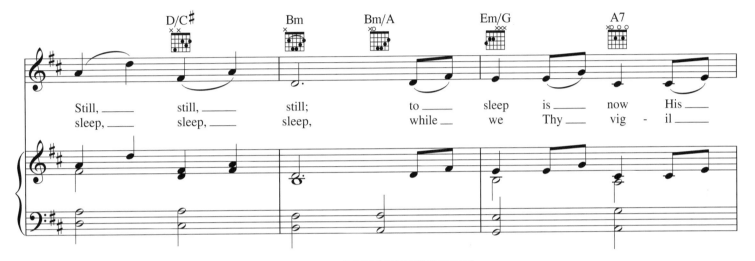

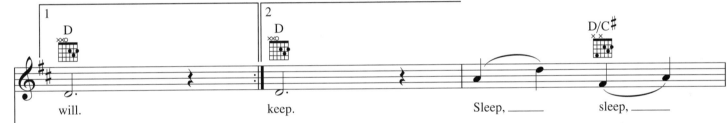

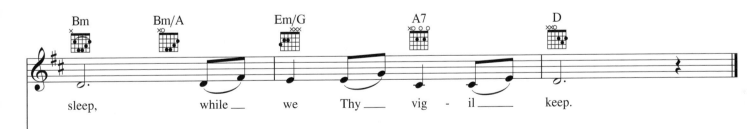

THERE'S A SONG IN THE AIR

Words and Music by JOSIAH G. HOLLAND
and KARL P. HARRINGTON

Flowing

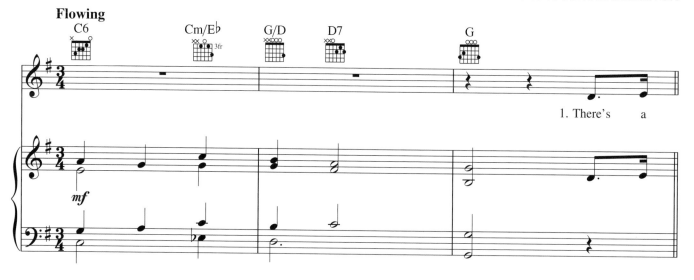

1. There's a

song in the air! There's a star in the
2. tu - mult of joy O'er the won - der - ful
3.,4. *(See additional lyrics)*

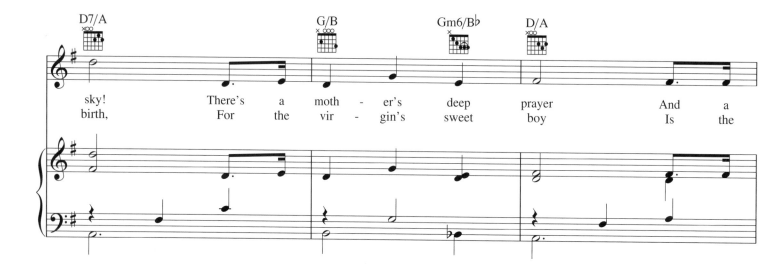

sky! There's a moth - er's deep prayer And a
birth, For the vir - gin's sweet boy Is the

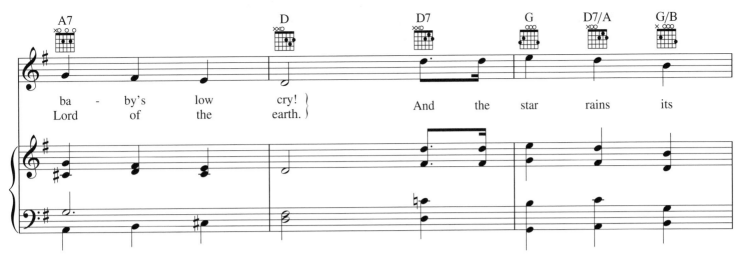

Additional Lyrics

3. In the light of that star
   Lie the ages impearled,
   And that song from afar
   Has swept over the world.
   Ev'ry hearth is aflame, and the angels sing
   In the homes of the nations that Jesus is King!

4. We rejoice in the light,
   And we echo the song
   That comes down thro' the night
   From the heavenly throng.
   Ay! we shout to the lovely evangel they bring
   And we greet in His cradle our Savior and King!

TOYLAND
from BABES IN TOYLAND

Words by GLEN MacDONOUGH
Music by VICTOR HERBERT

Lilting Waltz

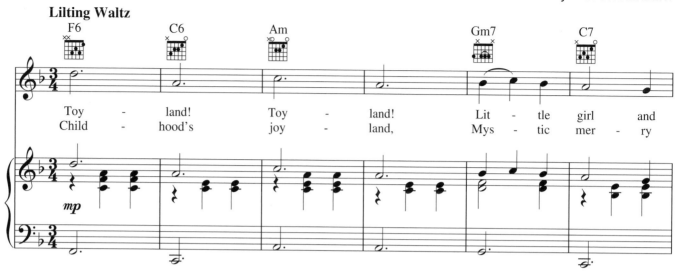

Toy - land! Toy - land! Lit - tle girl and
Child - hood's joy - land, Mys - tic mer - ry

boy land, While you dwell with - in it. _____ You are ev - er hap - py
joy land, Once you pass its

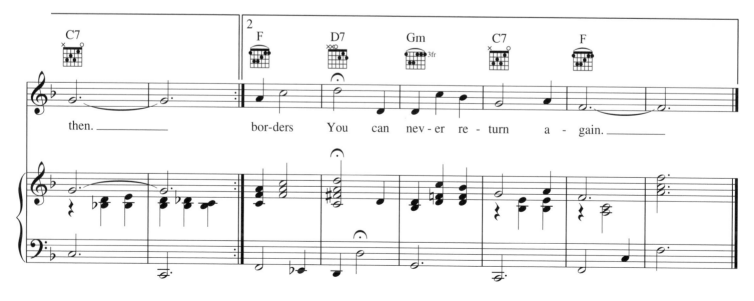

then. _____ bor - ders You can nev - er re - turn a - gain. _____

'TWAS THE NIGHT BEFORE CHRISTMAS

Words by CLEMENT CLARK MOORE
Music by F. HENRI KLICKMAN

Additional Lyrics

3. With a little old driver so lively and quick,
I knew in a moment it must be St. Nick.
More rapid than eagles his coursers they came,
And he whistled, and shouted, and called them by name:
"Now, Dasher! Now, Dancer! Now, Prancer! Now, Vixen!
On, Comet! On, Cupid! On, Donder and Blitzen!
To the top of the porch, to the top of the wall!
Now dash away, dash away, dash away all!"

4. As dry leaves that before the wild hurricane fly,
When they meet with an obstacle, mount to the sky,
So up to the house-top the coursers they flew,
With the sleigh full of toys, and St. Nicholas, too.
And then in a twinkling I heard on the roof
The prancing and pawing of each little hoof.
As I drew in my head, and was turning around,
Down the chimney St. Nicholas came with a bound.

5. He was dressed all in fur from his head to his foot,
And his clothes were all tarnished with ashes and soot;
A bundle of toys he had flung on his back,
And he looked like a peddler just opening his pack.
His eyes how they twinkled! His dimples how merry!
His cheeks were like roses, his nose like a cherry.
His droll little mouth was drawn up like a bow,
And the beard of his chin was as white as the snow.

6. The stump of a pipe he held tight in his teeth,
And the smoke, it encircled his head like a wreath.
He had a broad face, and a round little belly
That shook, when he laughed, like a bowl full of jelly.
He was chubby and plump, a right jolly old elf,
And I laughed when I saw him, in spite of myself.
A wink of his eye, and a twist of his head,
Soon gave me to know I had nothing to dread.

7. He spoke not a word, but went straight to his work,
And filled all the stockings; then turned with a jerk,
And laying his finger aside of his nose,
And giving a nod, up the chimney he rose.
He sprang to his sleigh, to his team gave a whistle,
And away they all fled like the down of a thistle;
But I heard him exclaim, ere he drove out of sight:
"Happy Christmas to all, and to all a Good-night!"

THE TWELVE DAYS OF CHRISTMAS

Traditional English Carol

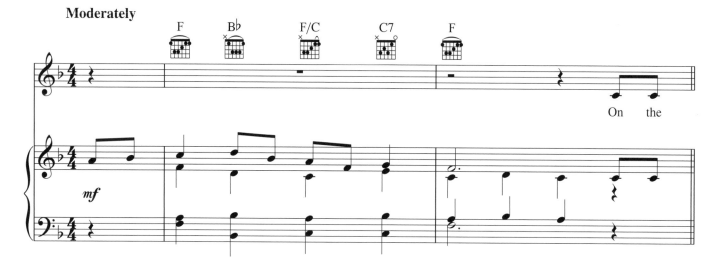

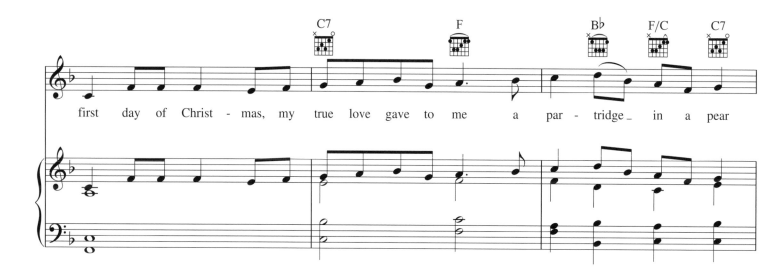

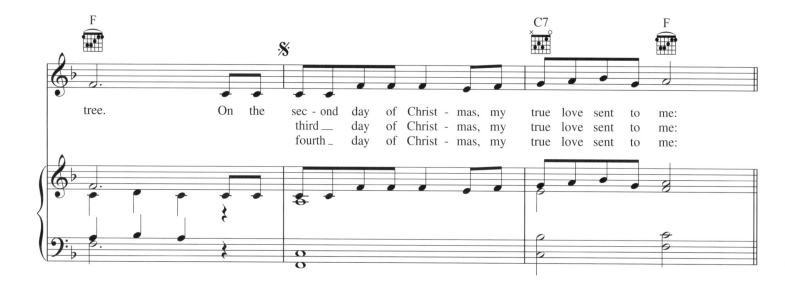

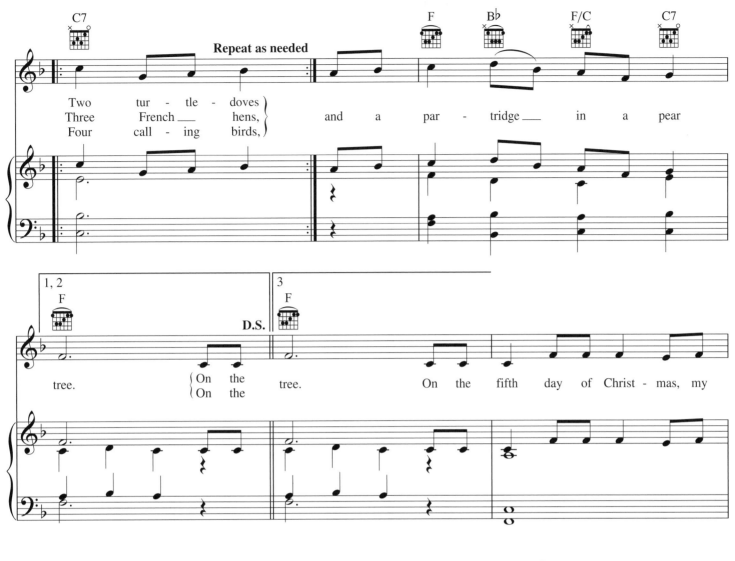

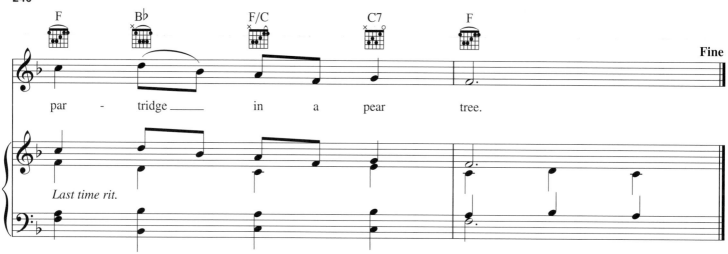

par - tridge _____ in a pear tree.

Last time rit.

Fine

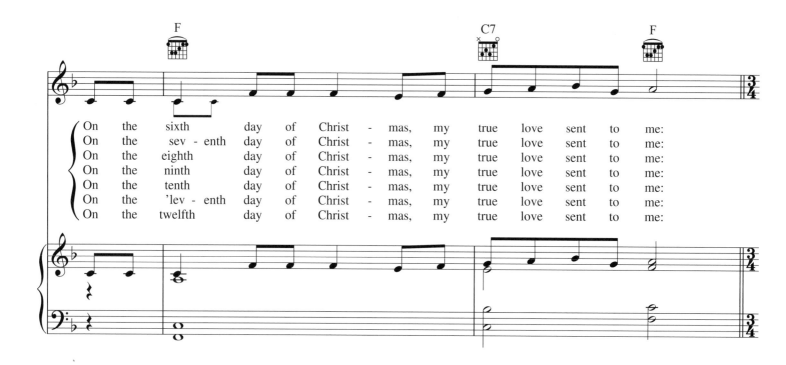

On the sixth day of Christ - mas, my true love sent to me:
On the sev - enth day of Christ - mas, my true love sent to me:
On the eighth day of Christ - mas, my true love sent to me:
On the ninth day of Christ - mas, my true love sent to me:
On the tenth day of Christ - mas, my true love sent to me:
On the 'lev - enth day of Christ - mas, my true love sent to me:
On the twelfth day of Christ - mas, my true love sent to me:

Repeat as needed

D.S.S
(Last time D.S.S. al Fine)

Six _____ geese a - lay - ing,
Sev - en swans a - swim - ming,
Eight _____ maids a - milk - ing,
Nine _____ la - dies danc - ing,
Ten _____ lords a - leap - ing,
'Lev - en pip - ers pip - ing,
Twelve _____ drum - mers drum - ming,
five gold _____ rings!

WE WISH YOU A MERRY CHRISTMAS

Traditional English Folksong

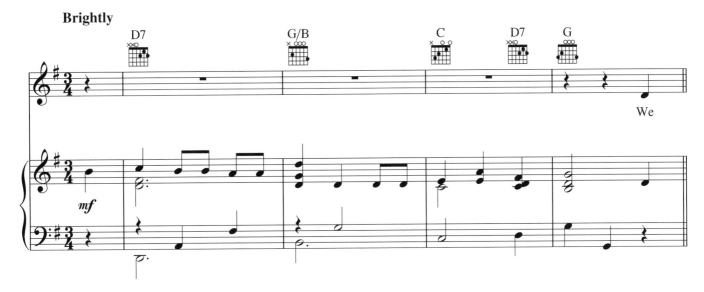

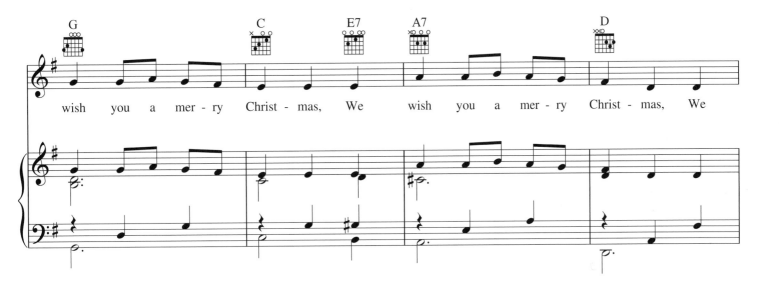

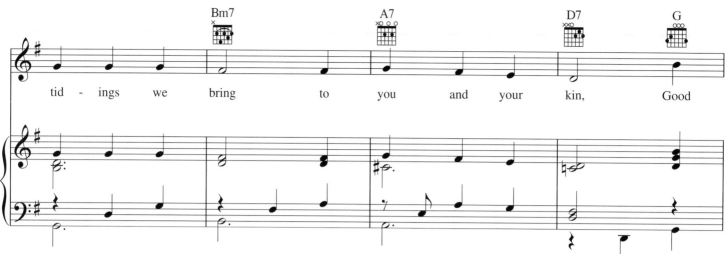

tid - ings we bring to you and your kin, Good

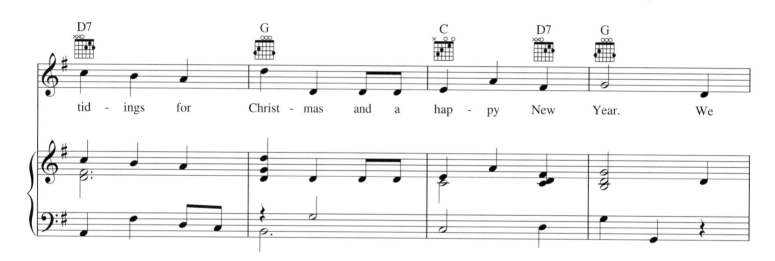

tid - ings for Christ - mas and a hap - py New Year. We

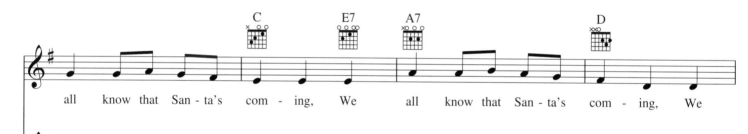

all know that San - ta's com - ing, We all know that San - ta's com - ing, We

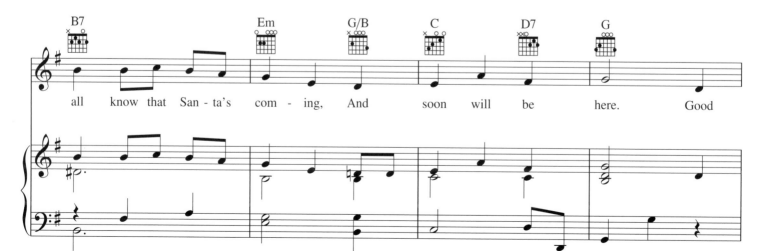

all know that San - ta's com - ing, And soon will be here. Good

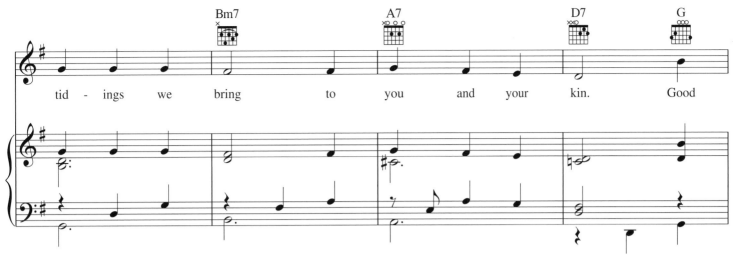

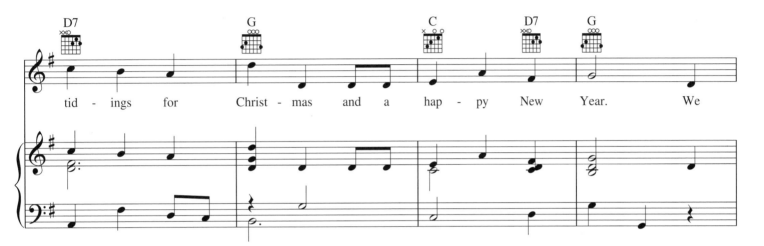

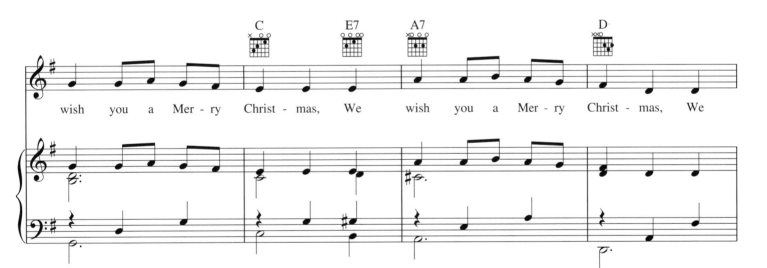

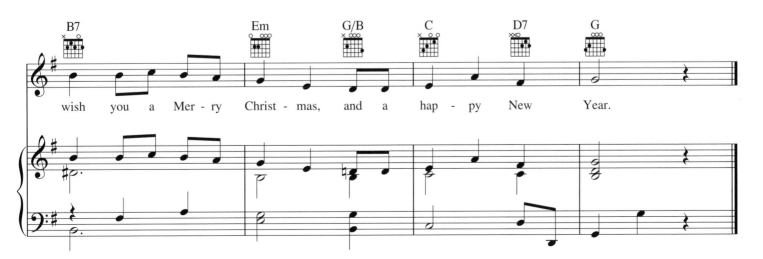

UP ON THE HOUSETOP

Words and Music by
B.R. HANBY

Up on the house-top ___ rein - deer pause,
First comes the stock - ing of lit - tle Nell;

Out jumps good old San - ta Claus;
Oh, dear San - ta, fill it well;

Down through the chim - ney with lots of toys,
Give her a dol - ly that laughs and cries,

All for the lit - tle ones, Christ - mas joys.
One that will o - pen and shut her eyes.

Ho, ho, ho! Who would - n't go! Ho, ho, ho!

Who would - n't go! ___ Up on the house - top, click, click, click,

Down through the chim - ney with good Saint Nick.

A VIRGIN UNSPOTTED

Traditional English Carol

1. A ___ vir - gin un - spot - ted, the ___ proph - et fore -
2. God sent an ___ an - gel from ___ Heav - en so
3.,4. *(See additional lyrics)*

told, Should ___ bring forth a ___ Sav - ior, which ___ we ___ now be -
high, To ___ cer - tain a poor ___ shep - herds in ___ fields ___ where they

hold; To ___ be our Re - deem - er from death, hell ___ and
lie, And ___ bade them no long - er in sor - row ___ to

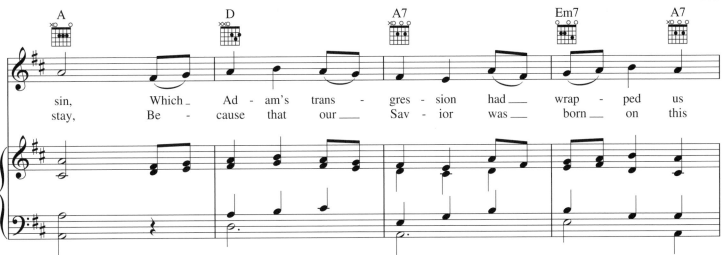

sin,   Which   Ad - am's   trans - gres - sion   had   wrap - ped   us

stay,   Be - cause   that   our   Sav - ior   was   born   on   this

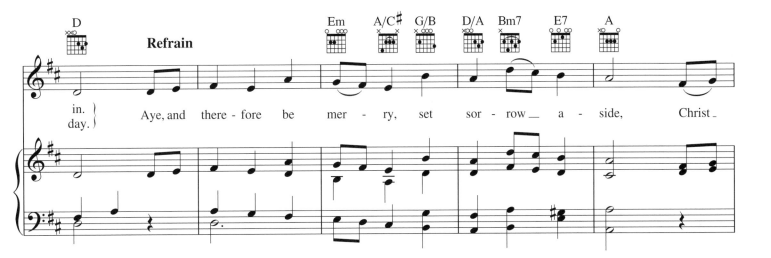

Refrain

in.   Aye, and   there - fore   be   mer - ry,   set   sor - row   a - side,   Christ

day.

Je - sus,   our   Sav - ior,   was   born   on   this   tide.   Then   tide.

Additional Lyrics

3. Then presently after, the shepherds did spy
   Vast numbers of angels to stand in the sky;
   They joyfully talked and sweetly did sing:
   "To God be all glory, our heavenly King."
   Refrain

4. To teach us humility all this was done,
   And learn we from thence haughty pride for to shun;
   A manger His cradle who came from above,
   The great God of mercy, of peace and of love.
   Refrain

WATCHMAN, TELL US OF THE NIGHT

Words by JOHN BOWRING
Music by JACOB HINTZE

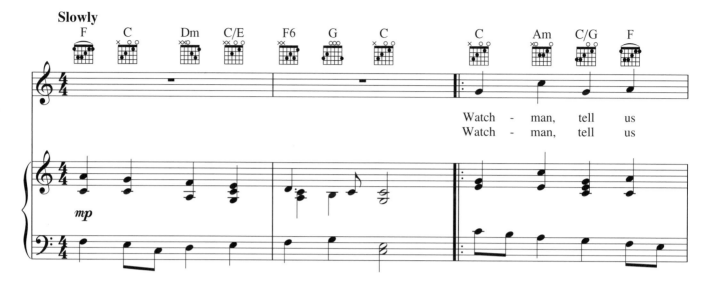

Watch - man, tell us
Watch - man, tell us

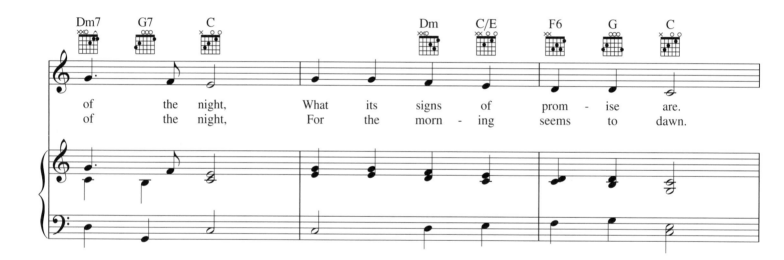

of the night, What its signs of prom - ise are.
of the night, For the morn - ing seems to dawn.

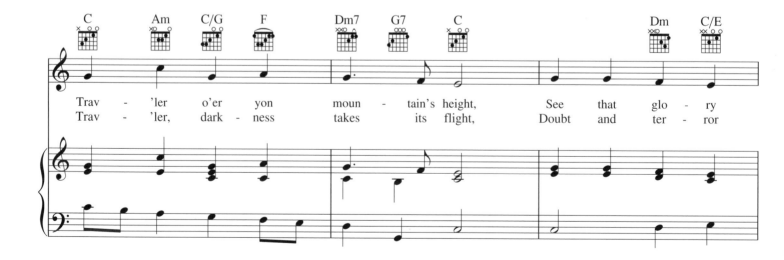

Trav - 'ler o'er yon moun - tain's height, See that glo - ry
Trav - 'ler, dark - ness takes its flight, Doubt and ter - ror

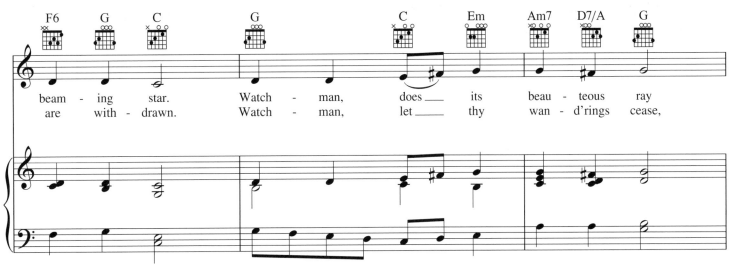

beam - ing star. Watch - man, does ___ its beau - teous ray
are with - drawn. Watch - man, let ___ thy wan - d'rings cease,

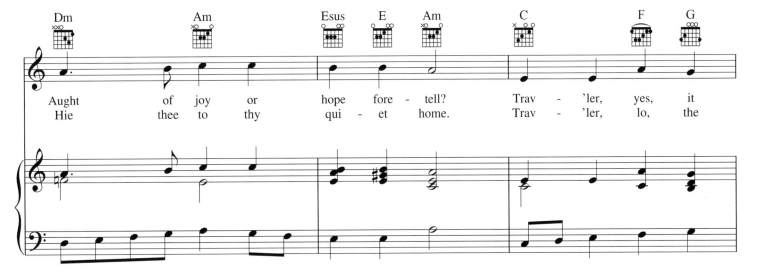

Aught of joy or hope fore - tell? Trav - 'ler, yes, it
Hie thee to thy qui - et home. Trav - 'ler, lo, the

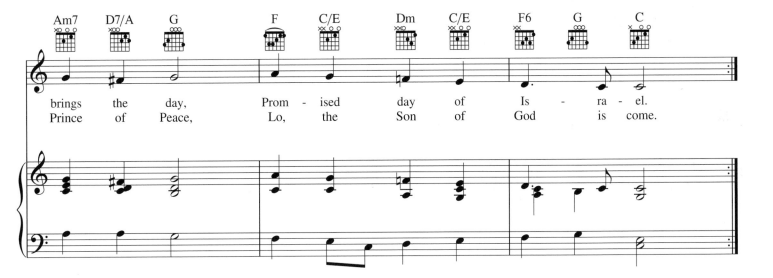

brings the day, Prom - ised day of Is - ra - el.
Prince of Peace, Lo, the day Son of God is come.

WE THREE KINGS OF ORIENT ARE

Words and Music by
JOHN H. HOPKINS, JR.

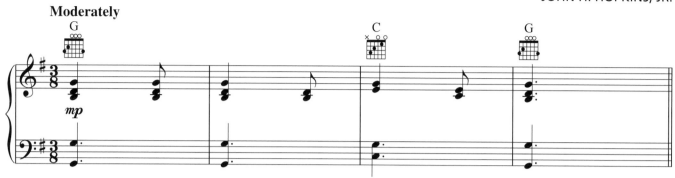

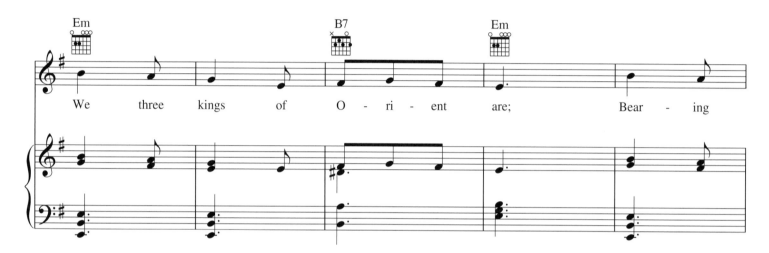

We three kings of O - ri - ent are; Bear - ing

gifts we tra - verse a - far, Field and foun - tain,

moor and moun - tain, Fol - low - ing yon - der

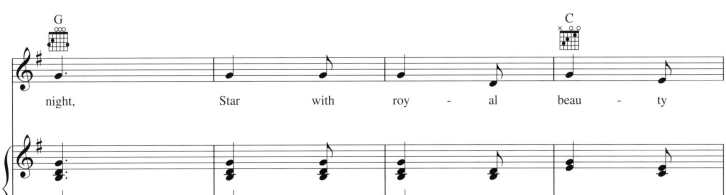

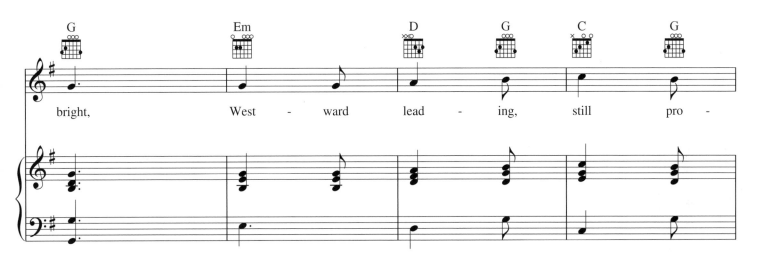

WEXFORD CAROL

Traditional Irish Carol

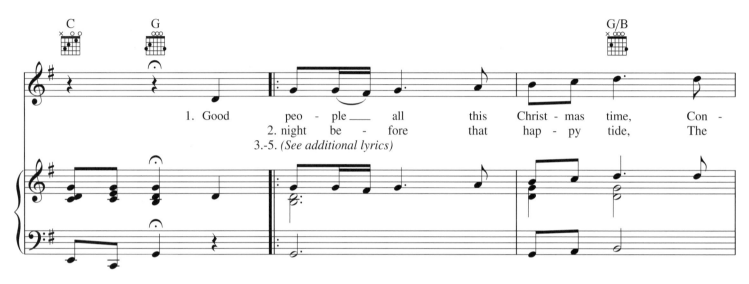

1. Good peo - ple ___ all this Christ - mas time, Con -
2. night be - fore that hap - py tide, The
3.-5. *(See additional lyrics)*

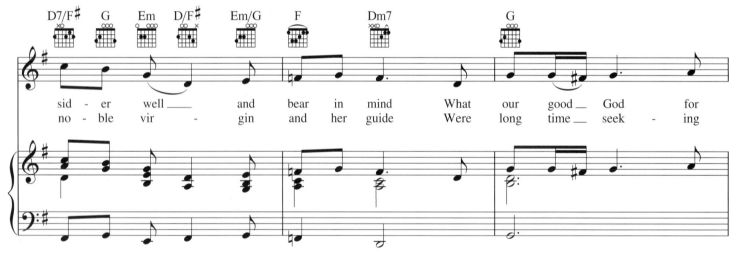

sid - er well ___ and bear in mind What our good ___ God for
no - ble vir - gin and her guide Were long time ___ seek - ing

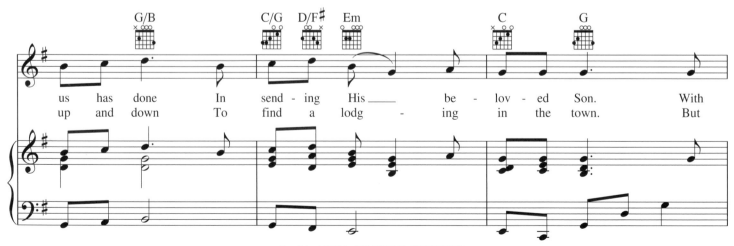

us has done In send - ing His ___ be - lov - ed Son. With
up and down To find a lodg - ing in the town. But

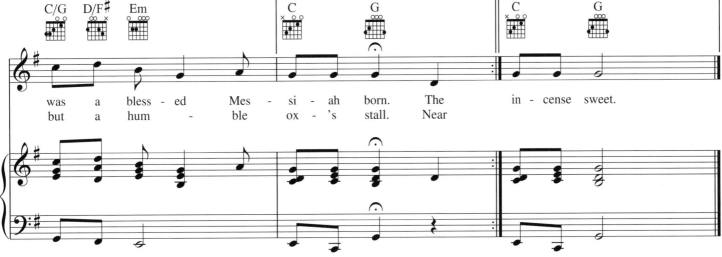

Additional Lyrics

3. Near Bethlehem did shepherds keep
   Their flocks of lambs and feeding sheep;
   To whom God's angels did appear,
   Which put the shepherds in great fear.
   "Prepare and go," the angels said,
   "To Bethlehem, be not afraid;
   For there you'll find this happy morn
   A princely Babe, sweet Jesus born."

4. With thankful heart and joyful mind,
   The shepherds went, the Babe to find;
   And as God's angel had foretold,
   They did our Savior Christ behold.
   Within a manger He was laid,
   And by His side, the virgin maid,
   Attending on the Lord of life,
   Who came to earth to end all strife.

5. There were three wise men from afar,
   Directed by a glorious star;
   And on they wandered night and day,
   Until they came where Jesus lay.
   And when they came unto that place
   Where our beloved Messiah was,
   They humbly cast them at His feet,
   With gifts of gold and incense sweet.

WHAT CHILD IS THIS?

Words by WILLIAM C. DIX
16th Century English Melody

Moderately slow

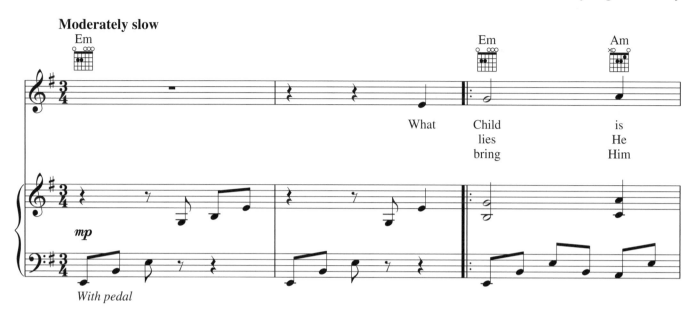

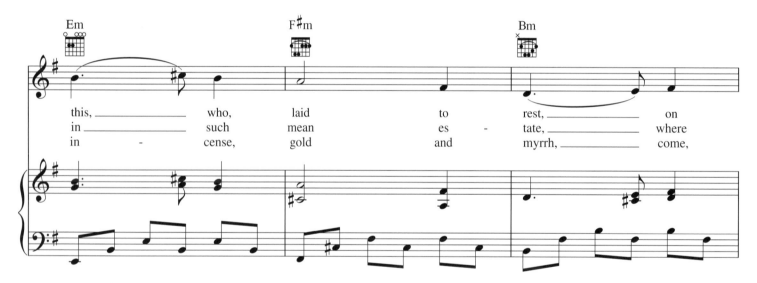

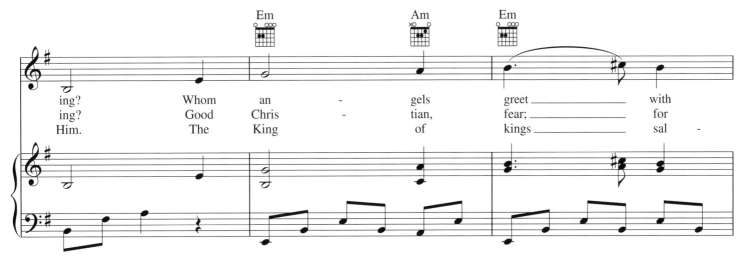

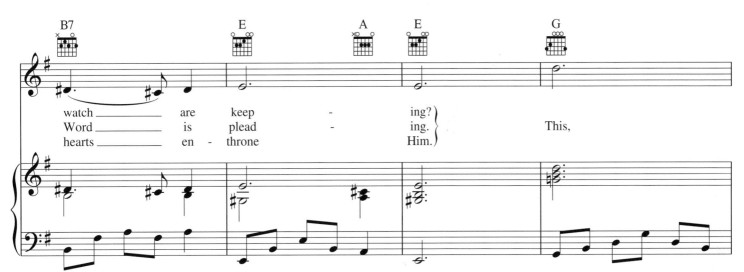

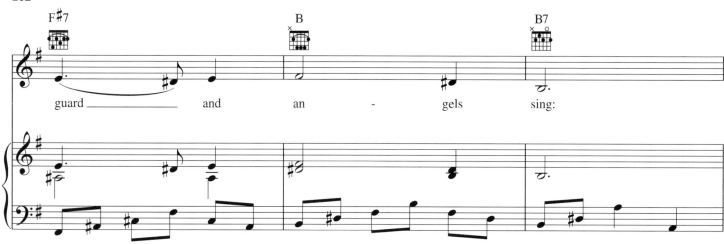

guard _____ and an - gels sing:

Haste, haste _____ to bring Him

laud, _____ the Babe, _____ the Son _____ of

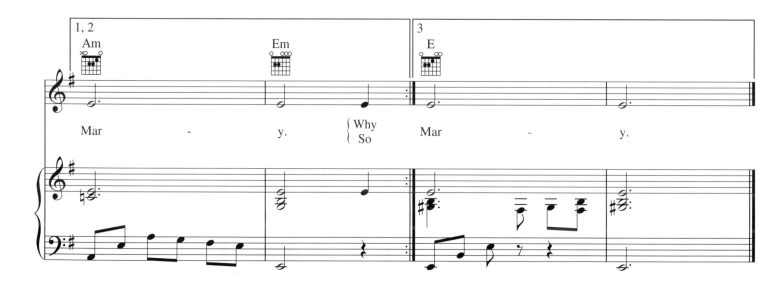

Mar - y. { Why So Mar - y.

WINDS THROUGH THE OLIVE TREES

19th Century American Carol

Winds through the ol - ive trees, Soft - ly did blow
Sheep on the hill - side lay, Whit - er than snow,
Then from the hap - py skies, An - gels bent low,
For in a man - ger bed, Cra - dled we know,

'Round lit - tle Beth - le - hem, Long, long a - go.
Shep - herds were watch - ing them, Long, long a - go.
Sing - ing their songs of joy, Long, long a - go.
Christ came to Beth - le - hem, Long, long a - go.

Long, long a - go.

WHEN CHRIST WAS BORN OF MARY FREE

Music by ARTHUR H. BROWN
Traditional Text, 15th Century

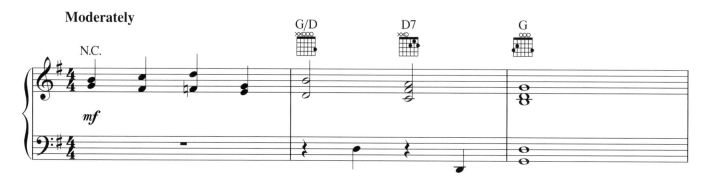

When Christ was born of Mar-y free, In
King is come to save man-kind, As
dear-est Lord, for Thy great grace, Grant

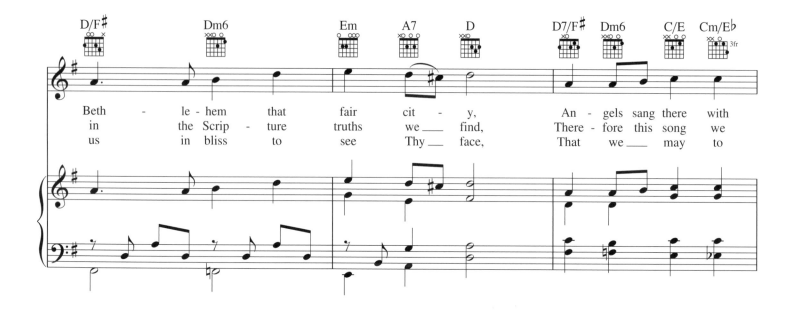

Beth-le-hem that fair cit-y, An-gels sang there with
in the Scrip-ture truths we find, There-fore this song we
us in bliss to see Thy face, That we may to

mirth and glee: }
have in mind: }
Thy sol - ace, }

In ex - cel - sis ____ glo - ri - a.

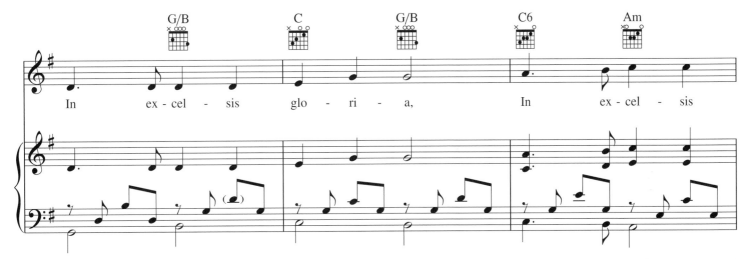

In ex - cel - sis glo - ri - a, In ex - cel - sis

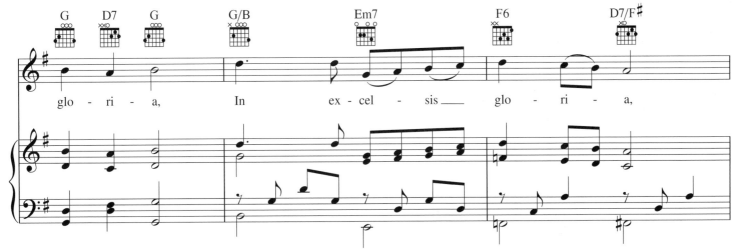

glo - ri - a, In ex - cel - sis ____ glo - ri - a,

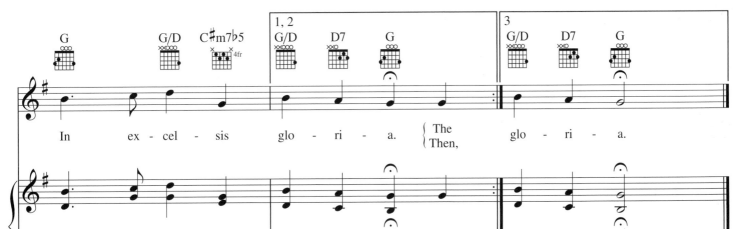

In ex - cel - sis glo - ri - a. { The
                                    { Then,   glo - ri - a.

WHEN CHRISTMAS MORN
IS DAWNING

Traditional Swedish

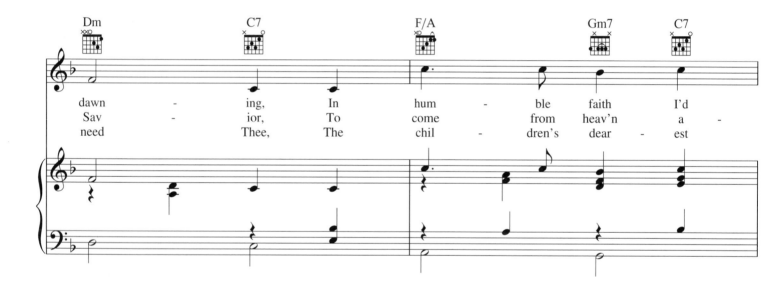

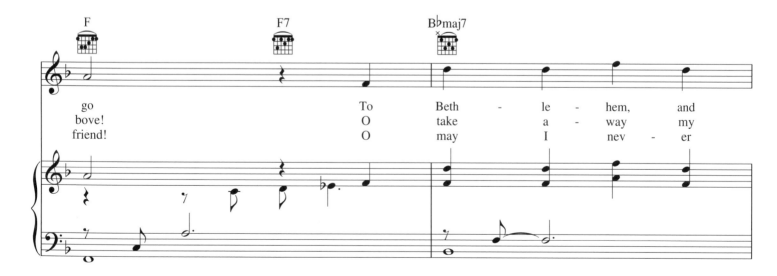

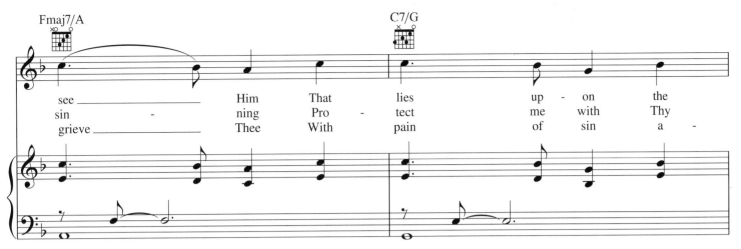

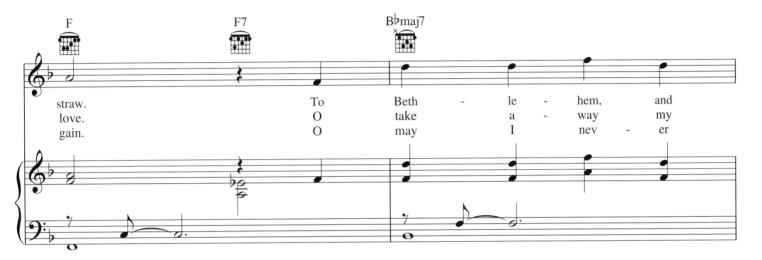

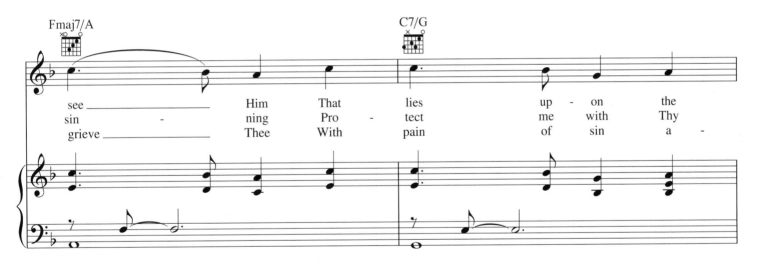

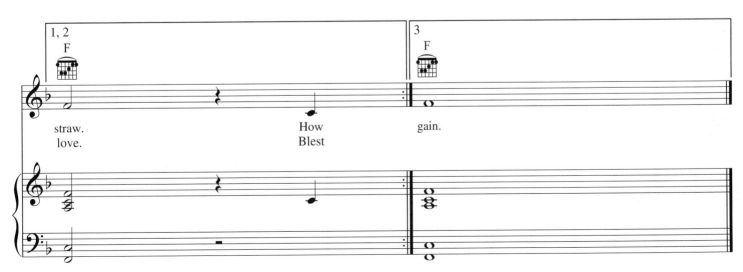

WHILE BY MY SHEEP

Traditional German Carol

While   by   my   sheep   I   watched   at
There   shall   be   born,   so   he   did
There   shall   He   lie   in   man - ger
Lord,   ev - er - more   to   me   be

night,   Glad   tid - ings   brought   an
say,   In   Beth - le - hem,   a
mean,   Who   shall   re - deem   the
nigh,   Then   shall   my   heart   be

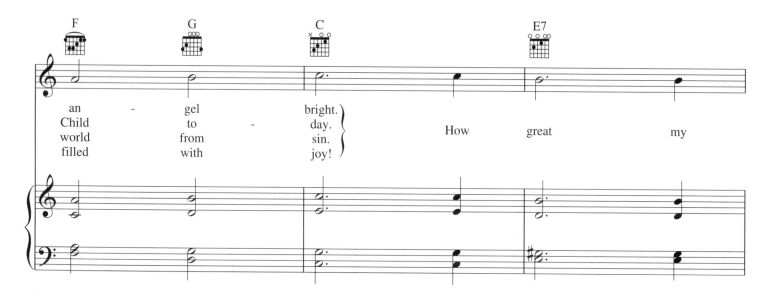

an - gel   bright.)   How   great   my
Child   to - day.   sin. }
world   from   with   joy!)
filled

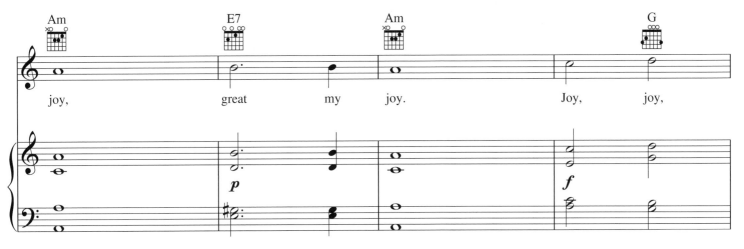

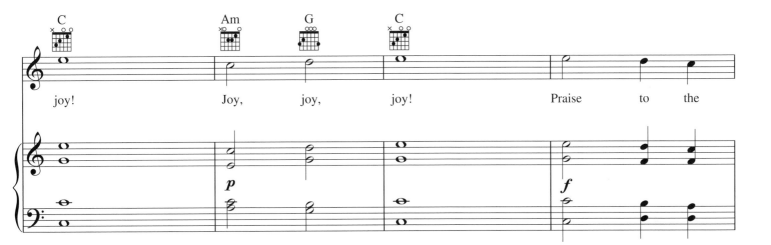

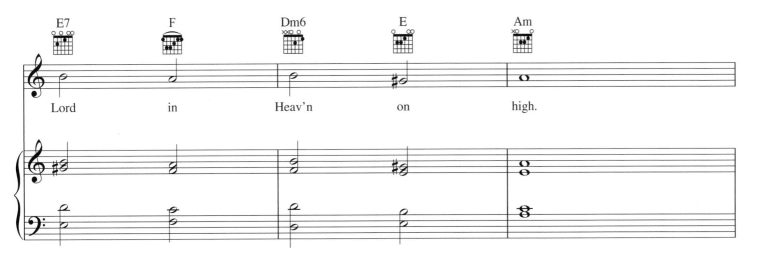

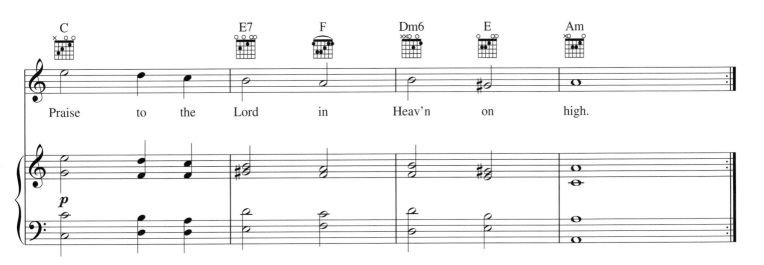

WHILE SHEPHERDS WATCHED THEIR FLOCKS

Words by NAHUM TATE
Music by GEORGE FRIDERIC HANDEL

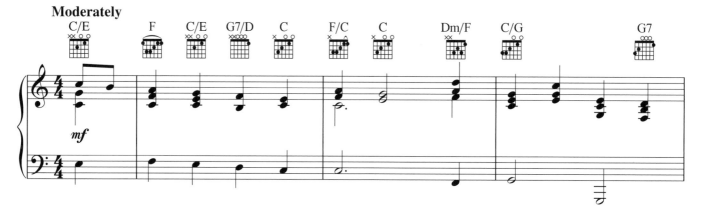

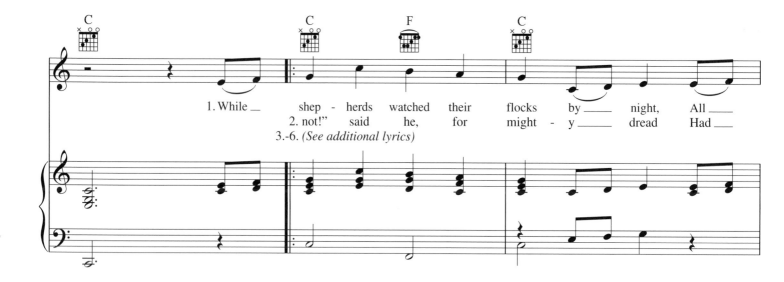

1. While ___ shep - herds watched their flocks by ___ night, All ___
2. not!" said he, for might - y ___ dread Had ___
3.-6. *(See additional lyrics)*

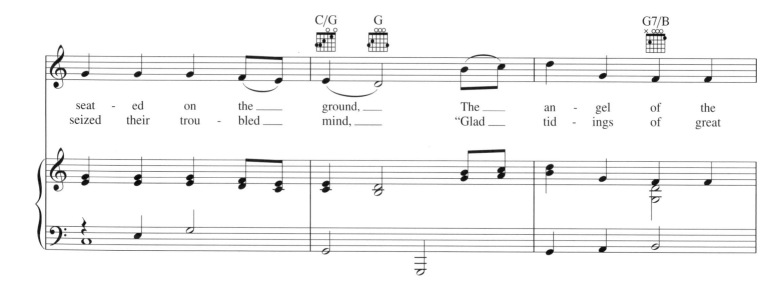

seat - ed on the ___ ground, ___ The ___ an - gel of the
seized their trou - bled ___ mind, ___ "Glad ___ tid - ings of great

Additional Lyrics

3. To you, in David's town this day,
Is born of David's line,
The Savior, who is Christ the Lord;
And this shall be the sign,
And this shall be the sign:

4. The heavenly Babe you there shall find
To human view displayed,
All meanly wrapped in swathing bands,
And in a manger laid,
And in a manger laid."

5. Thus spake the seraph; and forthwith
Appeared a shining throng
Of angels praising God on high,
Who thus addressed their song,
Who thus addressed their song:

6. "All glory be to God on high,
And to the earth be peace;
Good will henceforth from heav'n to men,
Begin and never cease,
Begin and never cease!"

Big Books of Music

Our "Big Books" feature big selections of popular titles under one cover, perfect for performing musicians, music aficionados or the serious hobbyist. All books are arranged for piano, voice, and guitar, and feature stay-open binding, so the books lie flat without breaking the spine.

BIG BOOK OF BALLADS
62 songs.
00310485 ....$19.95

BIG BOOK OF BIG BAND HITS
84 songs.
00310701 ....$19.95

BIG BOOK OF BROADWAY
70 songs.
00311658 ....$19.95

BIG BOOK OF CHILDREN'S SONGS
55 songs.
00359261 ....$14.95

GREAT BIG BOOK OF CHILDREN'S SONGS
76 songs.
00310002 ....$14.95

FANTASTIC BIG BOOK OF CHILDREN'S SONGS
66 songs.
00311062 ....$16.95

MIGHTY BIG BOOK OF CHILDREN'S SONGS
65 songs.
00310467 ....$14.95

REALLY BIG BOOK OF CHILDREN'S SONGS
63 songs.
00310372 ....$15.95

BIG BOOK OF CHILDREN'S MOVIE SONGS
66 songs.
00310731 ....$17.95

BIG BOOK OF CHRISTMAS SONGS
126 songs.
00311520 ....$19.95

BIG BOOK OF CLASSIC ROCK
77 songs.
00310801 ....$19.95

BIG BOOK OF CLASSICAL MUSIC
100 songs.
00310508 ....$19.95

BIG BOOK OF CONTEMPORARY CHRISTIAN FAVORITES
50 songs.
00310021 ....$19.95

BIG BOOK OF COUNTRY MUSIC
63 songs.
00310188 ....$19.95

BIG BOOK OF DISCO & FUNK
70 songs.
00310878 ....$19.95

BIG BOOK OF EARLY ROCK N' ROLL
99 songs.
00310398 ....$19.95

BIG BOOK OF '50S & '60S SWINGING SONGS
67 songs.
00310982 ....$19.95

BIG BOOK OF FOLK POP ROCK
79 songs.
00311125 ....$24.95

BIG BOOK OF FRENCH SONGS
70 songs.
00311154 ....$19.95

BIG BOOK OF GOSPEL SONGS
100 songs.
00310604 ....$19.95

BIG BOOK OF HYMNS
125 hymns.
00310510 ....$17.95

BIG BOOK OF IRISH SONGS
76 songs.
00310981 ....$19.95

BIG BOOK OF ITALIAN FAVORITES
80 songs.
00311185 ....$19.95

BIG BOOK OF JAZZ
75 songs.
00311557 ....$19.95

BIG BOOK OF LATIN AMERICAN SONGS
89 songs.
00311562 ....$19.95

BIG BOOK OF LOVE SONGS
80 songs.
00310784 ....$19.95

BIG BOOK OF MOTOWN
84 songs.
00311061 ....$19.95

BIG BOOK OF MOVIE MUSIC
72 songs.
00311582 ....$19.95

BIG BOOK OF NOSTALGIA
158 songs.
00310004 ....$19.95

BIG BOOK OF OLDIES
73 songs.
00310756 ....$19.95

BIG BOOK OF RHYTHM & BLUES
67 songs.
00310169 ....$19.95

BIG BOOK OF ROCK
78 songs.
00311566 ....$22.95

BIG BOOK OF SOUL
71 songs.
00310771 ....$19.95

BIG BOOK OF STANDARDS
86 songs.
00311667 ....$19.95

BIG BOOK OF SWING
84 songs.
00310359 ....$19.95

BIG BOOK OF TORCH SONGS
75 songs.
00310561 ....$19.95

BIG BOOK OF TV THEME SONGS
78 songs.
00310504 ....$19.95

BIG BOOK OF WEDDING MUSIC
77 songs.
00311567 ....$19.95